GUIDE TO MANAGING FINANCIAL CRISES & RESTRUCTURINGS

IN THE UK

ALAN GULLAN

Copyright © 2019 by Alan Gullan

All rights reserved.

No part of this book may be reproduced in any form or by any electronic or mechanical means, including information storage and retrieval systems, without written permission from the author, except for the use of brief quotations in a book review.

CONTENTS

Introduction					v

PART I

1. Overview					3

PART II

2. Managing crises					17
3. The fundamental technical issues					29
4. Financial advisers					43
5. Independent restructuring professionals					52
6. Interim executives					58
7. Private equity					62

PART III

8. The immediate response					73
9. The initial lender engagement					79
10. Leadership					83
11. Hiring a Ringmaster					89
12. Legal advisers					105
13. Personal risks					109
14. Financial advisers					114
15. Engaging with other stakeholders					123
16. The board's essential survival tools					126
17. Achieving stability					134
18. The financial restructuring process					138

PART IV

19. Gaining access to establish the causes					151
20. Unreliable numbers: no hiding place					158
21. Deciding whether to stay or resign					166

PART V

22. Early actions — 179
23. Governance of the process — 193
24. Governance of the business — 199
25. Stakeholder management — 205
26. Operational: liquidity management — 212
27. Operational: other — 234
28. Operational: fixing the finance function — 242

PART VI

29. Introduction — 249
30. The background — 254
31. What we see — 260
32. What we do not see — 293
33. So where did it all go wrong? — 301
34. An alternative ending — 316

PART VII

35. More effective governance: prevention and cure — 325
36. The fundamentals of governance — 327
37. The board's monitoring of financial performance — 333
38. The board's influence on the quality of financial management — 339
39. Changes in laws, regulations and behaviours — 349

Appendix — 369

INTRODUCTION

What, you may ask, is an independent restructuring professional? And why can their services not be bought from branded advisory firms? And how can large organisations facing major challenges put their trust in people who sell their services as individuals?

The reality is that independent restructuring professionals, like specialist medical consultants and surgeons, can establish successful practices built on their reputations. And find work through introductions from a network of specialist referrers, without the need for any publicity or recognition in the wider world.

The key difference is that independent restructuring professionals cannot learn their craft in a structured way, only by gaining experience and through the mentoring provided by colleagues.

A senior independent restructuring professional, therefore, is a highly experienced individual with a metaphorical toolkit who is introduced into a business facing survival challenges and has to rapidly work out what tools will be needed: first, to keep the business alive and, second, to restore it to health.

And someone who can commit to ethical behaviour and speak truth to power without having to consider whether that is in the commercial interests of an employer or fellow employees.

I am immensely proud to be an independent restructuring professional, but I am concerned that the breed is heading for extinction. In 2001, it was imagined that the UK market could support 50 of us. But now we are down to perhaps 15, and around half of those are considering retirement.

If we were giant pandas or snow leopards, our slow but steady demise would be ascribed to shrinking habitat and greater competition for food. The unprecedented volume of money sloshing around in the post-financial crisis markets reduces demand for ailing businesses to be fixed. And many of those on whom we have traditionally relied to introduce us to new opportunities have resorted to eating our lunch as a response to the challenges that they themselves are facing.

The more senior independent restructuring professionals are surviving by diversifying, but today's crop rising through the ranks is set to return a meagre harvest tomorrow. The risks in the current environment are too high for a young professional who, over a sustained period, has to put food on the table, educate children and provide adequately for retirement.

These are some of the factors that motivated me to write this book. Another is a strong empathy for directors going through their first financial crisis and restructuring wholly unprepared. I remember my own, when my start-up foundered: the menacing phone calls, the outrage when the sheriff attached the office heater and the fax machine, the determination to buy them back at auction and the sense of disbelief when some suckers paid more for them than I had originally!

And yet another motivating factor is my frustration at how the ignorance of directors in such positions can be, and is, arbitraged by a minority of professionals for ill-deserved financial gain. They do this not necessarily for sinister or unscrupulous reasons but because, in my opinion, parts of the business world have become unhealthily obsessed with revenue generation at the expense of putting clients first. This has wreaked havoc with the moral compasses of otherwise decent and honest cogs in the machine.

When a financial crisis is triggered, inexperienced and fearful directors have to make unfamiliar decisions with little information and naturally they look for advisers to help them fill that gap. There are household-name firms that offer such advice, but the reality is that the bulk of their restructuring businesses are built on serving lenders. This reflects London's place as a leading financial centre where lenders provide repeat business and insolvency can be enormously profitable.

So when anxious directors reach out to a branded firm, do they have the necessary experience to assess where the vested interests of that firm lie: in its long-term commercial relationships with lenders? In maximising its own fee revenue? Or in the health and survival of the business in crisis?

And is the senior person offering them soothing solutions

simply someone selling their firm's brand? Or is it an individual relying on their own reputation, established over a long period and built on a track record of working for the boards of businesses and achieving successful restructuring outcomes? What would be the consequences of that person failing to deliver? Against what standard would they be judged, by whom and with what powers?

As there is virtually no free information about these vital issues in the public domain, the board often finds itself operating in a vacuum when making its own inquiries and trying to satisfy itself as to the validity of the answers to those questions. And all this is often done in haste, at a time when the board members are desperately looking for people known to the company's lenders who can compensate for their own inexperience.

Until, say, three years ago, the workout teams in the large banks could be relied upon to save directors from making risky advisory appointments. But the high-profile scandals in recent years, in particular the Reading unit of Lloyds Bank and the GRG division of the Royal Bank of Scotland, have made such banks extremely sensitive to conduct risk – and rightly so – but unfortunately that has killed some good in the course of addressing the bad.

Restructuring advisers can and do earn eye-watering fees, and it is the very inexperience of the directors, combined with the insecurities of the senior executives, that provides them with the opportunities to do so. If the restructuring process develops an unpromising trajectory, the level of advisory fees can become turbocharged and even run out of control. By then it is too late to change advisers, because the board has become locked into the relationship, like a macabre embrace as the company hurtles to the end of its life.

An important factor in this, I believe, is that the relevant parts of the legal and regulatory regime are unbalanced and unfair, because when a restructuring fails and ends in insolvency, an adviser to the board will likely face no sanctions, whereas the directors could be in for an expensive and painful few years, from which their reputations might never recover.

Undoubtedly, the directors should be held responsible for what has happened up to the point that the financial crisis is triggered. But also for what happens after that point, if they lack relevant experience, are told they have no option but to soldier on and have to do so by relying heavily on advice? When there is very little material available to guide them in an area of business life in which there are no established standards? Is this really any different from the Victorians putting debtors in prison? Would enormous benefits not flow from incentivising directors to appoint a director with restructuring experience, immediately a crisis breaks?

As will be evident when you read this book, a senior independent restructuring professional is the closest thing to a panacea for directors who find themselves in such crisis situations. They bring an enormous body of legal, financial, operational and governance knowledge to the table, as well as a highly specialised network within the shadowy restructuring community that operates out of the public eye. As the health and survival of a business that hires them is (or ought to be) their only interest, that knowledge and those relationships are instantly available for the benefit of the board and management team.

That, allied to the individual's ability to rapidly diagnose the situation and sketch a way up and out, should, and does, provide immense relief to their new colleagues. Human nature being what it is, there will of course be others who find that threatening, some for healthy, understandable reasons and others out of self-interest.

All of which brings me to Carillion, the £5 billion UK construction and outsourced public services business that caused shockwaves throughout British society when it collapsed into liquidation in mid-January 2018. The company's predicament had hit the news six months earlier with the announcement of an enormous profits warning.

Because it is my business to track distressed company situations such as Carillion, I watched with interest from the sidelines. As is typical, not much information was made publicly available. Instinctively, it seemed to me that the direction taken by the board would not result in the company being rescued. Hence I took a deeper interest when, subsequently, two parliamentary committees conducted a joint inquiry into the collapse of Carillion and produced a report within four months.

From an academic point of view, the information made publicly available by the parliamentary inquiry was an unprecedented 'lifting of the veil' of restructuring: board meeting minutes, correspondence, advice, and both written and oral testimony. Moreover, the value of some of the information was greatly enhanced by how soon after the event it was made available: not only were recollections fresh but the parties involved had not yet had much opportunity to have their advisers dilute the information that they provided.

Soaking in all of this, I drew three conclusions:

1. The minimal attention that the parliamentary inquiry paid to the board's management of the situation in the company's final six months highlighted how the UK's business community, politicians, regulators and press have very little idea of what is involved in managing a company's financial crisis and restructuring, and there are no standards or benchmarks to help them.
2. Writing the book that was in me would make a contribution to filling this knowledge vacuum, and the public interest in Carillion would improve the prospects of being successful in that aim.
3. The availability of relevant material offered an unprecedented opportunity to illustrate the principles of managing financial crises and restructurings with a real-life example that many readers would already be familiar with.

One of the challenges in writing a book like this is the diversity of situations in which financial crises and restructurings need to be managed, ranging from a small family-owned business with a single lender to a very large multinational with a complex capital structure and a diversity of providers.

Broadly speaking, the guidance in this book will be most appropriate for directors of businesses with total debt ranging from £50 million to £1 billion. I have therefore addressed principles generically and have only highlighted how small and large situations might differ when I consider it would aid clarity. And, aside from a brief explanation in the chapter on private equity, I have not delved into the complexities of the situations in which debt is widely held.

On a technical note, I apologise for any confusion that arises from me using the word 'business' when it could easily, and might more properly, be substituted with the word 'company'. I have done this in the interests of simplicity, in particular to avoid having to be specific in the description of each situation.

So, who do I hope will find this book valuable? Most definitely company directors and executives going through their first crisis. I expect that a single read of this book will enable them to see the bigger picture and start to build a mental jigsaw puzzle that will help them better understand the situation they are in. A second read should help them to make more sense of specific challenges, develop a clearer vision of the outcome – good or bad – and focus more sharply on what they need to do as individuals.

The next group of readers is those financial stakeholders who have to deal with a company in a financial crisis or restructuring – investors, lenders, pension trustees and possibly regulators – and who will have access to information, to the leadership and the advisers. They will need a strategy and tactics for protecting the positions they are managing. I hope this book will be valuable to them in terms of being able to evaluate how well or badly the board is doing and to have clearer ideas of how they could improve. And to assist them in developing their own options for actioning and influencing.

Outside that inner circle will be potential solution providers – buyers, investors and lenders – who might be monitoring the situation as an opportunity and, if they are offered access, assessing and then diligencing the information they receive. The majority of such providers that I know have an abundance of legal and financial expertise available but zero situational experience personally and little appreciation of the people issues. I hope that the information in this book assists them to enhance their investment decision-making and better mitigate their downside risks.

A variety of professionals in different disciplines will be advising these various groups. I do not expect that the very senior people will learn much from this book, but there will be thousands in the ranks who I hope would benefit to at least some extent from the perspectives that I offer.

Then there are the stakeholders outside the tent, so to speak, who will lack access to information produced by the board. These include employees, landlords, customers, suppliers, and tax and other authorities; possibly regulators and unions, too. I hope this book helps them to evaluate the little information they do receive and to make better inferences about what they are not seeing or hearing.

I hope, too, that politicians, regulators, business forums and journalists – all concerned with the zeitgeisty topics of directors' failings, weak corporate governance, excessive executive pay, greedy advisers, the value of audits and safeguarding pension benefits – will find this book beneficial. Particularly the chapters at the end that outline my thoughts on how more effective governance and changes in laws, regulations and behaviours could help to avoid financial crises and, if they do happen, to improve the outcomes.

At the time of writing, there are two high-profile public inquiries in progress for which the parliamentary Carillion inquiry was the catalyst: a competition inquiry into the Big Four accounting firms' dominance of the audit market; and an inquiry led by Sir John Kingman into the possible reform of the Financial Reporting Council, the regulator responsible for overseeing the conduct of directors and professional advisers. In my view, these are important and long overdue, and I hope they prove to be building blocks towards genuine reform.

And finally, there are business students who have traditionally found elective courses on restructuring and turnaround appealing. Not only do I hope that my sharing of ideas and experience will enhance their education, but also that some will be inspired to become the independent restructuring professionals of tomorrow. Your country needs you!

My last words are to remind you that nothing in this book should be regarded as a substitute for legal advice from a reputable lawyer or law firm.

PART I

About this book

1
OVERVIEW

In this book, we are dealing specifically with situations in which a business very quickly changes from a normal existence to one in which its survival is threatened by a lack of liquidity (in simple terms, money). This is unlikely to include circumstances in which the owner has deep pockets or in which the maturity of debts in the medium term lights a long fuse.

It is the suddenness of the switch, the stark choices, the urgent need to adapt (or die), the newness of it all and the compressed timescale in which to secure the support of stakeholders that, in combination, create enormous pressure. And if the trigger for the crisis is the exposure of financial misstatements and irregularities, then the pressure will be even greater.

The theory

That pressure will, or ought to be, felt first and foremost by the board of directors of the business in crisis. Dealing with it will need the directors to climb a steep learning curve because survival will depend on them mastering numerous new and complex subjects, the board will need to be run in a different way and relationships at the top of the business may need to be reset.

Failure would result directly from insufficient liquidity. Understanding the mechanics of how that would happen is helpful and enhances an appreciation of how critically important liquidity forecasting is. Not only as a means to maintain confidence that failure can be avoided but, if failure becomes inevitable, to inform the decision about when to stop trading by seeking the protection of formal insolvency. There is a direct link between the losses that creditors are likely to suffer and the directors' personal risks.

In financial crisis situations, the stakeholders of a business naturally become concerned that they will incur losses. A subset of them are 'financial stakeholders', who may be in a position to force the business to stop trading. In most cases, secured lenders will be the most important financial stakeholders and therefore best positioned to both control a business's destiny and to provide additional support.

It is important, therefore, to identify who the financial stakeholders are, understand their respective rights and obligations, and carefully manage the relationships with them in order to maintain their confidence and secure their support. The resulting closer interaction will inevitably require the business to provide bespoke and timely information about a range of issues.

To remain supportive, the financial stakeholders will need assurances that the board is focused on what they have at risk and is committed to developing a plan to address that as a priority. Usually, the two main routes to doing so are to put the business back on an even keel with a stronger balance sheet or to make disposals to fund paydowns.

At the outset, it is vital to understand how each financial stakeholder's current exposure compares with the value of the business, under various scenarios, and its ability to pay. This analysis facilitates the board's development of clear strategic goals for the ensuing restructuring, along with a set of fallback options.

But, unless the board's plan is to sell the whole business as soon as possible, the financial stakeholders will only support a restructuring if they have confidence in both a revised business plan and the team that the board proposes will deliver it.

A business plan is difficult to prepare in an unstable environment. Hence, before a restructuring can be embarked upon, the financial crisis has to be stabilised. To create true stability, it is necessary to temporarily neutralise threats from financial stakeholders and to secure adequate liquidity support for the duration of the financial restructuring process.

Directors require at least a working knowledge of a variety of technical issues before the board can set about creating stability. First, there is acquisition term debt, a staple of modern debt markets that is likely to be at the very core of the majority of the restructuring processes. Second, there are the downside protection options that UK lenders will have – including formal insolvency – which will be built into lending agreements at the outset. It is highly relevant to understand what 'triggers and tripwires' are built into the facility agreement, whether breaches have occurred, and whether a state of default actually or potentially exists.

It will also be important for directors to understand how lenders are likely to manage their positions in situations of financial crisis or restructuring. If lenders are larger deposit-taking institutions, it would be usual for the relationship – or at least the credit aspects of it – to be taken over by their workout banking teams who rely heavily on legal and financial advisers.

For financial advice, lenders typically use the insolvency and lender advisory specialists provided by accountancy-based firms, spin-offs and hybrids. This is a product of the UK's insolvency framework, and a distinguishing feature of the UK market is a long history and a strong symbiosis between bank lenders and their advisers.

Those same firms opportunistically offer restructuring advisory services to borrowers. Their intelligence-gathering structures feed off their internal and external networks to identify new business opportunities which they then skilfully chase down. But if their long-term interests lie with lenders, that presents serious potential pitfalls for the board of a borrower who buys a brand-name adviser because 'no one ever got fired for buying IBM'.

Restructuring is a very expensive process and the borrower is responsible for funding its stakeholders' advisory costs as well as its own, plus increased borrowing costs.

Traditionally, UK lenders have been aware of the costly – and potentially fatal – downside of inexperienced borrower boards making inappropriate advisory hiring decisions. Hence they have taken comfort from the involvement of highly experienced independent restructuring professionals, who are hired by the boards of UK companies in financial crisis and restructuring situations, to help deliver a solution other than insolvency.

Many of them rely on bringing in battle-hardened interim executives with specialist skills and experience, both to bolster the business at a difficult time and thereby to support the executive team. Under the right leadership, interim executives can make a vital and durable contribution in key areas, in a flexible and cost-effective manner.

A director in a financial crisis and restructuring can feel under threat and therefore chronically stressed. This will almost certainly be exacerbated if the situation involves private equity ownership, complex debt structures, multiple stakeholders, a public listing, public debt, trading of debt, distressed buyers with predatory agendas and/or a plethora of advisers.

The practice

Given the interaction between stakeholder confidence and the credibility of the board and executive team, the board has to step up and swing into action once a financial crisis has been triggered.

The directors have to decide on a roadmap at a very early stage. A common error is to dive right into a wholesale transformation, depleting scarce liquidity and distracting from the vital priorities. Essential triage that demonstrably benefits liquidity in the short term should be tackled immediately, however.

Deciding on a roadmap has to be done in conjunction with associated judgements that it is essential for directors to make before they even engage with lenders for the first time.

One such judgement is an initial assessment of liquidity: how bad is the situation? How long has the board got? What can it do to buy more time? If there is headroom available on debt facilities, should it be drawn down to pre-empt it being removed?

Next, the board has to break the news to the lenders, in a considered way and ideally before they hear from any other source. If possible, the board should delay appointing financial advisers until after there has been a mutual sharing of views on the situational experience and bandwidth of the board and executive team.

Then, the board has to make possibly the most important decision of all: leadership. The leader's scope will have three components: governance, stakeholder management and operational. Ringmaster is a term I have created in this book to describe such a leader, in order to avoid the confusion caused by terms in use such as Chief Restructuring Officer (frequently referred to as CRO) and Turnaround Director. A Ringmaster is often a senior independent restructuring professional.

In hiring a Ringmaster, a board will be at a disadvantage if it does not seek candidates with appropriate qualities and experience and/or if it disregards the potential risks of involving advisers in the selection process. Guidance is provided on these aspects, as well as on how to settle on the scope of work, agree contractual terms, communicate the appointment to stakeholders and make upfront practical arrangements.

A board needs specialist legal advice but has to be circumspect in finding the right law firm. If the board needs to be advised separately, on matters including the directors' personal risks, it will be necessary to engage a different firm. The key principles of personal risk are not too complex for most experienced directors to understand and there are pragmatic steps that can be taken to deal with them and to avoid individuals becoming rabbits in the headlights.

If it is necessary to engage a financial adviser – and it should not be assumed that it always is – the subject should be approached cautiously. A board can expect a Ringmaster to provide valuable in-depth knowledge of the various financial advisers, to be aware of their strengths and weaknesses, and to point out the drawbacks, downsides and dangers of over-using them or, even worse, getting locked into them.

Usually, the right time to appoint financial advisers is in the window between initially notifying lenders and making a formal presentation to them. The Ringmaster is the obvious person to set up and lead the processes.

With leadership and advisers in place, the first objective is the creation of a stable platform. Stakeholders other than the lenders can play a very important role and there is usually a valuable golden window early on, in which it should be easier to win their support.

A liquidity forecast will be essential for this and it is important to begin working on three-year integrated forecasts as early as possible, because the next objective – the financial restructuring – cannot start without them.

The director's dilemmas

The demands of delivering the restructuring may comprise only part of the picture: the underlying causes may have to be addressed by the directors as well; and if numbers produced by the business are unreliable, that problem has to be confronted.

The circumstances may make it important to rapidly gain direct access to meaningful information from within the business, in order to establish reliably the causes of the crisis, to plan remedies and to rapidly improve the reliability of numbers. The character of the management team, the quality of the administration and options for remedies are all factors that will bear heavily on the prospects of success. And it may be essential to share such information with stakeholders, particularly lenders.

A director in such a position has to assess a host of issues, both individually and collectively, which may necessitate a more direct involvement and a longer-term commitment than hitherto. It may be in the best interests of all concerned therefore if, at the outset, incumbent directors were to conduct a considered evaluation of whether to remain on the board or to resign, based on a searching two-part self-examination.

The Ringmaster's art

Once appointed, a Ringmaster has to bring order to the situation as quickly as possible. This involves working rapidly to set numerous plates spinning, including legal analysis, appointing advisers, engaging interim executives and setting up a positive relationship with the finance team, so that various workstreams can be commenced. One of the early deliverables is the all-important management presentation to lenders and the liquidity ask.

The Ringmaster has to establish governance of the process, including the creation of a temporary platform within the board framework and at the top of the business, to facilitate management of the project, enable the board to oversee it (including by using survival KPIs) and control restructuring costs.

In parallel, it is important for the board to improve its own effectiveness by adapting to the changed circumstances, reconfiguring the division of responsibilities and, if necessary, adding to its members' bandwidth, skills and situational experience. One area in which the board has to be on the top of its game, despite everything else going on around it, is monitoring ongoing trading performance, against realistic forecasts.

The management presentation to lenders is an important watershed. It should signal that the board is now sufficiently well organised to manage the financial crisis and subsequent financial restructuring, set out what will be needed to create a stable platform, provide a framework within which the board's proposals will be negotiated – or rejected – and detail the timetable.

This will enable the lenders to formulate their own strategy in response and there may be some to-ing and fro-ing before a course is mutually agreed upon and a stable platform put in place.

As the business plan creation and, thereafter, the financial restructuring are proceeding, it is important to address triage – liquidity management, cost cutting and disposals – in parallel. And also to begin tackling the causes of the crisis, in particular permanently upgrading the capabilities of the finance team.

Many executives are surprised that liquidity management is

more complex than they routinely assume and most do not realise that many of the inefficiencies and obstacles in an organisation that impact adversely on liquidity are deep rooted and have been self-inflicted over a long period. Rapidly and decisively remedying these impediments requires craft and leadership and a failure to do so can, and frequently does, make the difference between the corporate surviving the crisis or dying.

It is important for the board to distinguish the vast difference between simply reporting, with increasing accuracy, when the Titanic is going to hit the iceberg and, instead, steering a course around it!

Liquidity management and reforecasting workstreams will naturally generate a host of cash mitigation and cost cutting opportunities for experienced Ringmasters and interim executives who will possess the techniques to successfully exploit them. Most will also be excellent at diagnosing the shortcomings in finance functions, designing remediation programmes and leading self-help implementation programmes.

Carillion plc: a case study

To illustrate the principles of managing financial crises and restructurings that are expounded in this book, I have included a case study that looks at how the Carillion plc board managed the company's financial crisis, by analysing relevant information among that made publicly available. As will be seen, although all parties were working towards a financial restructuring, the process never got that far and its stakeholders suffered enormous losses when it collapsed into liquidation.

Mitigation

Thus, the failure of Carillion provides a high-profile example of the costs of an adverse outcome. In the final part of the book, I provide my views about what could be done in mitigation either to prevent crises or, if they do happen, to achieve better outcomes and provide durable cures for common root causes.

There are three chapters that look at effective governance and a final one in which I share my views on how changes to laws and regulations, in conjunction with changes in behaviour driven by investors, lenders and business leaders, could also help to achieve better outcomes.

And thus save the country billions!

PART II

The theory

2

MANAGING CRISES

Under UK law, particularly section 172 of the Companies Act 2006, the directors of a company are responsible for managing a financial crisis and restructuring. This derives from their duty to promote the success of the company, which is owed to the company and cannot be delegated.

Essential changes

Obviously, no one wants to find themselves in a financial crisis and restructuring, but once it has happened then the directors *in situ* at the time have to get on with the job to the best of their ability. Much as they might be tempted to delegate the responsibility to professional advisers, that would be incompatible with their legal duty to exercise independent judgement and also to exercise reasonable care, skill and diligence.

To do their job effectively, directors will need to change the way the board operates and commit considerably more time, quite likely without a pay increase. They will also need to rapidly acquire specialist knowledge, because their experience and acumen, accumulated in conventional business circumstances, will be insufficient.

Of course, for everyone in the senior team and on the board, there will be the additional personal dimension in the form of increased personal risk that individuals will have to get comfortable with, and the threat to careers and reputations. Perversely, some might see in the situation opportunities that they will hope to exploit.

These divergent interests and conflicts have to be managed, all of which might mean resetting existing relationships among the non-executive directors and between them and the executive team. The relationship with shareholders might also need to be altered.

Should a director stay or go?

The practice prevailing in the UK is that, once a financial crisis and restructuring has been triggered, a director ought to stay on the board no matter what. However, there is no strict legal reason why that should be the case (although a resignation that harmed the interests of the company could risk a breach of duty). Perhaps the pressure is social or reputational in that a director who resigned might be labelled a deserter.

But, as I explain in Chapter 21, I believe that directors who find themselves in such a position and lack the necessary experience should nonetheless consider whether resigning would be in the best interests of the business.

If they were hired in normal times for their experience in widget making, certainly the survival prospects of the business would be improved if they were replaced on the board by a director with years of experience in managing financial crises and restructurings.

Directors with no prior restructuring experience will inevitably find the opaque world of restructuring, with its complex technical issues, arcane practices and esoteric skillsets, unfathomable. At least at the outset.

These are all a concomitant part of the UK's creditor-friendly insolvency regime, which facilitates the availability of myriad debt products on terms that provide lenders with greater downside protection than in most other jurisdictions. This is one reason behind London's strength in financial services and its concentrated cluster of expertise in all matters related to debt.

Failure to successfully manage the crisis

As they transition mentally from normal to crisis mode, it is likely that the board will spend time considering the full range of adverse effects the crisis might produce. However, it is important from the outset for the directors to have a peek over the edge, in order to understand how failure would happen and what developments might hasten that journey.

Failure will not be anything technical, like a legal judgement or an adverse ruling by a regulator. Rather it will be real and visible when a once lively company will wake up one day to find that the people that made the business work will no longer report for duty, the equipment they operated will fall silent and the sites and offices they occupied will be virtually empty – possibly because they are aware that they are not going to be paid. But a more likely scenario is one in which the directors will have filed for insolvency before the bank accounts are completely empty and the insolvency office holder will have swung into action and told employees whether or not to report for duty.

In the most obvious, open-and-shut cases, an insolvency filing will be needed immediately a financial crisis has been triggered. But more often, there is a lead-up to the insolvency filing during which the board will have access to a liquidity forecast.

It is not the case that the cash balance will simply deplete in a straight line leaving the directors with the decision to file for insolvency as it gets closer to zero. Far from it. The directors have an obligation to minimise the creditors' losses.

This means that even when forecasts show that there is sufficient liquidity to fund operations for some time to come, if suppliers are continuing to give the business credit then, by doing so, they might be increasing the amount that they would lose if and when the directors file for insolvency. In such a case, the likelihood of having to file becomes a very important consideration.

A decision to file for insolvency will be founded on a number of important assumptions, not only about whether efforts to raise additional liquidity or secure the ongoing support of incumbent lenders will be successful, but also about downside risks, including credit insurers restricting or withdrawing cover, suppliers reducing payment terms, and customers terminating contracts or sourcing their supplies elsewhere.

For directors, these are not academic questions: firstly, because under the law they could be held personally liable for creditors' incremental losses beyond the point at which they knew, *or ought to have known*, that insolvent liquidation was unavoidable; and secondly, because if the tax authorities have incurred losses, that could have an adverse impact on an assessment of their conduct by the Official Receiver, who in due course will receive confidential reports from the insolvency office holder.

Key issues to manage

To start with, there are the capital providers, usually shareholders and lenders.

In a publicly listed company, individual shareholders cannot have privileged access to relevant information, and the need to communicate such information through market announcements can create a real conundrum when managing a crisis. Directors have to be mindful of the risk of regulatory scrutiny, especially if the outcome is insolvency and questions arise as to when the market was informed of difficulties and whether it should have been earlier.

But the company's public status can help to box in its lenders, particularly high-profile banks who will be fearful of board pushback and shareholder recriminations in the event of a debt for equity transaction or an insolvency.

On the other hand, a company owned by private investors will be expected to involve its shareholders in the borrower–lender dialogue. Lenders will look for the shareholders to fund any equity needs and, if they are willing, the crisis can usually be resolved quickly.

Given the proliferation of debt products, there are many different types and configurations of lenders. The main distinctions in debt products are firstly between public (traded on a public exchange, e.g. bonds) and private debt, and between secured and unsecured debt. A further distinction is between term debt and working capital facilities. Among lenders, senior lenders (least cost, lowest risk, highest priority upon insolvency) are at one end of the spectrum and subordinated lenders at the other.

In a restructuring, it is critically important to manage the legal rights and obligations of lenders. A host of additional considerations can add to the complexities, for example, where the assets and debt sit in the legal structure and if there are inter-creditor agreements, guarantees or cross-default provisions.

Dealing with lenders can become more complex if some of the original lenders sell out, especially if those who have bought in have different agendas, particularly ones that involve converting their debt into equity. And lenders that have bought in at a discount will view restructuring proposals differently than those who are in at par.

There may be other creditors to manage as well, including credit card merchants, defined benefit pension funds that the business sponsors (represented by trustees), hedging counterparties and providers of sureties, bonding, indemnities and trade finance.

In addition, there may be one or more industry regulators. Some regulators have the power to terminate the ability of a business to continue operating, based on their duty to protect the interests of non-financial stakeholders such as the clients of a law firm. And the pensions regulator may take an interest in a situation if there are pensions issues that warrant its involvement.

Some or all of these financial stakeholders will demand access to information and a seat at the table and they will have one or even a suite of their own advisers. The regulator, or regulators, may be active or passive depending on the circumstances, and in any event will have access rights to at least some of the information that the borrower provides to other financial stakeholders.

Then there are the non-financial stakeholders, including customers, suppliers, employees (and possibly unions) and landlords. If the suppliers have trade insurance cover they will generally be happy to continue supplying as long as the cover remains in place, but if it is reduced or withdrawn, they will have no flexibility.

Strategic and tactical imperatives

To begin managing a crisis, it is critical for the board: to start shaping its strategy and developing its tactical focus; to get rapidly up to speed on the fundamental technical issues that are going to dominate the process; to identify and commission development of the essential tools; and to adopt new priorities and ways of working without delay.

The strategic aims

A crisis is only the first phase of a process that will involve a financial restructuring and possibly an operational restructuring as well.

In the simplest terms, the aims of a financial restructuring are to give back the lenders either their money or their confidence. Even when the outcome is a liquidation with a pitiful return, the most senior lenders will get some of their money back. Needless to say, capital providers will want as much of their money returned as is possible in the circumstances.

The strategic goal for the board, therefore, can be summed up as to maximise value for capital providers. If the debt exceeds the value of the business, then throughout the restructuring, the capital providers will be mindful of all the options available to them and will probably be working on more than one at a time. They will be ready to switch at short notice and will expect the same from the board.

Unless the business is to be sold or liquidated, a prerequisite for lender support – in order to complete a financial restructuring – is a fresh business plan backed by fully integrated financial forecasts. Such a plan will demonstrate the ability of the business to service debt in the future and this will determine its debt capacity and, by elimination, the equity required.

Determining the equity is not formulaic, because the incumbent or new shareholder(s) will be looking to optimise the terms of any deal through negotiations (conducted by the board in the case of a publicly listed company) and this may involve lenders – with different risk-reward appetites or different strategies – being found to bridge funding gaps with money that is more expensive. If the incumbent shareholders are unable to fund the equity they will almost certainly be relinquishing control.

Value enhancement is driven directly by an improvement in performance and an operational restructuring can be a significant factor in achieving that. Typically, this might involve changes to strategy, mergers and acquisitions

(M&A), discontinuing businesses or product lines, improving margins, cutting overheads or closing sites. Implementing all of these changes will incur costs and the funding required will, therefore, have to be included in the business plan.

Capital providers will need to have confidence in the team that will deliver the new business plan, including in their ability to successfully implement the operational restructuring and deliver the forecast benefits. If the incumbent executives have been tainted by the crisis, then, unless a new owner is going to need them, management change may become a very thorny issue for the board to manage. Of course, the same may apply to the board itself, or at least to certain of its members.

The timing of any personnel changes will be a key consideration. On the one hand, the executive team responsible for delivery should ideally have played a big part in formulating the plan, and they should be very conversant with the operational restructuring and its expected payback and be able to sell it to the capital providers. On the other, the best quality candidates as replacement hires may not be willing to leave the relative comfort of their existing, secure and well-paid roles before the future of the business has been assured.

When a crisis is triggered, most boards have more time, runway and headway than seems obvious. However, it is very easy for them to throw this advantage away. And if they are in denial about the existence of a crisis, or about how bad it really is, they will fail to see or use that advantage in the first place.

Clearly, the option that all stakeholders will want the board to deliver is the one that maximises value. Understandably, most time and effort is usually spent working on that very option. But, in practice, the outcome actually delivered sometimes turns out to be the one ranked third or fourth at the outset of the process. Unless it is influenced by significant external events, there is a strong correlation between the outcome and the board's competence in managing the financial crisis and restructuring.

Restructuring tactics

With the strategic aims established, how does a board get from the onset of the crisis to the completion of a financial restructuring and mitigate the risks of failing to deliver the optimal outcome?

There are two sequential phases, each a distinct process: crisis stabilisation and financial restructuring.

Stabilisation provides the platform for a fresh business plan to be produced and negotiated with capital providers and for the agreed commercial terms to be legally documented. When the parties execute those documents and implement their terms, the financial restructuring will have been delivered. Unless the business is sold, the outcome should be a fully funded business plan, usually with a team in place to deliver it.

Any stabilisation that does not secure sufficient liquidity until the deal closes is almost certain to fail. Just as a human cannot survive long without oxygen, so a business will die if starved of liquidity even for a short period of time.

But, as outlined earlier, failure will manifest itself as a fatal lack of confidence some time before the bank accounts are actually empty. So actual liquidity is often less important than confidence in liquidity. It is essential that the board, the lenders and the other financial stakeholders have – and maintain throughout the financial restructuring phase – high confidence that there will be a comfortable cushion of cash right up until the deal is complete.

This liquidity issue is the most likely cause of a board failing to deliver the option that maximises value.

For example, if the business is being sold and there is an orderly process already under way – involving a crop of quality buyers and producing competitive bids – the sudden imposition of a liquidity-driven deadline that precludes sufficient due diligence will likely result in the process being abandoned in favour of an accelerated process involving distressed business buyers who will offer much less and possibly transact via a pre-packaged insolvency process.

The process can also be threatened by underestimating how difficult a transaction will be, a lack of realism about the value of the business, what increment in value can actually be achieved in the circumstances and confidence in the personnel. However, the time to put those assumptions to the test is once stabilisation has been achieved.

Putting adequate liquidity in place is, therefore, a very demanding challenge for a board and it should be addressed very early on in the process. The directors' lack of experience and the danger that they will use flawed information to support their judgements in new and difficult circumstances will increase both the risks and the challenges.

One pitfall to avoid is doing things out of sequence,

especially embarking on the operational restructuring when the priority should be to create stability as rapidly and as convincingly as possible. That is not to say that triage or piecemeal disposal opportunities that demonstrably benefit liquidity during the restructuring should be ignored.

3

THE FUNDAMENTAL TECHNICAL ISSUES

Acquisition debt and its role in crises

In the UK, the debt landscape has changed enormously in the past 30 years. Until the mid-1980s, acquisitions were funded with equity, while debt was used mainly to fund hard assets and working capital, making it straightforward for a secured lender to lean on shareholders to fund a cash shortfall and to realise its security if they did not.

Nowadays, debt is commonly used to fund acquisitions and the target businesses acquired are used as collateral. The targets are valued by reference to the cash they are expected to generate, on the basis that if secured lenders have to realise their security they can do so by selling the business as a going concern to third party buyers.

Publicly owned businesses will raise acquisition debt on the assumption that refinancing risk is low as there will be lenders willing to fund refinancing at maturity. This relies on sensible gearing and sustained growth in enterprise value, underpinned by sound governance.

Private equity-owned businesses, on the other hand, are acquired with debt raised on the basis that the businesses being bought are expected to be sold for a higher price within, at most, five to seven years.

A number of key metrics have grown up around acquisition debt. Earnings before interest, tax, depreciation and amortisation (EBITDA) is a proxy for the cash flow generated by the business. Enterprise value is the product of EBITDA and a multiple that reflects the growth potential of the business, typically between three and 10. Lender appetite for risk will be expressed as a 'turn', or multiple, of EBITDA. Leverage is the sum of those turns. The gap between leverage and enterprise value is equity.

To provide an example, a business with an EBITDA of £100m, valued using a multiple of 8, will have an enterprise value of £800m. If the most risk-averse (i.e. senior) lenders are willing to lend 3.5x EBITDA (£350m) and junior lenders are willing to lend a further 2.5x (£250m) giving total leverage of £600m, the equity to be provided by the private equity investor will be the balance of £200m.

In liquid market eras (such as those before and since the global financial crisis), private equity acquisition debt will not be amortised. In other words, no portion of capital will be repaid until the business is sold. In the example above, there is clearly a risk that the business will be sold for less than £800m. If the proceeds from a sale are less than £600m, at least one of the lenders is going to suffer a loss.

As lenders would prefer to find out as early as possible if the business is on course to leave them facing a loss, they set covenants that the business has to test and report on quarterly. The most common covenants are leverage and interest cover, which are based on EBITDA in the last 12 months. The covenants are set by reference to the medium-term forecasts that are the basis for the negotiation of the commercial terms of the loan.

Covenant levels typically correlate inversely with the debt cycles: in a liquid cycle, a senior lender might be comfortable with 6x leverage but in a recession that might shrink to 2.5x.

To a lender, a covenant is a control mechanism that flags up when a closer look at the performance of a business is needed.

The insolvency framework

As already mentioned, the UK has a creditor-friendly insolvency regime. It is important for directors going through a restructuring to understand the basics, especially if they are used to doing business in other countries, where insolvency processes are court-driven and lenders have much less control.

When a lender takes security under UK law, it is possible for that to cover every source of value in a business as well as everything necessary to control it. Without this, lenders would not have the ability to realise their security by delivering a business to a third party. And consequently, lending to fund acquisitions would be a much higher risk for them.

Where a borrower has two or more sets of lenders, lending on different terms with the highest ranking taking priority over the security, they and the others enter into an inter-creditor agreement, to which the borrower is a party. This sets out the various parties' rights and obligations.

Generally, if the most senior lenders are repaid the second-ranking lenders will acquire their rights.

It is common for certain collateral to be carved out of the security package, especially property and fixed or movable assets that have been separately funded by another lender. And if a specialist lender provides funding secured by inventory or receivables, that collateral would also be carved out.

Generally speaking, formal insolvency processes in the UK are contract-based, with the lending agreement being the contract. A court oversees the processes from a high level but does not get involved in the specifics. Lenders with security over substantially all of the assets will have the final say over the appointment of the insolvency practitioner(s) who will control the process.

It is important to understand the distinction between a company and a business. A company is an artificial person that is easy to incorporate and the business is the totality of its assets, liabilities, contracts, and so forth. The company administers the business and the two are separable. Only a company can be the subject of an insolvency process and a sale of some or all of its business may be the purpose of that process.

Selling the assets and liabilities of a company can be messy. One way round this is to create at the outset a structure of shell holding companies (referred to as holdcos) above the companies that own the business (referred to as opcos), lend to the holdcos against the security of the opco shares and through insolvency deliver the business by selling them. If done this way, only the financial creditors suffer losses and the business's employees, suppliers, the tax authorities and other creditors are unaffected.

A state of insolvency is an essential ground for a UK court application. The two recognised states of insolvency are balance sheet (liabilities exceed assets, fairly valued) and cash flow (inability to pay debts as they fall due). Under UK law, providing insolvency is not unavoidable (and that will be judged with hindsight), there are no adverse consequences per se of trading while balance sheet insolvent.

The mainstream insolvency processes are a Company Voluntary Arrangement (CVA), administration and liquidation. The CVA was designed as a means of reducing unsecured liabilities and/or stretching the period over which they are settled. It was adapted beyond its originally intended purpose and nowadays makes the headlines because a tenant can use it as a tool to force landlords to either cancel leases or reduce rents. Creditors and shareholders have to approve a CVA, which can only affect a specific class of creditors (e.g. landlords). Secured creditors cannot be bound by a CVA.

Administration effectively removes the directors and replaces them with an insolvency office holder whose objectives are, in order of priority: to rescue a company as a going concern; to achieve a better result for creditors than they would get through a wind-up; or to realise property in order to make a distribution to one or more secured or preferential creditors.

Insolvency office holders are personally liable for losses incurred in an insolvency, so if sufficient funding cannot be provided up front, they are not going to trade a business in administration. This immediately eliminates the first objective, leaving them, in reality, with the task of selling the business and realising any other assets that the business buyers do not want.

It is logical that if an administrator is appointed without funding, the alternative to a sale is the cessation of trading. Unless the business comprises purely non-trading assets this would destroy significant value at a stroke. Which is where the pre-packaged administration insolvency process (or 'prepack') comes in.

This involves an insolvency practitioner being lined up in advance and conducting a process to market the business or businesses to potential buyers, very much 'under the radar'. Once bids have been agreed, the sale and purchase agreement is negotiated and documented. The appointment of an administrator is followed, potentially within minutes, by the execution of the sale and purchase agreement.

Liquidation is the process of bringing a business to an end and distributing its assets to its creditors. It is commonly used as a kind of corporate funeral for companies that have been emptied by an administration process. But businesses can be placed directly into liquidation if they are in such a dire state that administration is not a feasible option.

(Readers may wonder what happened to receiverships, which were in the news in the 1980s and 1990s. Receivers were appointed by secured creditors and, in essence, their duties ended once they had maximised the return for those secured creditors. In the early 2000s they were replaced by administrators, who have a duty to serve the interests of all creditors.)

Because 'debtor in possession' funding is not available in the UK, until a financial refinancing is successfully implemented, the most senior-ranking lenders are likely to be the only realistic source of funding. Hence they will have the de facto ability to control a situation in which a business is reliant on lender support.

As mentioned above, in a restructuring process, they and other lenders will be constantly sizing up their options and these will usually include insolvency in its different forms.

UK lending agreements

A standard secured lending agreement for acquisition debt – most term loans nowadays – will have three elements: good times; bad book (i.e. for the lenders, the borrower has become a high risk); and plenty of boilerplate provisions to provide belt and braces. It is likely that during the good times, most directors will not have paid much attention to the bad book element.

Leaving aside non-financial causes such as serious regulatory issues and natural catastrophes, the status of a lending relationship will transition from good times to bad book because the performance of a business has gone badly off plan.

If routine reporting has previously presented the business as performing within tolerable parameters, an admission that this was not the case would be likely to make a difficult situation much worse.

Numerous mechanisms will be built into the agreement, to automatically activate the transition from good times to bad book. Lawyers refer to these as triggers and tripwires. In theory, from the point that they are activated, the borrower is at the mercy of its most senior lenders for its survival.

The *coup de grâce* might come in the form of a demand for repayment which would almost certainly create both statutory states of insolvency. This in turn would leave the directors with no alternative but to file for formal insolvency.

From the perspective of a borrower, either already in or on the cusp of bad book, it is essential to understand rapidly what triggers and tripwires the lending agreement contains, whether any have already been activated, and whether others will or might be.

Covenants tend to be the triggers that receive the most focus, but there are others, such as misrepresentation, that should not be ignored. Under the lending agreement, routine loan management events such as interest payments and drawdowns can mean that representations are automatically repeated. One of the representations is likely to be that no event of default has occurred or is subsisting!

Some breaches are capable of being cured. Others are technical. The critical issue is whether a breach will be an event of default, either automatically or if called by the lenders.

A failure to make a contractual payment of capital and/or interest is an altogether more serious breach and if this happens there may be little time or runway to manage the situation.

Interest can be fixed or floating. If the latter, then typically the rate will have two components: the London Inter-bank Offered Rate (LIBOR) and a margin. LIBOR is set and published daily by a rate-setting body in the London market. There are rates for different currencies and time periods.

For loans denominated in Euros, there is also EURIBOR (as distinct from Euro LIBOR) which the rate at which European banks are prepared to lend to each other.

Understanding lender behaviour

Although lenders with the contractual right to force a business into insolvency following a breach of a lending agreement are able to do so, an unplanned insolvency is very destructive of value and will almost certainly crystallise their losses.

It is rational, therefore, for them to keep the business alive while they gather information and perform analysis, to enable them to evaluate and prioritise their options. Except in the most adverse circumstances, they are likely to support the business. This remains the case even if it appears that their position will be worsening, provided that doing so could potentially improve their outcome on insolvency, for example, by enabling their advisers to start planning an insolvency and begin discreetly marketing the business. But they will be sensitive to other creditors improving their positions at the lenders' expense.

The lenders may quickly discover sound reasons to confirm their support for the business with minimal fuss, but that falls outside the scope of this book on managing financial crises.

If a business needs new money to survive, the first and easiest option for the lenders is to look to the equity. This is much simpler with private company shareholders, although publicly listed businesses usually have the ability to place some shares without involving all shareholders or having to issue a prospectus. If new equity is not available, it follows that the shareholders have little to offer and cannot realistically demand a seat at the negotiating table. This puts them at risk of seeing their shareholdings being diluted, perhaps heavily.

From the perspective of the lenders, the backstop value of their security is what a third party would pay to buy the business, whether in a solvent transaction or via insolvency. Whatever their other options, they will want to maximise the value from this one. For the uninitiated, this has two implications, or consequences, for borrower-side incumbents that may not be obvious.

Firstly, the ability to sell the business out of the company means the key elements in the current configuration may be separable, in other words, the board and/or the management may not go with the business to a new buyer.

Secondly, lenders will be sensitive to any damage that the business might suffer, which would reduce its value, for example, regulatory sanctions or a loss of reputation, brand value, market share, major contracts or customers.

What this means is that the directors and senior executives may be more dispensable than they assume, because if they become threats to the lenders' recovery value, they may find themselves being shown the door.

The lenders will be more comfortable with key personnel who are focused on finding a solution to the predicament that the business is in and who do not assume, perhaps blithely, that the lenders have a duty to continue supporting it.

The kind of behaviour that undermines lender confidence includes not adapting to the changed circumstances quickly enough or remaining in denial, producing unreliable numbers, serially deceiving, being wilfully obstructive, giving the lenders unwelcome surprises, misleading the lenders as to the support required and not adequately managing their conflicts.

There are also grey areas, most particularly in relation to directors and senior executives pursuing unlikely or unfeasible alternative solutions or strategic options that would personally benefit them. While lenders would be delighted if such outcomes could be delivered, they have the experience to make realistic assessments and understand the correlation between time wasting and value destruction.

Lenders tend to handle such situations by imposing milestones as conditions of their support, for example, if new, lower-ranking funding does not materialise within 60 days, the board will abandon its fundraising efforts and focus on selling the business. They might also impose a tougher condition, requiring the board to constitute a strategic options committee which will have sole responsibility for considering all alternatives, making its recommendations to the board and providing its minutes to the lenders.

The reason that lenders have to go to such lengths, in such a circuitous fashion, is that they are fearful of becoming shadow directors, which would be embarrassing for the institutions and possibly leave the individual employees open to personal liability. Shadow directors are generally regarded as people from whom the directors (of the borrower) are accustomed to taking instructions.

There is greater sensitivity where the borrower is a public company, because there is the additional reputational risk in that investors could claim that the lenders' actions had exacerbated their losses.

The costs of restructuring

Directors experiencing their first financial crisis and restructuring can often be surprised at how expensive the process is. Some are naïve enough to complain to the lenders, hoping that they can shame them into somehow reducing the costs. This is guaranteed to seriously dent the complainant's credibility!

But in addition, and as we will see later, there is a strong (inverse) correlation between how effectively the borrower's directors manage the crisis and conduct the restructuring on the one hand, and the cost of the process on the other.

The fact is that restructuring is a very costly business. It used to be said, anecdotally, that the cost averaged 4% of the annual turnover of the business being restructured. One business I was engaged by had, in a prior restructuring, incurred restructuring costs nearer to 20% of turnover!

To the costs incurred directly by the borrower for its own advisers must be added the fees charged by the various advisers to the lenders (which in terms of the facility documents will all have to be borne by the borrower) along with fees and additional interest costs that the lenders impose.

Likewise, the other financial stakeholders who, if they do

not already have the contractual right to have their advisers' fees paid by the business, will likely soon acquire such a right as a condition of their continuing support.

From the lenders' perspective, any new money is going to be at much greater risk than it would have been before the crisis and if they are exposed to equity risk they will seek equity-type returns. They also need to be compensated for the intensive work put in by their risk people, who bring specialised skillsets.

What used to happen behind the scenes is that the lenders who led the syndicates and resourced the restructuring received a greater share of the fees than those lenders who remained passive. Nowadays the picture is mixed and it is not uncommon for advisers to take on a co-ordination role.

In a sense, the process whereby the borrower pays the advisory costs is smoke and mirrors. In fact, although the borrower is bearing the costs, the lenders are funding them through increasing the debt in the final restructuring. What they are in effect doing is increasing the share of value that will be theirs if the equity value recovers.

Hedging agreements

Having a hedging agreement in place allows a business to manage the risks of volatility, typically in commodity prices, interest rates and exchange rates.

A common example, ahead of the global financial crisis, was that over the life of a term loan the LIBOR rate would not move out of the band 2% to 7%. Hence, if LIBOR dropped below 2%, which it subsequently did, the borrower would be disadvantaged by having to pay interest to lenders based on the spot LIBOR rate and in addition the difference between that rate and 2% to the hedge provider. The assumed capital balance of the loan at each interest payment date, until maturity, was built into the hedging agreement.

Such a contract would be described as 'out of the money', and the only way it could be broken would be for the borrower to pay out, in cash, a break fee calculated by reference to its remaining life and the differential between LIBOR and the spot rate at the time. In many cases, that amounted to a material sum.

It is common to find that such hedging contracts are structurally either the most senior of all the borrower's debts or rank *pari passu* (a Latin term that means on an equal footing) with the most senior lenders. This in turn means that no debt restructuring would be possible unless the agreements were settled by paying the break fee in full. This usually takes place just before completion of any transaction.

4

FINANCIAL ADVISERS

The London restructuring advisory market is opaque, even to those working within it.

There are firms that offer restructuring services to borrowers and firms that offer them to lenders.

The former tend to be niche, high-powered and very expensive financial advisory boutiques, housed within investment banks. They work almost exclusively on large, complex cases.

By contrast, firms that advise lenders and take insolvency appointments are accountancy firms, spin-offs or hybrids. In terms of the size of the businesses they serve, most cover the whole spectrum. I have worked opposite some of the leading lending advisory professionals and they are very capable people who do an excellent job for their clients, sometimes under difficult circumstances.

Within their restructuring businesses the lender advisory firms may have established niche practices that advise borrowers. But some advise borrowers on an opportunistic basis.

Such firms have always needed to maintain large permanent establishments to win lucrative insolvency mandates, which can appear suddenly or unexpectedly. Offering lender advisory work is a way for them both to win formal insolvency appointments and to generate more revenue in a smoother fashion, off the same cost base, using employees with transferable skillsets.

But this entails committing to significant fixed costs and therefore high operational gearing. Consequently, a cyclical reduction in the volume of bank lender work and increasing regulatory restrictions on work that individual firms cannot do – as has happened in recent years – means a way has to be found for these expensive heads to earn revenue from other sources. This has been exacerbated by the spin-off and hybrid firms and the financial advisory boutiques gaining a significant share of the growing non-bank lending market.

Hence the opportunistic offering of restructuring advisory services to borrowers. But, understandably, their long-term interests lie with lenders who, unlike corporates facing a one-off crisis, will be a source of repeat business. This presents serious potential pitfalls for the board of a borrower that buys a brand-name adviser because 'no one ever got fired for buying IBM'.

The large accountancy firms tend to take on and train both graduates and recently qualified accountants, making use of the 'leverage model', in other words, deploying teams with a mix of experience. By contrast, the staff in spin-off and hybrid firms tend to be more experienced.

The role of the senior people is to win work and oversee its delivery by their teams. In my view, the firms' incentive models keep them under constant pressure to bring in work and maximise fees from the engagements they have won through 'scope creep' and by introducing specialist colleagues.

The boom in the preceding 25 or so years had resulted in the marketplace carrying a sizeable number of insolvency and lender advisory professionals. However, the sharp market contraction has left a considerable number of them facing an increasingly uncertain future.

In response, some of the accountancy firms have aggressively downsized their restructuring practices. The spin-offs and hybrids have recruited selectively from the accountancy firms. Many individuals have simply left the profession.

One tactic of the advisory firms to defend revenue has been what might be termed the Trojan Horse: a firm will start acting for a borrower and then switch to taking an insolvency appointment, with lenders in the driving seat.

Another defensive tactic has been to create a borrower-side restructuring advisory offering. I believe this has a number of serious shortcomings, which can prove expensive, even fatal, for unwary borrowers.

Firstly, firms that provide insolvency and lender advisory services do not employ independent restructuring professionals. Over the years, a few firms have run experiments, but these have been short-lived. Furthermore, there are regulations, introduced in the wake of Enron, that prohibit audit firm employees from making executive decisions within client organisations.

Secondly, in my view, the requirement that these firms have to make the leverage model work is simply incompatible with the needs of borrowers in restructuring. And, given the rates that are charged, this offers poor value for money.

Thirdly, I believe only a limited subset of the skills that insolvency and lender advisory professionals possess may be relevant to a borrower's needs.

All of this is borne out by the fact that between roughly 2000 and 2015, when the vast majority of restructuring work by accountancy firms was performed for lenders, they maintained panels of independent restructuring professionals and introduced them to borrowers, without charge, both directly and via banks. This was a practice driven by the UK lending banks.

Until the current oversupply of such advisers is addressed, either by an increase in demand or a reduction in supply, the market is likely to continue evolving, all the more so if politicians and regulators follow through on threats to break up the Big Four accountancy firms.

Unsuccessful M&A attempts have offered clues to potential future developments. A few years ago, Alvarez & Marsal's offer to acquire KPMG's restructuring services was rebuffed. More recently, it is rumoured that FTI Consulting's offer to acquire PwC's restructuring business was voted down by the firm's wider partnership.

To recap, restructuring advisory firms in the London market, with their roots in accountancy and insolvency, principally serve lenders and this is reflected in the skillsets of the vast majority of the senior individuals that work for them.

These insights into the restructuring advisory community may be helpful.

It is a relatively small community, in which news travels fast through personal networks, and where people exchange intelligence under the radar about potential opportunities. It is not dissimilar to the African savannah, where, once word gets out that a pride of lions is stalking a herd of wildebeest, every animal in the vicinity, from the hyenas down to the ants, starts to lick its chops.

Advisers know that every financial stakeholder in a sizeable restructuring will likely appoint at least one adviser: not just the borrower and the lenders, but every class of lender, the pension trustees and any other stakeholders with material interests, such as surety providers, regulators and major customers. So they will keep probing and pressing until all the slots are filled.

Advisory firms will go to great lengths to win a role. They receive high quality sales training and are likely to support their pitch with slick presentations, prepared by specialist teams.

All the larger advisory firms have teams that immediately mobilise when the jungle drums start beating. If a business suffers a crisis, its name will be added to the list of hot leads. A profile will be built using research gleaned from Companies House, Google, LinkedIn and other sources, including expensive subscription services that provide financial histories and calculate distress indicators.

The senior people will start working the phones, calling

lenders and complementary professionals, as well as competitors that are known to have already secured a role. They will also seek to establish whether colleagues in their firm's other service lines have existing relationships with any of the borrower's directors, senior executives or stakeholders and they will look to leverage off those by securing introductions to decision-makers. If a firm is conflicted from taking a role, buddies will pass on intelligence to their competitor buddies, under informal reciprocal arrangements.

If a borrower's situation is large and complex, it could soon feature in Debtwire and Reorg, subscription-only restructuring industry news services that are very skilled at gathering intelligence through their networks. Advisers have been known to use such publications to promote their expertise or even go on fishing expeditions.

Act in haste, repent at leisure

The appointment of the wrong financial adviser can prove to be a costly, or even fatal, error for a borrower. If their shortcomings in the early stages do not become apparent until the intense final phase it will be too late to replace them. This can and does lead to the best option being abandoned in the home straight, after months of work, and a suboptimal outcome being pursued instead.

If that involves the business entering an insolvency process, the directors will get the blame and be left to deal with the fallout while the advisers will walk away with their fees, unless an element of them was linked to a successful outcome. If part of the cause was the rate at which the advisory fees consumed the available cash, then that would add insult to injury.

While lenders have been known to conduct reviews into work that their advisers have done – and complaints about lawyers can be made to the Law Society – there is no corresponding mechanism for routinely exposing substandard financial advisory work in restructuring. Advisers thus have little to fear except some reputational damage in the lending community and fleeting adverse publicity. They might also find themselves being pursued by a liquidator, but this is highly unlikely.

Even if an adviser's work for a borrower was to be reviewed, being able to say that they had acted on instructions from the directors would probably hold water as a credible defence. All of which underlines the need for a borrower's directors and executives to be robust in directing advisers and overseeing their costs. Advisers cannot act in a vacuum; they need clients from whom to take instructions.

Lender-side advisers

For a borrower entering a financial crisis or restructuring, it is highly relevant to know which firms its lenders are considering appointing, not least to avoid informal conversations with firms that are pitching for a lender-side role, because there will be nothing to stop them using to their advantage any information they can glean.

If the lenders are predominantly UK-based banks, only firms that could take an insolvency appointment would make the shortlist and both the financial and the legal advisers would have to be members of the lenders' panels in order to be considered. This arrangement is aimed at ensuring that the advisers have a threshold level of capabilities. It also reduces costs as panel firms have to charge discounted rates.

The lenders' shortlist would almost certainly include those Big Four accountancy firms that are not conflicted, for example, as auditors of the borrower. But some of the other names may be unfamiliar to a director experiencing their first restructuring.

FTI Consulting is highly regarded in the London restructuring market and of late has been enjoying spectacular success. The firm does not do audit, does not advise borrowers and nor does it provide operational consulting. The insolvency services it offers are tactical. Its ability to lead and coordinate syndicates is also valued by lenders.

AlixPartners is a consultancy that expanded from the US in the early 2000s and originally did only borrower-side operational consultancy work. After losing key staff in Europe, it bought a London-based insolvency and lender advisory firm and now offers a spectrum of non-audit services to both borrowers and lenders, including insolvency.

Alvarez & Marsal had the same origins and offers similar services. Since its unsuccessful attempt to buy KPMG's restructuring services it has begun building a Big Four-type advisory business.

The financial advisory boutiques, mainly housed in investment banks, also advise non-bank lenders and bondholders in large and complex situations. They do not do insolvency or consultancy and typically provide a small team to work strategically.

Norms, protocols and tips

Under the lending agreement, the borrower will be

responsible for paying the lenders' advisers. Other stakeholders may have similar contractual rights. Those without such rights may negotiate similar arrangements during the course of the restructuring. To give effect to this, the borrower will usually be a party to the contractual arrangements between each stakeholder and its advisers.

If the adviser is on a lender's or other stakeholder's panel, it would be reasonable for the adviser's rates charged to be in accordance with panel rates.

VAT invoiced by stakeholders' UK-based advisers is not recoverable by a borrower, as it is not the party to which the services have been supplied.

A payment to an adviser is not a preference if it is a condition of the adviser performing the work that its fees will be paid on specified terms. Indeed, you should not be surprised if an adviser tells you they will need to suspend work if they are not paid on time.

Lenders will expect to have matching advisers involved in any meetings or conversations. So, unless it has been agreed in advance, do not expect them to meet you if you arrive with an adviser and theirs is not present!

5

INDEPENDENT RESTRUCTURING PROFESSIONALS

Independent restructuring professionals are individuals who are hired by the boards of UK companies in financial crises and restructurings to help deliver solutions that keep businesses out of insolvency. In the distant past, they were known as company doctors. Vaunted predecessors include Lord David James, the late Peter Middleton, the late Sir Alastair Morton and Sir Michael Edwardes.

Are CROs and independent restructuring professionals synonymous?

The term CRO is frequently used in restructuring. It is vague and is understood to be an acronym for Chief Restructuring Officer. It does not help that the term CRO is also used in the pharmaceuticals industry (Chief Research Officer), in financial services (Chief Risk Officer) and in corporates generally (Chief Revenue Officer)!

In the world of restructuring, the term originated in the US, where it has a precise legal meaning. In that country, CROs are officers of the courts, appointed when a business is either in or on the brink of insolvency. At the time of writing, the Wikipedia entry only describes the US concept.

It gained currency in the London restructuring market in the mid-2000s and today is used imprecisely alongside synonyms such as 'turnaround director' and 'turnaround practitioner'. Branded restructuring advisory firms and retired insolvency practitioners offer CRO services - typically these are relatively narrow stakeholder management roles, sometimes in combination with ancillary services such as cash forecasting.

What would be a less confusing description of what independent restructuring professionals do?

As detailed in Chapter 10, the board's appointment of a leader with a scope tailored to the situation is possibly the most important decision it will take. At its widest, the scope of such a leader's responsibilities would encompass governance, stakeholder management and operations. To provide clarity in this book, I have referred the person who fills this leadership role as a Ringmaster.

Although others could fill the leadership role, independent restructuring professionals make ideal Ringmasters.

What roles do independent restructuring professionals take?

Today there are perhaps 15 independent restructuring professionals capable of taking on large and complex Ringmaster assignments, all of them London-centric and based at home.

There are also independent restructuring professionals, many of them based in the regions, who take on the

Ringmaster role in smaller situations and who, in the role of point person, could support the Ringmaster in larger and more complex situations.

Independent restructuring professionals' modus operandi

By definition, independent restructuring professionals are not branded; their names are their brands and typically they have spent decades honing their craft and building their networks.

In the London market they are known by their individual reputations, built on a track record of serially and successfully delivering outcomes that have protected, even on occasions unexpectedly created, value.

They are authentically independent, in that they are interested only in the health and survival of the business. In financial crisis and restructuring situations, their agenda is simply to help the board achieve a successful outcome. And, once that is achieved, all of them would expect to leave. But, if asked, some might stay involved, either as pure non-executive chairmen or directors or in hybrid roles to help remedy the causes of the financial crisis or oversee the implementation of a break-up or an operational restructuring.

Finding independent restructuring professionals

Headhunters are unlikely to have independent restructuring professionals on their books, not only because their esoteric skillsets will not be in demand under normal circumstances but also because the appointment timescale and the bespoke and unconventional nature of the job spec tend not to be compatible with the way headhunters typically work.

As it would not be feasible for independent restructuring professionals, who operate from home under their own individual brands, to market their services directly to corporates, they find their work through word-of-mouth recommendations, typically from investors, lenders and restructuring advisers. Hence, networking is an important activity for them.

For many years, introductions flowed to independent restructuring professionals from firms that advise lenders; the larger firms maintained panels and introduced individuals to borrowers, without charge, both directly and via lenders. But, as explained in Chapter 4, these introductions largely dried up along with bank-introduced work in about 2015. Since then, some of the lender advisory firms have taken to offering their own employees in the place of independent restructuring professionals.

Partly in response to this development, 12 senior and reputable independent restructuring professionals, all well-known and highly regarded in the London restructuring community, set up the London Restructuring Network (LRN). I must declare my interest: I am a founder member of the LRN.

It is an informal and non-commercial organisation that exists primarily to enable its members to showcase their capabilities and to maintain a profile with those in the restructuring community who might potentially introduce them to work opportunities. This is done by arranging several discreet and low-key networking events each year, the majority hosted by financial advisers and law firms.

The LRN does not operate a website, because the majority

of its members have found it expedient not to court publicity.

How do boards benefit from hiring them?

Later in this book, particularly in Chapter 10 on Leadership and in Part V on the Ringmaster's art, the roles that they can fill are outlined and there is detailed coverage of the work that typically forms part of their agreed scope. The benefits of boards hiring independent restructuring professionals are also explained.

How does the appointment of independent restructuring professionals benefit lenders?

Independent restructuring professionals have never been engaged by lenders, only by borrowers. Nevertheless, their appointment mitigates lenders' concerns about a borrower's board and executive team not being able to successfully deliver an optimum outcome in challenging circumstances, in particular, if they lack the skills, experience or bandwidth.

Despite the sound logic of appointing an independent restructuring professional to the role of Ringmaster, borrowers can sometimes be reluctant to do so. Possibly because incumbent senior executives feel threatened or exposed by the prospect of experienced individuals joining the board or senior team in unfamiliar circumstances. Mostly, such fears are visceral and can quickly recede once the benefits of the Ringmaster's experience, expertise, network and relationships become evident.

If lenders have concerns that would be allayed by the appointment of a Ringmaster, they will generally wait for a borrower's board to act first. If the board is slow or reluctant to do so, lenders might raise the issue. If the board still does not act, the lenders will have the option to force the issue by making such an appointment a condition of their continuing support. However, they would typically insist on the principle of the appointment but not an individual and they might introduce up to three independent restructuring professionals to the board as Ringmaster candidates. In such circumstances, a borrower's board would usually be free to introduce its own candidates into the process and if such a candidate were preferred the lenders would have to be satisfied as to the suitability of that candidate before the appointment could be finalised.

How do independent restructuring professionals charge?

Independent restructuring professionals are paid fees by the day, week or month. And if a way is found to align interests, that is measurable, transparent and mutually fair, then it is common to reduce the time-based rate and introduce an element that is linked to progress or outcomes.

6

INTERIM EXECUTIVES

In the UK, there are a small number of battle-hardened interim executives with specialist skillsets, expertise in fixing broken back offices and experience of working in restructuring situations.

They are able to climb a learning curve quickly while staying above corporate politics. For them, a new project is not a career move, it is a job to be done, which they will do to the best of their ability and which they intend to leave as soon as they have delivered a durable fix that has put the right people in the right roles, well trained and with capable leadership.

They comprehend the pressures of time and money in distressed situations. They understand the lenders' mindset. They are versatile and possess a very well-developed sense of what good looks like. All of this enables them to diagnose problems rapidly, design pragmatic solutions and implement them, hands-on and leading from the front.

The way they design and implement a solution will not

involve detailed project plans, Powerpoint presentations and long meetings. Rather, they operate mainly by changing how the people above, below and around them work. When they step into a situation they immediately acquire a number of direct reports, the majority of whom take to them within days and get right behind them, recognising their valuable experience and their commitment to making things better.

They work closely with and mentor those people, identifying and addressing gaps in knowledge and training. They fix systems and processes and introduce meaningful KPIs, so that backlogs are reduced and more reliable management information is produced more quickly. From that base, they look at resourcing, structures and leadership.

Then, with the involvement of HR, they draw up proper job descriptions, recruit as necessary, and work to ensure that all the roles are filled by people with appropriate skills and experience, who are paid fairly, incentivised sensibly and have up-to-date employment contracts.

When this has been delivered, they can go home for a well-earned rest and wait for the next call.

Finding such high calibre specialists is not easy. They tend to be in constant demand. Moreover, they tend not to do any networking of their own or to be on the books of mainstream agencies. They can be confident that those who know what they are capable of will keep them busy.

There is a misconception that interim executives are more expensive than permanent staff. To do the comparison, it is necessary to calculate the fully loaded cost of hiring a permanent employee for three years, including recruitment fee, salary, bonuses, employer's pension and payroll costs and any termination costs at the end of the three years. Then calculate a day rate, working on 44 weeks a year and five days a week, which accounts for public holidays, statutory holiday entitlement and a week a year off sick.

A useful ready reckoner is to multiply an interim executive's day rate by 150. To illustrate this: an interim executive on a day rate of £1,000 would cost the same as a permanent employee on a base salary of £150,000 with a 20% annual bonus. This gives a very different answer from somebody inexperienced who immediately multiplies the day rate by all the weekdays in the year – no holidays, no sick leave – and, in the example given, would arrive at an equivalent base salary of £260,000!

What also needs to be taken into account is that the day rate is not the interim executive's take home pay or even gross salary: it has to fund pension and payroll taxes, too, and a portion has to be set aside to fill the income gap between jobs and when on holiday.

Caveat emptor!

These specialists should not be confused with the tens of thousands of interim executives in the UK, most of whom work in vanilla situations, typically filling gaps, resourcing projects and providing maternity cover. I would like to think that most agencies handling such interim executives would be honest enough to say the people on their books were not suitable for a financial crisis and restructuring.

However, there are several pitfalls for the unwary. An agency may simply be a body shop seeking to maximise its revenue. It may proffer ineffective interim executives who are really looking for a permanent role and who will milk any situation for as long as they can, without actually fixing anything. Even worse, interim executives supplied by such agencies may have concealed conflicts of interest in the form a share of the margin on all placements that they introduce. Some agencies will gouge the truly naïve still further. I was shocked to come across a situation in which a business had signed up to a rolling 12-month commitment on each interim executive, a 30% margin, a 'search surcharge' in the initial six months and break a fee of £50,000 if the interim executive was made permanent! As there were a dozen or so interim executives from this agency in place when I arrived, I suspect the first few through the door had a tidy little earner on the side so that the business was getting a raw deal twice over!

.

7

PRIVATE EQUITY

In dealing here with private equity, we are talking about buyout investors, rather than those interested in venture or growth capital.

The acquisition debt market

M&A activity sponsored by buyout investors has become a significant feature of the investment landscape in the UK economy. The business model relies on the availability of acquisition debt. Lenders love the new business volumes that private equity generates for them and also the fact that, as professional investors, the private equity managers fill the 'sponsor' role: finding deals, funding advisers and arranging debt, with the objective of growing the value of the business acquired and typically exiting within five years.

In effect, private equity investors use lenders' balance sheets for the period that they hold an investment, for the purpose of turbocharging their returns through the operation of the leverage effect. Their downside risk is limited by the lenders securing only the assets and future cash flows of the business being acquired.

Buyout M&A activity is cyclical. Through the global financial crisis, markedly fewer deals were done because acquisition finance was scarce and buyout firms had to commit a higher proportion of equity. But the quantitative easing that was introduced in the aftermath has seen a proliferation of new, non-bank lenders enter the acquisition debt market, deploying funds invested by institutions and family offices hunting for fixed-income yield in a low interest rate environment.

At the time of writing, the acquisition debt market is still in this very liquid part of the cycle. The competition between lenders has suppressed their returns and the abundance of supply has shifted bargaining power to private equity investors who have been able to negotiate progressively weaker lender protections in the form of lighter covenants and fewer (or no) triggers. When (not if) things go wrong again, these lax lending terms will make it difficult for workout bankers to do their jobs.

(As an aside, this bears similarities with the market in 2007, ahead of the global financial crisis. However, it is not clear whether the next downturn would have as dramatic an impact, because much more of the money at risk belongs to insurers, pension funds and wealthy families. Any losses would cause them solvency rather liquidity issues, which in 2007/08 caused debt holders to rush for the exit in order to liquidate the loans they had taken to fund their leveraged bets.)

Because private equity invests on a portfolio basis, with losses limited by the total equity in each, it is reasonable to expect that a proportion of their deals will go sour and therefore that some proportion of the debt provided will never be recovered. As competition for deals pushes up acquisition prices and investee companies are more thinly capitalised in a liquid debt market, it may become evident when the cycle next turns that credit fund managers have been mispricing new debt issuance.

When the equity is wiped out

Inexperience and a lack of business acumen on the part of individual fund manager employees who make investments and are responsible for the investees' governance can be significant factors in deals going sour. This can happen in a number of ways: through overpaying, selecting the wrong management team or being oblivious to back-office shortcomings. But there is also sometimes a failure to understand the direct causal link between good governance and value and the enormous contribution that a properly functioning board can make to value creation.

Over the years, I have experienced shocking negligence in this sphere. Admittedly, I have not been exposed to a representative sample as I only get involved in situations that have gone badly wrong. What is concerning is that a management consultancy mindset seems to have progressively permeated some fund managers' thinking. This sees individual investments being managed by a team of fund manager employees interacting one-on-one with the senior executives in pursuit of a short-term value creation plan, with the board existing on paper only.

It may be that such 'light-touch' governance arrangements appeal to management teams that have grown weary of the bureaucracy of life in a public company. And, of course, there may be some success stories which I would be unlikely to be aware of. But, of course, success for the selling fund might mean disaster for the buying fund if the music stops in the markets and underlying problems in the investee business have never been addressed.

Someone I interviewed recently told me about a situation like this that they had worked in. It had been a very stressful experience. A big-name investor had bought a distressed business but did not operate a board at all. The only formality was a weekly sales call attended by dozens of people, who spent a significant proportion of the call arguing about where the reported numbers had come from! When the business was failing, there was a leadership vacuum and a financial adviser brought in provided what might charitably be described as very expensive palliative care.

In theory, when there is an equity shortfall, a private equity investor could cure it by injecting new money equity, and it is common for debt facility agreements to contain terms that permit covenant breaches to be cured in this way. But the investor may have reasons for not wanting or being able to do so, some of which are understandable. For the directors of a private equity investee business in a financial crisis and restructuring, the loss of equity value and a refusal or inability by the investor to provide more can create a difficult dynamic.

This can be exacerbated by the fact that, for as long as it owns the majority of utterly worthless equity, a private equity investor retains a free option through its ability to control the board and to change the directors and management. Moreover, if its representatives constitute a majority of directors, the board may be prevented from fulfilling its proper role, especially if the employees of the fund manager try to usurp the role of the board in managing the financial crisis and restructuring despite their inexperience and conflicts.

Essentially, the issue here is a divergence of interests. The investor may lack any motivation to resolve the situation. Perhaps because in terms of the impact on the portfolio, there would be no economic benefit to putting any effort into a lost cause. Or it may not want unhelpful details to be discovered by potential investors conducting due diligence on its current efforts to raise a new fund. Conversely, the investor may be very aggressive, perhaps because a poor outcome will impact directly on its carry in a fund nearing or beyond the end of its realisation phase. This might result in attempts to achieve unrealistic outcomes in a restructuring, such as a sale at a good price to an unwitting buyer or the lenders taking a haircut.

The latter expectation would most likely be based on the commercial leverage that the fund manager enjoys over particular lending institutions, in view of their targets for new loan origination business that would be harder to achieve if the relationship soured.

Lenders can be susceptible to this and it can therefore become an internal issue that interferes with the effective management of a situation by a professional workout manager. One of the changes they have had to live with in recent years, driven by sensitivity to conduct risk, is relationship colleagues remaining involved in a situation where previously it was typical for the management of all aspects of a lending relationship to be moved to workout.

For a workout manager this results in the need to manage another stakeholder, with a different angle, giving the borrower opportunities to divide and conquer.

The position of directors

Private equity sponsors tend to appoint non-executive directors from their own ranks or from among current or former executives who possess sector experience. When everything is going swimmingly, it can be a satisfying and rewarding experience. But when the equity has been wiped out, or there is a need for new money and the sponsor cannot or will not inject cash, the resulting crisis and financial restructuring can be very uncomfortable.

The main difficulties are rooted in the behaviour of the private equity sponsor and its failure to properly manage its conflicts. Legally, all of the directors, both individually and collectively, will have duties under the Companies Act to promote the success of the company and protect the interests of all stakeholders, not just the shareholders. And when a company enters the zone of insolvency, the directors' primary duty switches from shareholders to creditors. In particular, they have a responsibility to minimise those creditors' losses.

At that juncture, a sponsor acting in a socially responsible way would be expected to withdraw to the wings, remove its people from the board, not extract any further cash from the investee and fully cooperate with the lenders in order to minimise their losses, if necessary finding and appointing a Ringmaster to help the independent directors fulfil their duties.

However, some sponsors consider their responsibilities to be narrow and to extend only to their investors, which leads them to behave in different ways. Each director has a personal decision to make about whether to stay on the board or resign. The guidance in Chapter 21 may be useful for those in such a situation.

Large and complex situations involving widely held debt

Established, deposit-taking lending institutions tend to limit their exposure to private equity deals by operating in a different way on larger deals because their risk and return are impacted, on the one hand, by the low margins prevalent in a liquid market and, on the other, by the potential difficulties posed by how sponsors would behave if the borrower businesses have to be restructured.

Their involvement in debt issuance on new deals or refinancings is limited to arranging and doing the deals and then syndicating them in the form of selling parcels to credit funds, which are deploying funds invested by institutions and wealthy families. This earns them fees both upfront and on an ongoing basis. In this, they compete with direct lenders who are credit funds willing to 'write the whole cheque', quickly but at a higher cost.

Lending institutions also provide revolving facilities, which credit funds are not able to do, on a very low-risk basis by taking the highest ranking priority in the security structure. Such involvement also gives them opportunities to offer the provision of other revenue-generating services such as money transmission and credit card merchanting services.

Thus, over time, deposit-taking lending institutions have had less and less involvement restructuring private equity-owned businesses. Instead, a borrower's board will find itself having to deal with either a direct lender that ought to do the same job as a traditional workout lender in an established institution, or with restructuring advisers acting for a group of credit funds that either participated in the syndication of the debt or more recently bought a par holding at a discount.

It can happen that one or a handful of such funds will hold a significant or dominant position, either because they are par lenders or because they have bought in with a loan-to-own strategy.

It can also happen that the par lenders and the secondary buyers will be separate groups each with their own advisers!

Debt buyers with more liquid strategies, who tend to be in the majority, will not want to adversely impact their ability to sell, which means that they do not want a significant stake that could potentially move the market or be difficult to sell quickly, and they do not want to 'go private'.

The opposite of going private is 'staying public', that is you possess no information not already in the public domain. Traditionally, this was only relevant to publicly traded debt such as bonds, but increasingly it can impact on private debt as well.

The board of a company involved in a restructuring of this sort needs to be very careful not to inadvertently supply private information to a debt holder who wants to remain public. If this happens, one solution is to cleanse the information by making it public, which can potentially prejudice the restructuring efforts.

The legal and financial advisers appointed by the debt

holders will, in part, take on the role of a principal in negotiating the terms of a restructuring.

It will feel like an odd process, in which lenders will stay public throughout the restructuring process until the home straight when, having locked up or agreed to not trade for only a small window, they will be taken 'over the wall' to scrutinise and hopefully bless terms that the advisers have negotiated on their behalf. Following which all the information they have seen will be announced, alongside the terms of the deal.

PART III

The Practice

8

THE IMMEDIATE RESPONSE

Unless the trigger is an act of God, the first casualty of a financial crisis is management credibility.

Confidence in the board will be shaped by the extent to which the directors knew what was coming – and, if they did not, whether they should have known. If the crisis developed over time, some may conclude that the board misjudged the risks or failed to manage the situation as well as it might have done.

Either way, the manner in which the board responds in the immediate aftermath of the crisis – sharing the information that it has, in particular, on what it has uncovered about the crisis and what remedial action it recommends – will be key to underpinning the confidence of capital providers.

Priorities for the board

There needs to be an initial assessment of how bad the situation is, how long the business is likely to survive and what can be done to improve survival prospects and buy more time.

In exceptional circumstances, the outcome may be a decision to file for insolvency as soon as practically possible. It is likely, however, that survival will be the more responsible course for the board to take, at least until there are sufficient facts available to make an evaluation with an acceptable level of confidence. Often, the board has more time in the initial stages than it realises. But, to use that time wisely, it should focus, in order, on three broad key issues: judgements, organisation and changes to the modus operandi.

Judgements

Achieving consensus on the way forward is essential. This should minimise the chance of setting misguided priorities that, if pursued, could waste such runway, time and headroom as the board has at the outset. A conventional 'roadmap' in response to a crisis involves: stabilisation; then financial restructuring (or business sale); and then operational restructuring, with each phase being concluded before the next is started.

The key stakeholders, and their likely major concerns, need to be identified and agreed upon. Where appropriate, the list should include pensions trustees, regulators and ratings agencies.

Critical survival information that will be needed by the board and financial stakeholders needs to be agreed and prioritised.

A provisional timetable to achieve stabilisation, in particular the schedule for the first two to three weeks, should be agreed.

Work on gaining access to information and identifying the causes of the crisis needs to start straight away.

Organisation

Ideally, the board should set up a small ad hoc committee to which day-to-day management of the restructuring is delegated. The committee's first task should be to assign responsibilities and plan delivery, based on the judgements agreed by the wider group. A key issue for the committee is going to be leadership of the crisis stabilisation and financial restructuring processes, to be provided either by an incumbent or by a specialist hired in from outside. In earlier chapters, such a leader has been identified as the Ringmaster.

That leader should spearhead the selection and engagement of financial advisers. An important consideration is whether work on gaining access to information and identifying the causes of the crisis will form part of the leader's scope. With guidance from the leader, the committee should also take the lead on selecting and engaging legal advisers and establishing what Directors and Officers (D&O) insurance cover exists. At the same time, a board communication protocol should be agreed so that the other directors, who will be anxious to be kept in the loop, can stay informed without getting in the way.

Modification of the modus operandi

If the executive team still enjoys the confidence of the board, it might be intuitive to give them a leading role in managing the financial crisis and restructuring. However, it will be more important than ever for them to be focused on managing the performance of the business and communicating with key non-financial stakeholders, including customers, suppliers, regulators and the unions. So a balance needs to be found and the chairman and some of the non-executives will have to both increase their own level of support to the executives and free up their time by de-cluttering the board's agenda and putting non-essential issues that survive on the back burner.

Another urgent task will be to identify and fill gaps in people, skills and experience – on the board, among senior executives and in the finance team.

If the non-executives have lost confidence in senior executives or the whole team, their decision-making will be more complex, particularly if those executives are under suspicion or if the board has decided to suspend, terminate or scaffold some or all them.

Engaging with lenders

When the bombshell of the crisis has dropped, it is important to maintain utmost confidentiality for as long as possible (and, if a listed company, permissible), so that the board can make an assessment. Other than equity owners in a privately owned business, the first people who should be informed are the most senior lenders. It is imperative that they do not hear from anyone else first so the time available for informing them may be as little as a few days.

Although there will be many different concerns, liquidity must be the most important, in particular, how long might the business last with the cash available to it? The answer to this question largely defines how big or small the problem is.

It is important to get this right at the outset. Lenders will not be impressed if facts emerge further down the line that contradict the board's initial assessment. It will be understood that time will be needed to gather the facts, but when they do become available it would be unhelpful if it transpired that the business had either cried wolf or underestimated the seriousness of the situation.

So the board's most urgent priority is to make an assessment of liquidity and the threats that would reduce what is available. There are three elements to this: cash balances and unutilised facilities currently available, such as headroom on overdrafts; breaches or potential breaches of the debt facilities, especially covenants, that could result in undrawn facilities being made unavailable; and incomings and outgoings in the short term.

Although it is difficult to gauge at this very early stage, a downside case should, if possible, also be developed to show what would happen if customers, suppliers, credit insurers and others in the marketplace were to react unhelpfully.

Avoiding a drawstop

A big early decision for the board to make will be whether or not to fully draw down existing available headroom if there are revolving facilities that are at risk of being 'drawstopped', that is when lenders make headroom unavailable. If the board considers going down this route, then it needs to decide whether to do so before the first engagement with lenders. There may be no time to take specialist legal advice.

The key grounds for drawstopping are usually misrepresentation (where past reporting to lenders has been materially misstated) or reporting covenants as having been passed when they that had in fact failed and were thus in default at the time representations were made. It is reasonable to assume that lenders will waive them in due course and, if required, deal with potential future covenant breaches as part of the arrangements necessary to achieve stability. But for the immediate future they are unidentified and therefore have not been waived.

The best interests of the business, which will be aligned with the interests of the lenders, may be served by drawing down the cash and having it securely in the bank, thereby removing doubts about whether the lenders will or will not drawstop a facility. Any doubt about access to cash would be likely to undermine the confidence of customers, credit insurers and others in the marketplace, once the news got out.

In my experience, providing the cash is not used to improve the position of equity or lower-ranking creditors, lenders are likely to silently thank the directors for not asking the question but instead going ahead and doing the deed, on the grounds that it will improve the business's survival prospects and also avoid both sides expending precious time and effort early in the process on what should be a no-brainer.

Although there is a downside risk of creating mistrust at the very start of the lender engagement, if the lenders feel very strongly about the issue, the business could volunteer to place the cash in a separate account and report on its use. In the worst case, it could simply be repaid.

9

THE INITIAL LENDER ENGAGEMENT

In planning the initial engagement with lenders, it is important to work out who will represent the business. If the non-executives have lost confidence in senior executives or, indeed, in the whole team, the non-executives will have to do so alone. If not, a mix of executive and non-executive directors would be the norm.

Dominant management teams will instinctively want to have the conversation alone, but that would send the wrong signals. Lenders rely on boards to protect their interests.

If the business is privately owned, the lenders would expect to hear from the shareholders as well, even if the message is simply that they remain supportive, will not draw any cash out of the business and will stay in the wings for the time being.

The agenda should be restricted to outlining the crisis, explaining how the board has mobilised in response, sharing an initial view of liquidity and agreeing the terms of a pause while the business pulls together better information and formulates a plan to achieve stability. If a drawstop is an issue, that needs to be discussed as well.

Lenders abhor shocks. But if bad news has to be delivered they will appreciate an early and thoughtful initial conversation that gives them more time to mobilise internally. More so if the meeting assures them that the directors are both gravely concerned and fully committed to resolving the situation.

As the board will not get a second chance to make a first impression, the planning and tactical approach to that initial engagement are critically important.

It is advisable to compress all of the initial contacts into a tight timescale. Usually contacting the relationship people first and then meeting with them along with any risk or workout colleagues they have invited. If someone representing the business has genuine restructuring experience and an authentic relationship with the lenders' senior workout people, a discreet call in parallel would be valuable.

It is vital to be well prepared for the first discussion with the lenders. The timing also needs to be finely judged. Do not go too soon. But do not wait too long – certainly do not delay until the board has engaged a full suite of advisers and started producing work, because that may look like an attempt to steal a march that has wasted valuable time that the lenders could have used to mobilise themselves.

Prepare and rehearse a succinct explanation that anticipates the questions the lenders are likely to have. Do not sugar-coat the story. Validate as many facts as possible beforehand, so as to have sufficient confidence in their veracity. It is acceptable to say you do not yet have all the answers, particularly about the precise cash outlook. The alternative is to create hostages to fortune that could hamper the board for a long time to come.

It is important to be aware of the very latest balances and available headroom on all bank accounts and facilities. Because that is the same information that the lenders will have checked on their way to the meeting.

At this stage, it would be both appropriate and advisable to share the board's early thinking about governance and advisers: the evaluation of its own restructuring experience and the possible need to bolster it; leadership roles and potential candidates; the advisers it is thinking of appointing; and its options or plans for strengthening the senior executive team and bolstering the finance team, in order to have sufficient situational experience as well as additional bandwidth.

The risk people involved will be quick to grasp the common threat inherent in the crisis situation and will thus be fully aligned in wanting to avoid value destruction. As such, they are likely to have valuable contributions to make in relation to these issues, which could have a critical impact on the eventual outcome.

A caveat to this is that workout bankers rely heavily on individual professionals in the insolvency and lender advisory firms and in a quiet market may have an interest in supporting those who have been short of work, to help them through the doldrums. This makes a second opinion, from someone independent, experienced and well networked, valuable.

At this early stage, both sides are still flying blind and will crave as much visibility as they can get. Hence, while the business works through the planned actions, there is considerable value to both sides in establishing a positive and constructive dialogue, aided by transparency and providing limited access to the lenders' advisers.

The initial engagement will usually conclude with a tentative date on which the board and the lenders will next meet and it is likely that it will be a formal engagement at which a comprehensive presentation will be delivered. It would be conventional for this to be prepared with assistance from the advisers to (be appointed by) the business and shared in advance with the lenders' advisers.

In parallel, developing information about liquidity will be shared on a regular basis.

10
___

LEADERSHIP

In managing a financial crisis and restructuring, possibly the most important decision a board makes will be in relation to leadership.

People in and around the situation will typically use various terms to describe this leader, including CRO and turnaround director. As explained in chapter 5, the term Ringmaster is used in this book, in order to provide clarity.

The Ringmaster could be either an incumbent – the chairman, a non-executive or an executive – or someone brought in from outside, such as an independent restructuring professional. In making the decision, it is important to recognise the additional time that the chairman and senior executives will need to spend on managing business performance and maintaining the relationships with key non-financial stakeholders.

Ideally, the Ringmaster will be a member of both the board and the executive team, have both the authority and the direct reports tailored for the needs of the situation and oversee all advisory and interim executive resources.

The Ringmaster should be a strong and decisive leader with deep business and situational experience and excellent organisational skills. Business transformation experience on its own, gained without being subject to the multiple pressures of time, dwindling liquidity and anxious, aggressive stakeholders, is unlikely to be a suitable substitute and could even be a disadvantage. Being known and respected by the lenders and their advisers would be an enormous advantage.

The leadership issue should have been on the board's agenda when it met to decide its immediate response and, again, in the initial engagement with lenders. Some early markers should thus already have been laid down. In some situations, a degree of consensus will have started to emerge.

There is little to be gained by delaying a decision for very long. Certainly, appointing financial advisers before deciding on the leadership could be a damaging mistake, perhaps even fatal.

The decision can be very challenging because it needs to be made quickly and under pressure, with little information to hand, by people lacking situational experience, while trying to balance the sensitivities and insecurities of the senior executives against the need to prevent them from inflicting further damage on the business (if it is believed that they are a big part of the problem).

Apart from anything else, this is a test of the board's authority and of its mettle. If the non-executives believe that the CEO bears prime responsibility for the crisis and have had growing concerns about performance or a failure to execute strategy, then in the interests of the business they need to be candid about what has to be done. The same applies to the CFO, although for possibly any number of different reasons. In addition, they need to consider whether the chairman is also part of the problem.

Clearly, any credibility problems are magnified if key stakeholders or the market at large share the board's views.

Leaving aside individuals' direct responsibility for the crisis (and consequent suspension or termination with cause) the difficulty the board faces is that it cannot feasibly part company with all three – chairman, CEO and CFO – at once, except in the most egregious circumstances. Scaffolding the executives (as explained in chapter 19) may provide a short-term solution; it is easier for a non-executive chairman to be sidelined.

In many situations, unless there are pressing reasons to part company with one or two of the three, the best course will be to resist the temptation to act hastily but instead, if possible, design the Ringmaster's scope to limit the downside risk pending a final decision on their futures. At the same time, they should be kept away from the leadership of the financial crisis and restructuring.

With a decision about that aspect made, it is important to consider very carefully what else should be included in the Ringmaster's scope and to create a unique and highly customised job spec. The starting point is an analysis of the situation. Then the weaknesses in both governance and executive management are overlaid. And finally the need to provide a pillar of support to the non-executives through a difficult period is factored in.

Getting from the job spec to the final appointment is likely to be a reiterative process. Most candidates in the tiny pool may be unavailable. Others may not be available immediately. Those on the shortlist will have different strengths and may have other time commitments.

More importantly, the initial job spec will be a long way from perfect and it will remain so until the chosen candidate has made an initial diagnostic assessment, which typically takes between three and six weeks. That should enable it to be finalised. It would not be unusual for the job spec to mutate into two or more. This is not as high-risk as it sounds, because suitable candidates will bring a wealth of experience. But, on the board's part, it does involve much more of a leap of faith than they will be used to.

Scope

The scope of the leadership role, or roles, can be summarised under the headings of: governance, stakeholder management and operational.

There are two facets to the *governance* element. One is overseeing and directing the processes and driving them from the borrower's side. The other is giving the stakeholders confidence that the governance of the business is effective, in particular that conflicts are being properly managed and the correct priorities are being focused on in challenging circumstances.

The *stakeholder management* role involves analysing and agreeing the borrower's needs and presenting and negotiating its position with its stakeholders. This is likely to cover the development of a revised capital structure, based on an updated business plan, the sourcing of capital, and varying the rights of numerous stakeholders.

The responsibilities within the *operational* role have at least four dimensions: the critical data that the financial stakeholders and the board will rely upon throughout the process; cash generation, cost cutting and other triage; a finance change programme that identifies administrative rot and delivers remedies in the very short term; and the permanent upgrade of the capabilities of the finance organisation. This is a hands-on role, so it is essential that it is filled by a decisive leader with deep business experience, a strong financial skillset, and a well-developed sense of what good looks like.

In smaller situations, it is usually feasible for all three elements to be included in the Ringmaster's scope. Conversely, in larger situations, one or more individuals might be appointed as the Ringmaster's point person, or people, each with responsibility for a specific element or parts of an element.

There is an art to calculating the capacity of the Ringmaster, to identifying the support that will be required and to judging which elements would best be provided by financial advisers and which by interim resources. In my experience, the only leadership role that financial advisers would have the credibility to fill is that of stakeholder management point person.

What titles are used?

Ringmaster describes the nature of the job and a person appointed to the role needs a specific title, which will likely reflect the sensitivities of a situation.

If the board wants to send a strong message in messy circumstances, it might plump for having the words 'restructuring' or 'turnaround' in the Ringmaster's title. But if the situation is ambiguous and it wants to avoid 'spooking' those in and outside of the business, the title would be anodyne, for example, 'independent director' or even 'planning manager'.

If appointed to the board, a Ringmaster's title would usually reflect the agreed authority and time commitment, covering the spectrum: non-executive chairman or director (part-time); executive director (full-time); or NED-Plus (a hybrid). A variation of the executive director title would be CEO, CFO or COO, if one of those positions were vacant and the relevant, associated responsibilities were incorporated within the Ringmaster's agreed scope.

A Ringmaster's point person with responsibility for stakeholder management could take the title CRO, as could a point person responsible for specified operational issues. If there were two or more point people, other titles would need to be found.

If no point people are appointed and the Ringmaster's role covers the stakeholder management and/or operational elements, in addition to governance, then, providing there were no sensitivities, the Ringmaster might take the title CRO.

One variation is Chief Restructuring Adviser, or simply Board Adviser, which would reflect non-director status and no element of executive responsibilities.

11

HIRING A RINGMASTER

In this chapter I am speaking directly to directors responsible for managing financial crises and restructurings. This is the advice I would give.

I appreciate that you may be reading this shortly after a crisis has been triggered and that it will be some time yet before the full extent of the implications for you, your board colleagues and the senior team become apparent.

If your instinctive reaction to the paragraphs below is that the candidate requirements recommended would be overkill in the particular situation in which you are involved, be assured that it is not uncommon for the initial scoping and needs assessment to rapidly expand, in response to unfolding reality.

The importance of a diagnostic

It is important to be aware that no one will fully understand what the Ringmaster's job spec is until the Ringmaster starts doing the job and reports back on initial findings.

Hence a board should seek an experienced Ringmaster who is capable of rapidly diagnosing the many different aspects of the situation, and reverting with a proposed scope of work that represents the art of the possible.

This opportunity to have a peek under the bonnet only slightly mitigates the risk that Ringmasters take on, knowingly, when they jump feet first into hairy situations from which many incumbents would run a mile. For reputational reasons, there is an unspoken commitment that, once signed up, the Ringmaster will stick to the task through thick and thin, no matter how much the reality turns out to be worse than what was described at the interview stage – and no matter what offers might come in for other, and possibly more lucrative, roles elsewhere before the job is finished.

Involving a restructuring advisory firm in the Ringmaster selection process

If the board feels an urgent and instinctive need to hire a brand-name advisory firm ('nobody ever got fired for buying IBM') it should bear in mind that it is not an either/or choice between a Ringmaster and a brand name. If hired first, the Ringmaster can help hire the brand name most suited to the situation, get the best out of them in terms of both effectiveness and cost, and provide a challenge to advice that may favour the firm's, rather than the client's, interests.

But if a board decides to hire an advisory firm first, on the basis that the firm will assist with the appointment of the Ringmaster, it should at least try to be aware of the risks of such an approach and the ways in which they can be mitigated.

If the firm hired is an advisory boutique, housed within an investment bank, the risks should be lower. It is very likely that such firms will suggest suitably experienced independent restructuring professionals and make introductions. The same would apply if the suggestions came from the lenders' adviser, which would be conflicted from taking a borrower-side role.

But if the advisory firm is one that has traditionally had a much larger insolvency and lender advisory business, caution should be the watchword. As explained in Chapter 4, in a shrunken lender advisory market some of these firms are looking to maximise their borrower-side revenues. It is not a clear-cut issue, however, because some such firms have established, credible practices that operate in market niches.

An obvious risk to a borrower is that such a firm will try to persuade the board and the senior team that an independent restructuring professional would not be such a good idea, perhaps on the grounds that, as individuals, they lack their own support resources or that they might be looking to take the executives' jobs.

They might go on to suggest that their own employees should be engaged instead. One of the features they might promote is that the individuals they would deploy to do the work have long experience of advising the lending institutions involved in the situation, they might even have deep personal relationships, possibly built earlier in their careers while on secondment in those very same institutions.

At the pitch stage, they might suggest that if the board appoints their firm quickly, that would remove any scope for the lenders to pressurise the board into appointing an independent restructuring professional. Such a suggestion might appeal to insecure executives, who will take comfort from remaining in control and thinking that the advisers will be gione when the problem is solved.

Until a few years ago, before their institutions became so sensitive to conduct risk, experienced workout bankers might have pushed back on such tactics.

If a board, having considered the suggestions, nevertheless insists on considering independent restructuring professionals, a less obvious pitfall is the risk that such an advisory firm could suggest candidates that they expect, if selected, would be helpful to their interests. They might, for example, suggest individuals who they would expect to provide no, or only weak, oversight of the advisers and the restructuring costs, or who would be so inexperienced as to need to engage considerable additional resources which the advisory firm would, of course, be in a position to provide.

Another pitfall is an individual with whom the advisory firm has an undisclosed reciprocal commercial arrangement. I have heard anecdotally of individuals who report back to the introducer firm with details of all the revenue they have generated for them, on each specific assignment.

Obviously, directors and executives might have come up with the names of independent restructuring professional as potential Ringmaster candidates from their own sources or from other advisers involved. The pitfall is that a financial advisory firm providing counsel might seek to keep those candidates off the shortlist, either by disparaging them or damning them with faint praise.

The best way for the board to mitigate these various risks is to independently compile a list of candidates, using as many sources as possible, and to make up their own minds by meeting or interviewing them personally. It may take more time, but it would be time well spent.

Selection, offer and acceptance

As someone who has made a living as a Ringmaster, I expect that the people I meet who are responsible for running the selection process will be one of two types: either they will want a Ringmaster to take the problem away and solve it; or they will want to use a Ringmaster to advance their own agenda. My advice to a board would be to ensure that the former dominate the selection process.

Very rarely, I have seen the process fronted by a senior HR executive. Which has told me that an insecure executive who dominates a docile board is looking for a patsy, to tick a box! In one case, the insecure executive also turned out to have a sinister agenda and the whole situation went to hell in a handcart because the conflicts were not properly managed.

It is important to confront the reality that Ringmaster candidates have considerable experience of how financial crises and restructurings develop and therefore their foresight and anticipation are going to be much more keenly developed than those of the people looking to hire them, who still have a steep learning curve to climb.

Take advantage of this by asking the candidates to share emerging thoughts and predict the course that the processes will take. Be careful not to reject analysis from such experienced people just because it contradicts the board's emerging views, causes discomfort and might require the chosen course to be adjusted.

And accept the likelihood that once a Ringmaster is *in situ*, facts will emerge that will challenge the board's views and expectations. In other words, it is naïve to expect that the board has made an accurate assessment in unexpectedly changed circumstances, of which its members have little or no prior experience, and that all that is needed is an extra pair of hands to fire the bullets that the board has hastily made.

Realistically, the board is looking for someone who can very quickly conduct a discovery exercise, provide them with a realistic assessment and make proposals for their own scope of work.

Inevitably, that is going to require the Ringmaster to get out and about in the business, meet people and take in information. If that prospect frightens the board, because all they want is someone to travel in the caravan of advisers, perhaps they should be looking for a lawyer, an accountant or an insolvency practitioner instead.

Effective Ringmasters are not warm and cuddly. If they flatter you, make out that the situation is definitely manageable and assure you that the major issues can be resolved with minimal stress, then you should probably move swiftly on.

And be careful not to be taken in by candidates who are best described as 'knee cartilage' – because their main benefit is to reduce friction between the board and the lenders – who everyone feels comfortable with, but who do not proactively crack on with getting the job done, if necessary by breaking a few eggs along the way.

Do not expect the Ringmaster candidates to automatically take on a role once it is offered. If a candidate feels that the hirers have their heads buried in the sand, or that their aspirations are unrealistic, that their approach is flawed, that they are looking for a patsy, or that they just want to rent that individual's reputation, then that individual will make their excuses and leave the process.

The hirers should also understand that a candidate will probably need to speak off the record with incumbent lenders and advisers before committing to accept an offer.

If I was on a board that was looking to hire a Ringmaster, my main requirements would fall under four key headings:

- commitment, reputation and independence
- personal qualities
- experience, expertise and network
- leadership.

Commitment, reputation and independence

I would not consider candidates who are either career executives between jobs, lenders' advisers trying to generate revenue from a new source to counter a weak market, or retired insolvency practitioners (unless they had gained considerable board experience after giving up their licences).

I would want the candidate to be an individual who could

demonstrate a commitment over a long period to operating as an independent restructuring professional. Someone with a hard-earned reputation built on a track record of serially and successfully protecting value and delivering outcomes that have restored it.

A board should be looking for a person with a singular interest in the health and survival of the business and with no agenda except helping the board to manage the financial crisis and restructuring, while in parallel identifying and addressing the causes of the crisis. I would definitely rule out someone who I felt would, if the situation were to go pear-shaped, see financial opportunities for themselves in the need to provide incremental resources.

I would not be concerned that the Ringmaster's name had been submitted by a lender. A Ringmaster is engaged solely by the borrower. The subtlety that needs to be appreciated is that if the lenders have the largest economic interest in a business and control its destiny, it is proper that the Ringmaster should be protective of their interests and that they, in turn, should take a direct interest in the Ringmaster's work. This means that there should be opportunities from time to time for the lenders and the Ringmaster to speak directly and privately.

I would quiz candidates about overlapping commercial interests, including reciprocity with any firm or individual. A Ringmaster with vested interests and conflicts will find it very difficult to be effective. I believe it is reasonable for a board to require prospective Ringmasters to disclose any reciprocal commercial arrangements they have with advisory firms and whether they have any revenue-sharing arrangements with advisers, interim executives, consultants and recruitment agencies.

I would not be squeamish about prohibiting such conflicts in a Ringmaster's contract.

Personal qualities

Integrity is enormously important. Situations vary and there are often forks in the road where the choice on offer might be between a path that will generate greater rewards for the Ringmaster and one that will bring a better outcome for the business.

The board does not want Ringmasters kicking the can down the road to prolong their stay, or going easy on an advisory firm in the hope that they will help them get work in the future.

It is important to bear in mind that individual directors, the senior team, the advisers and the stakeholders are all likely to develop their own vested interests as a situation develops. Almost inevitably, these will become conflicts that have to be managed. In this context, it is important to realise that in due course the Ringmaster may end up being one of a few people, or perhaps the only person, whose interests will be completely aligned with those of the company.

Boards should ask themselves some key questions about Ringmaster candidates. Will an individual care passionately about a successful outcome and take personal responsibility? Will their commitment extend to living away from home, travelling at unsociable times and, if necessary, foregoing family holidays? Are they no-nonsense? Can they get to the heart of the matter? Will they bring a laser-like focus to the role? Within the business, will they risk unpopularity by displacing myths with facts? Will they see through titles, hierarchy and rituals, in order to expose any incompetence and vested interests? Will they challenge dysfunctional regimes to improve?

Are they an individual who, when called upon to do so, will pugnaciously defend the business and those with stakes in its success? Will they have the courage to take on others' negligence, greed and unprofessional behaviour if they threaten those interests? Will they persevere doggedly and unflappably, no matter how bleak the outcome may look from time to time, sometimes prevailing through sheer force of will?

Will they be a person with empathy for the people in the business caught up in the situation? Will their commitment and approach inspire confidence in the second and third-tier managers, who hold the key to discovery of problems and to the design and rapid implementation of solutions?

Experience, expertise and network

I would consider it essential that Ringmaster candidates possess meaningful business experience, both on a board and as an executive – as CEO, CFO and/or COO – and situational experience. Sector experience is seldom more than a nice to have.

The successful candidate will be someone with a diversity of experience and skillsets who has a well-developed idea of what good looks like, from the coalface to the boardroom, someone who knows where to look and what questions to ask in order to conduct the initial diagnostic effectively.

They also need the intellectual horsepower to rapidly assimilate all of the discoveries and forge a plan for delivering the best outcome possible, and they should possess a toolkit from which the tools required for each specific set of circumstances can be selected and employed.

It needs to be someone who will earn the respect of the stakeholders and their advisers and can work collaboratively with them to diagnose key issues, identify priorities and agree a workable plan, by being candid where necessary and by buying time if more is needed to produce credible numbers.

A successful Ringmaster is someone who can help the board stay at least one step ahead of stakeholders and on the front foot, by being well prepared for meetings and anticipating what is coming next. They can make judgements about what is and is not important to build confidence in the borrower-side team, particularly by ensuring that it never has cause to be embarrassed by its numbers turning to dust.

The Ringmaster should be someone whom the board can quickly accept as a valued new colleague: a mentor who, by becoming a director, accepts the same risks as the incumbents; a guide through the minefield, with expertise in all the areas that a non-executive has to master after a crisis has been triggered; the point person on tackling all the thorny new areas that fall within the board's expanded responsibilities, including addressing unreliable numbers and gaining access to the business to make an honest assessment of the senior team and the quality of the administration.

The Ringmaster should be a source of invaluable assistance in rapidly evaluating and improving governance, as well as dealing with thorny issues such as accounting irregularities, executive misconduct and litigation.

Through the Ringmaster's network and relationships, the board and the senior team should be able to gain instant access to unfamiliar, esoteric skillsets in the shadowy restructuring community. They can help to scope advisory roles, shortlist suitable candidates, lead the selection processes and oversee their work and costs, as well as identify and source specialist interim executives who can fill key gaps and bolster the finance team at a critical time.

Leadership

Chapter 10 detailed the elements of a Ringmaster's scope – under the headings of governance, stakeholder management and operational – and explained that the size and complexity of the situation will determine whether either or both of the stakeholder management and operational roles will need to be delegated to point people.

In whichever way the three roles are resourced, the Ringmaster needs to lead, and be seen to lead, all aspects of the management of the financial crisis and restructuring. Having a web of bilateral communication channels and back channels can be destructive, not least if it serves to undermine the Ringmaster.

In the governance role, the Ringmaster ought to chair the committee which the board has established and to which it has delegated responsibility for the management of the financial crisis and restructuring. That will necessarily require the Ringmaster to set up a series of recurring activities, informed by bespoke reports, which will invariably involve advisers.

If the stakeholder management role has been delegated the firm or individual appointed can and should be the face of the business in its dialogue with stakeholders, presenting and negotiating the business's needs. However, it should be clear that the reporting line is to the Ringmaster or the committee, not to the board.

In the operational roles the individuals appointed will each report to the Ringmaster, either directly or via an operations point person. And it is a good idea for the senior interim executives engaged by the business to have a dotted line reporting relationship with the Ringmaster.

The contractual terms

Ringmasters are very different from vanilla consultants hired directly by the business. They are an interim executive, a director or an NED-Plus or any permutation thereof. The practicalities of any work they will need to do inside the business should be catered for in their contract. Some Ringmasters have a preference for a separate director's service contract, in which case the executive elements will usually be covered by a consultancy agreement.

You should expect Ringmaster candidates to offer their own bespoke contractual terms, that they have developed over time, and fine-tuned each time they have suffered a bad experience!

It is important to agree and document the Ringmaster's

initial scope upfront and to build in the flexibility to review it following the initial diagnostic. Title, authority and reporting lines, both upwards and downwards, are a concomitant part of the scope and need to be included in the review. This is usually dealt with by either a short, fixed-term initial contract or by a rolling contract with a review by a fixed date.

If the financial position of the business is precarious, it would be normal to agree short payment terms, usually weekly upon presentation of invoice, and possibly also to lodge a deposit sufficient to cover two fee invoices and, say, a month's expenses. And in a group situation, a guarantee from the parent or a subsidiary in which funds are held would be a reasonable request.

The Ringmaster will want to be included on the D&O insurance and any run-off policies.

The confidentiality clauses should be bespoke if part of the Ringmaster's role is to provide information to stakeholders, third parties and their advisers. If direct lender communications are a serious concern, that aspect can be dealt with in the contract.

Keeping the stakeholders informed

If the hiring of a Ringmaster is a board initiative, rather than one instigated by the lenders, keeping the key stakeholders informed is an opportunity to share positive news. The content of the communication should be agreed with the Ringmaster. And details of the scope should be shared.

Practical arrangements

A Ringmaster with executive responsibilities will need

access, equipment, facilities and support. Lining all of this up before the start date is important, so that the Ringmaster can hit the ground running and not suffer an embarrassing loss of credibility in the early stages, for example, by sitting around in meeting rooms in the early days, clearly in a holding pattern.

A company email is important, otherwise using the Ringmaster's personal email will involve the company's data sitting on servers outside its control.

In my experience, the visibility that these arrangements bring is one aspect that allows a Ringmaster and any direct reports to be much more effective than an adviser, in any operational role. That effectiveness derives from being a director; having a title, a reporting line, and being allocated an office or desk; using a company computer and a company email address, and having access to colleagues' calendars; being a member of key mailing lists and executive committees; and having direct reports and administrative support.

It is important to make an internal announcement about the Ringmaster's arrival. The text should be agreed with the Ringmaster. Inevitably, the announcement sets hares running and tongues wagging in the business – both helpful and unhelpful – that are invisible at the centre.

To capitalise on the interest that the announcement will generate, it is therefore important for the Ringmaster to get out and about as soon as possible because (unlike their reaction to the appointment of A N Other adviser) many employees will be eager to see, hear from and speak to the newly appointed Ringmaster.

There is a saying among experienced workout lenders that a Ringmaster 'provides adult supervision'. In an organisation that has suffered a financial crisis, there will be a sizeable number of employees who are invested in the company and care very much about it. They will feel the same way and many will be relieved to hear that a 'grown up' has arrived.

12

LEGAL ADVISERS

In a financial crisis and restructuring, the appointment of a law firm is usually a priority, as the directors of a business will need specialist legal advice as quickly as possible. The board may handle the process of identifying suitable firms or it may delegate to one or more senior executives, or possibly the company secretary, responsibility for drawing up a short list.

Legal advisers: to the company

Given how specialised the subject matter is, and how important it is for a borrower to be advised by a firm with strong credentials in the restructuring arena, a poor choice sloppily made can carry serious risks. The board should not feel under an obligation to engage any firm based on an existing relationship.

Those conducting research would be well advised not to have unguarded conversations with people they do not know well, unless they either trust the person who introduced them or have researched them carefully in advance. There is a risk that such people will contact the lenders involved to try and get the lender-side engagement. This could be very unhelpful, especially if the directors have yet to engage with the lenders.

It is important first to establish which law firms have acted for the lenders in the past. If there is doubt, existing facilities documentation should be looked at. These firms can be eliminated, as they will be conflicted and there is a strong possibility that they will be appointed by the lenders.

Law firms that the business already has a relationship with should then be identified. By using Chambers and other online legal directories, in conjunction with the law firms' own websites, their capabilities can be researched. This process should include any law firm used only for debt advisory work.

The research should then establish whether those firms have restructuring advisory credentials and eliminate those that do not, digging deeper to identify individual partners who predominantly advise borrowers, and being careful to distinguish between those who advise borrower entities and those who advise the boards of borrowers. The latter can be dealt with at a later stage. Those that advise lenders and insolvency practitioners can be eliminated. If an individual has a foot in each camp, caution should be exercised, especially if their credentials include qualified insolvency practitioner status and the firm highlights that it is on lender bank panels.

The research should also establish the type and value of work that each firm has done for the business recently, for example, over the past year, and by which partners. A client service partner, if there is one, should also be identified.

Based on findings from the research, it may be that a law firm already used by the business has relevant expertise and, based on work it has done in the period covered, would be conflicted from acting for lenders to the business or other stakeholders. If so, caution is needed before contacting banking partners who advised on the debt in good times, in case they try and hang on to the work rather than refer it to their restructuring colleagues. Named individual partners that advise borrowers should be identified and contacted, either directly or via the client service partner.

Without revealing any details, it is important to establish whether that law firm acts for the lenders involved, or for other significant stakeholders, if the situation is sizeable. If so, a definite answer should be sought as to whether the law firm could advise the borrower, emphasising that the matter is to be regarded as highly confidential and urgent. Getting the answer is likely to take a few days.

If it can be established that the firm is free to act, then it should be safe to engage with a partner, either the one identified in the course of the research or another put forward by the firm. As the stakes are high, it is important to be both comfortable and confident about the choice of individual, therefore there should be no concerns about offending the firm or the individual.

It should be borne in mind that partners in professional services firms are incentivised to win work but might actually have minimal involvement thereafter. Clear and concise information about who will actually lead the assignment should be requested. Directors do not want to be paying school fees. They should ask for a CV and meet the candidate, if necessary more than once. They should ask for off-the-record conversations with directors or executives of borrower entities that the individuals have previously advised. And they should satisfy themselves that the individuals will have adequate bandwidth, by reference to their other commitments, current and expected, to clients and court proceedings – and whether they are planning a sabbatical in the next six to nine months.

Other law firms and individuals within them can be identified in a similar way. Unless there are compelling reasons not to, directors should shortlist at least three firms and have initial conversations with them, bearing in mind that each will need to run conflict checks, which also can also take between a day and a week.

Legal advisers: to the board

It is usually necessary for the board, as a body rather than as individual directors, to be advised separately by a different law firm from the one that is advising the business. This is particularly important in relation to personal risks and possibly also conflicts.

As the former is not regarded as lucrative work, the larger law firms will not want to be boxed in. It is, therefore, common for a smaller firm with a specialism in the field to be appointed.

The timing of an appointment is usually driven by the directors' concerns about their personal risks. This is covered in the next chapter.

13

PERSONAL RISKS

Understandably, most directors who find themselves in a crisis are concerned about personal risks. Myths abound about how difficult their position is at the outset, and naturally there is a genuine desire not to sleepwalk into making that worse.

As outlined earlier, if the directors want or need legal advice about their personal risks a specialist firm will need to be appointed as legal adviser to the board. The firm that is advising the company cannot also provide this.

Most firms acting in that role will provide pre-prepared, standard guidance for directors of a company in the zone of insolvency ahead of an initial consultation.

The frequency of contact after that will be correlated with how close the business is to insolvency. If it is teetering on the brink, several meetings might be held in a single day.

However frequent the contact, once a firm has been engaged, it is sound practice to have the firm represented at every board meeting and on every board call and to have them draft, or at least review, the minutes.

At an early stage, the appointed firm should be asked to evaluate the existing D&O insurance cover and to make recommendations for any areas in which it could be strengthened. This should all be done in writing. D&O cover is quite a complicated subject, but in summary it indemnifies directors for liabilities to third parties and for their defence costs. It is important for directors to acquaint themselves with the terms of the cover and, if the business is to be sold, to ensure that before completion, run-off cover is bought for the maximum available period.

Not surprisingly, D&O insurers are reluctant to make amendments once a business is in distress and any they do agree to are likely to be expensive. It should not be assumed that an existing insurer will renew and, if they do, renewal premiums are likely to be significantly higher. There are a handful of specialist insurers and brokers in the market and it is a good idea for one of the directors to get to know at least one of them (even at the risk of upsetting the business's incumbent broker).

Some transactions in the zone of insolvency can be attacked subsequently, by an administrator or a liquidator, the main ones being preferring individual creditors and selling assets at an undervalue. A range of fraudulent acts are criminal offences.

If the company goes into administration or liquidation, the former directors of that company, assuming they have conducted themselves in an honest fashion, face the risk of attack from two sources: creditors and the Official Receiver.

Creditors

As mentioned earlier, one downside of making an inappropriate decision – and it will be judged with the benefit of hindsight – is that the directors could end up with personal liability for the incremental losses of the business's creditors incurred beyond the point at which they knew, *or ought to have known*, that insolvent liquidation was unavoidable.

If you examine that risk in detail, it is going to need determined creditors, willing to risk throwing good money after bad by putting the liquidator in sufficient funds to pursue a civil action against the directors, not only to finance the legal fees but also to undertake the forensic exercise both to establish the critical point and to calculate the creditors' exposure at that point, which will then be used as the base for calculating the increment that will constitute the directors' theoretical liability.

The Official Receiver

The conduct of directors (including de facto and shadow directors) of a company in the three years prior to it being placed into administration or liquidation will routinely be investigated by the Official Receiver.

Evidence will be provided by the administrator or liquidator in a confidential report, based in part on a questionnaire that each director will be required to complete, that has to be provided within three months of the insolvency. Adverse representations from the tax authorities will also be factored in.

The Official Receiver, under the authority of the UK government's business ministry (Department of Business,

Energy & Industrial Strategy – BEIS) can ban individuals from holding directorships for up to 15 years. It is often cheaper and easier for them to volunteer for a ban.

Defences

Effective defences to legal attacks from either of these sources include taking appropriate professional advice and being able to produce evidence of meetings in which the situation was evaluated in a considered fashion, as often as necessitated by the circumstances. In particular, the evidence will need to show that the directors formally considered it was responsible to continue trading and incurring credit.

Personally, I am relaxed about knowingly putting myself in the line of fire by joining a board, the exception being where a business is at risk of its industry regulator causing a catastrophic outcome, for example, by shutting it down or transferring its assets for no value, and thereby utterly negating any restructuring efforts. Obviously, I also need to have confidence in my fellow travellers.

As a precaution, I always make a point of saving the meeting minutes and all the associated papers (in particular the liquidity forecasts and analyses) because if it ever became necessary to defend an action, I expect it could be a nightmare to try and access those papers years after a company had been placed in insolvency. I also keep copies of all the documentation in relation to D&O and run-off insurance cover.

The critical issue for me is a less worse position for creditors on an ongoing basis. Pragmatically, if the directors are working to mitigate the situation, and creditors benefit as a result, then it is difficult to envisage circumstances in which it would be considered more responsible to cease working and instead file for insolvency.

However, as I will illustrate with a hypothetical situation, 'creditors' and 'position' are not straightforward concepts and individual creditors can be worse off while all creditors as a whole are better off.

On the positive side, the potentially precarious legal position of directors in such situations and the need for them to be kept 'comfortable' does provide a means to pressurise the lenders. To make a restructuring work, it is necessary for individuals to sit on the board – and obviously it is not going to be the lenders' employees – and, by so doing, the individuals serving as directors are putting themselves at risk for the benefit of the lenders.

A sensible balance is required. There is always the possibility that some of the directors involved will stoke the fears of the others by acting like Chicken Licken. What benefits no one is directors who act like rabbits in headlights, unhelpfully retarding the whole process by insisting on formally meeting and taking advice at every possible opportunity.

14

FINANCIAL ADVISERS

If possible, a decision to appoint financial advisers should not be rushed or taken before the board has worked through the leadership issue and identified the resourcing needs of the processes. In certain circumstances, the services of a financial adviser may not be needed at all.

The inputs needed from financial advisers are a function of how the borrower's board is going to resource the key leadership roles. The Ringmaster will naturally fill the governance role and either fill the stakeholder management and operational roles as well or oversee others in them.

In certain circumstances, it is feasible for advisers to resource the whole of the stakeholder management role. This is something that the advisory teams housed within investment bank specialise in, working in very small teams. Prominent names in this space are Evercore, Gleacher Shacklock, Goldman Sachs, Greenhill, Houlihan Lokey, Lazard, Moelis, Morgan Stanley, PJT Partners and Rothschild.

These advisers usually charge success-related fees with monthly retainers that are deductible from the final fee. As their fees usually run to seven figures, only the larger and more complex situations can accommodate these advisers' costs.

In my experience, the staff provided by advisory firms with accountancy and insolvency roots can do a good job supporting the Ringmaster and stakeholder manager with organisational and analytical tasks and monitoring activities. Their numerical, technical and presentational skills come to the fore, especially if they are supplemented with situational experience.

However, in my view they tend to be weak in the operational sphere; they are often ill-equipped to recognise, diagnose and remedy weak and non-functioning systems and processes and are unable to deliver improvements. To use an analogy, they could tell the captain of the Titanic, with increasing accuracy, when the ship was due to hit the iceberg, but not devise a course to steer around it.

I put this down to them lacking any experience of having worked in a business. It is typical in large firms for recently qualified accountants and graduates in other fields to be employed in restructuring roles. I believe the quality of such staff can be very variable and the unwary borrower can end up being charged several thousand pounds a day for employees who are new to restructuring or perhaps have only minimal finance skillsets.

That said, timing and stakeholder confidence at the outset are issues that need to be factored in. Liquidity management will be an urgent and high-profile priority and, in the initial stages, the board and key stakeholders will be comforted if brand-name advisers have been brought in.

All such firms provide a commodity offering in this space – input templates, a model, a report format, resources of variable experience – and their involvement quickly elevates liquidity as a priority within the upper levels of the organisation.

However, such work should not be confused with the need for actually driving cash mitigation and unlocking cash from working capital, which the operational point person will take charge of, overseen by the Ringmaster. In terms of effectiveness, therefore, such employees are likely to hit a glass ceiling quite quickly.

The pitfall here for a board is that an advisory firm that gets its foot in the door will seek to expand into all the other roles, perhaps (as explored in Chapter 11) even discouraging the board from appointing a Ringmaster.

The firm may suggest that it should act with a joint duty of care to the borrower and the lenders. While this might indeed have cost benefits by eliminating the need for each side to appoint separate advisers, the hidden agenda might be ensuring that the firm is not precluded from taking an insolvency appointment. It would be able to do this by 'flipping' to a sole duty of care to the lenders if the process starts heading towards an insolvency outcome.

This may be perfectly proper under the rules and regulations, but a board may not be anticipating it at the outset. This gap in expectations was illustrated by a quote in a national newspaper from an insider who claimed that an advisory firm appointed by the board of a company in financial distress had a conflict of interest in that they started out advising the company, quickly began working with the banks and were then appointed as administrators. Aside from that, there is the reality that once a firm flips to the bank side, the board is left without advice at a crucial stage.

Given that certain firms' long-term commercial interests lie with lenders and that borrower clients are far less likely to provide repeat business, in my experience it should be taken as read that they will establish a back channel to lenders involved in the situation. With a sole duty of care, but not with a joint duty, in theory it should be possible to put in place safeguards that would prevent the individuals involved from having side conversations with lenders. However, at any given time, the firms and the lending institutions will have lots of other reasons to be in almost daily contact and as the details of a borrower's situation are confidential to the firm, not only to the individuals within it, I believe it would be practically impossible to prevent de facto back channels from developing.

If a board feels it has to appoint a firm to get started on liquidity management, the conversation should be strictly limited. If the directors are concerned about the risk that an adviser might 'flip' to the lender side at a critical juncture, it should consider hiring the firm that does the company's audit, as that firm would not be able to take an insolvency appointment. Engaging a handful of their restructuring people with a very narrow scope and for a limited period should not present a problem in terms of exceeding the non-audit fee threshold (which only applies to publicly listed companies). Whichever firm is eventually engaged, any mission creep should be stoutly resisted until the Ringmaster is in place.

It is advisable for the board, or the restructuring committee if one has been set up, to be involved in the adviser selection and appointment processes, under the leadership of the Ringmaster. And it is essential also to maintain 'radio silence' until the appointments have been finalised.

In Chapter 4, I explained how every adviser with the situation on its radar will hunt avidly for information. They will be working their networks, seeking informants and sponsors in the selection process. If people who receive calls can give away no information, directing callers instead to the Ringmaster, then the integrity of the process will be safeguarded.

A structured, objective and professional approach to the selection and appointment of advisers is far preferable to a knee-jerk reaction that involves senior individuals lacking in restructuring experience shooting from the hip. There may be opportunities in due course for them to call people in their own networks and to speak to advisory firms that are already used for other services.

A Ringmaster who is an active member of the restructuring community will be very well networked and should quickly and easily narrow down the list of suitable candidates. Legal advisers will possibly have some suggestions, but these should be treated with caution because they may be based on reciprocity, for example, lawyer x and accountant y regularly introduce work to each other.

As I detail in a subsequent chapter, it is important to make a start as soon as possible on the forecasting that will support the new capital structure. If advisers are tasked with designing the models, sourcing the inputs and producing the consolidated outputs, they will be off to a promising start. But it is impossible to predict what the exercise might unearth, and there is always a high risk that the end product will be delayed or severely limited in its usefulness.

And, of course, they will not be involved in consideration of whether the additional workload would be too much for an organisation already under considerable strain. The best use of advisers would be to support elements that require heavy lifting on a short timescale, for example, analysing specific areas of the balance sheet or cataloguing potential cost savings.

In my experience, high calibre senior finance interim executives with specific experience will do a much better job.

Good Ringmasters will either have such people in their networks or know where to source them. They can have a crucial role to play, in terms of providing the Ringmaster and the CFO with battle-hardened officers and NCOs to buttress the finance operations at a critical time. Without this, the finance capacity can be stretched to breaking point, which would risk undermining the whole restructuring effort, with potentially disastrous consequences. Foot soldiers will be needed, too, but they can be sourced quickly and cheaply.

Advisory firm staff are not a viable substitute for the foot soldiers, as they have no experience of working in a business, cannot provide leadership and will cost 10 to 20 times as much as a temporary or a contract worker. If the lenders or the board feel they need some specific analysis from a brand-name adviser, to shore up confidence, that can be procured on a rifle-shot basis.

However, swamping the finance team with an army of advisory staff in response to some confidence-denting episode for the purpose of reassuring the board and the lenders will risk simply overloading the overworked finance team and could endanger the restructuring process and perhaps even the entire business.

As I said earlier, the borrower many not need a financial adviser at all. I have been involved in situations with unexpectedly good outcomes for all stakeholders that were resourced by independent restructuring professionals – on the board and in the executive team – supported by specialist finance interim managers who leveraged off and mentored existing employees.

As outlined in Chapter 9, when engaging initially with lenders, the issue of advisory appointments should be on the agenda. There will be a strong alignment of interests, especially if the lenders are going to be providing new money, because a portion of the need will be to fund the borrower's professional fees.

The lenders' workout people will understand this minefield very well and have valuable contributions to make with regards to the suitability of firms and individuals, with whom they are likely to be familiar.

If they have had bad experiences of a firm or individual they will be able to give the borrower a steer, albeit without going into specifics. And if the senior advisory people pitching have spent their careers advising lenders and are being sold as company-side restructuring advisers on the premise that their skills are transferable, the lenders should point out the pitfalls.

Transparency in both directions will help the borrower to avoid considering candidates who are trying to ride both horses, by having discussions with the board while participating in lender-side pitches.

To recap, in my experience the directors should strongly consider not appointing restructuring advisers before the initial engagement with lenders, but instead compile a list of candidates that they are considering, share it with lenders and hear their views, which are likely to be expressed laconically.

However, if advisers are engaged without any lender input then, unless the choice is so manifestly bad, in my experience the lenders would be unlikely to make any comments, especially if the borrower is a publicly listed company. They would simply recognise that a choice they consider inappropriate had unfortunately been made and then try to compensate for that through the choice of their own advisers and the scope that they agree with them.

Other advisers and consultants

Other services that might be needed include tax, corporate finance, M&A and debt advisory, as well as management and strategy consultants. The need to engage any or all of these will depend on the circumstances. I would be sceptical of claims that there would be benefits in procuring multiple services from the same firm.

In a publicly listed business, brokers – and possibly a nominated adviser (NOMAD) – and PR advisers will already be in place and their suitability for the circumstances will be a matter for the board, including the Ringmaster, to judge.

15

ENGAGING WITH OTHER STAKEHOLDERS

Following the initial engagement, the lenders mobilise and appoint their advisers, while the business appoints its restructuring leadership and additional resources and engages its own advisers. In parallel, work commences on the all-important liquidity analysis and outlook.

If the early cuts show an imminent threat of the cash running out, the business will have no option but to share the forecast with its lenders. The pitfalls of this are outlined in Chapter 16.

If the lenders do agree to provide a temporary increase in facilities ahead of the management presentation, that is likely to prove helpful in negotiating support from other stakeholders in order to start making progress towards stabilising the financial crisis.

As explained earlier, lenders will usually be willing to provide additional support under most circumstances, but they will be sensitive to others with a lesser priority improving their positions at the lenders' expense.

A tactical judgement needs to be made about starting a dialogue with other financial stakeholders to secure in-principle, conditional expressions of support. Major customers and suppliers, the tax authorities and pension trustees, all have a strongly symbiotic and shared interest in the business living to fight another day. If all that is being requested is different timing, the ask is not a very large one, especially if the stakeholders have big balance sheets.

In my experience, the earlier this dialogue starts, the better the prospects of achieving a helpful outcome. The lack of clarity and the stakeholders' visceral fear of the business failing are an advantage, especially when individual employees with the necessary discretion identify the personal risk that the finger of blame may point at them if they obstruct the provision of help, leading to their employer organisation suffering criticism as a result.

There is also the benefit of information asymmetry: positioned in the centre, the Ringmaster or stakeholder management point person will be working with a group who are not permitted speak to each other, each of whom will be more inclined to be supportive if they know (from information provided by the business) that the others are as well.

I have found that there is a golden window within which to rally stakeholders to give support. The prospects of receiving it later in the restructuring process will invariably be much weaker, especially if the information available then shows a poor outlook, leaving the stakeholders feeling that their expectations have been mismanaged. The risk is that a request at that stage, made by people in whom confidence has ebbed away, will be perceived as desperation. And if customers have worked in the intervening period to find new sources of supply, a request will probably drive yet more nails into the business's coffin.

The requests for stakeholder support will necessarily be conditional on lenders providing increased support. Being able to provide definite details in the management presentation to lenders should help to speed up the lenders' decision-making process, by eliminating a step and reducing uncertainty.

If it turns out later that the support requested is not actually needed, I would be inclined to still take it, not only because you never know what nasty surprises are around the corner, but also because saying you do not actually need it will not be good for credibility. This could be costly if you need to ask for support later on.

16

THE BOARD'S ESSENTIAL SURVIVAL TOOLS

Like an explorer's map and compass, the short-term cash flow forecast (STCFF) and the three-year three-way integrated financial forecasts are essential survival tools for a board managing a financial crisis and restructuring. Although the longer-term forecasts become much less important if the likely outcome is a sale of the business to a trade buyer or to a distressed investor.

The STCFF

Unlike the top-down cash flow statements published in financial statements which, in effect, bridge one balance sheet to another, a STCFF is based purely on receipts and payments. It reports and predicts bank balances, available headroom and cash movements, and with the passing of time it provides a growing historical record.

The raw forecast meshes elements of the opening balance sheet unwind with the near-term trading forecasts and relies on assumptions about the timing of working capital movements. It is then finessed with judgements about mitigations, downside risks and juggling of cash.

The standard forecast period is 13 weeks. But it is advisable to maintain a forecast for 26 weeks for internal use. In practice, an 18-week forecast is updated monthly so as to align with both the latest balance sheet and any trading forecast updates. In the intervening weeks, the forecasts are maintained by updating the most recent week to reflect actual figures, making adjustments to future weeks and adding one more week

When starting out, extreme care should be taken in sharing developing information with lenders because the earlier versions, which inevitably will have much room for improvement, are at risk of becoming the baseline for their internal reporting, against which they will always have to reference every update. The trick, therefore, is to heavily caveat early versions, refer to them as drafts and prototypes, and share them formally only when there is a reasonable level of confidence in them.

This should be reinforced by numbering the first version in which there is sufficient confidence 'CF1' and referencing all future analysis back to CF1 rather than to any earlier version. An essential feature of the process is strict version control and this can be achieved by giving the final version of each week's update the next number in the sequence.

The updated reports that are sent to the lenders and other stakeholders every week, possibly via their advisers, are an output from a recurring weekly process of producing a fresh forecast and analysing and explaining variances from the preceding weekly forecast. It is conventional to have a call with the lenders on the same day each week, at least until initial anxieties about liquidity have receded.

In the course of the restructuring, a variety of ad hoc analyses and reconciliations will be called for and this necessitates maintaining a reasonably sophisticated cash forecasting spreadsheet model.

As a rule of thumb, from a standing start it takes six weeks of very hard work, overseen by someone with a wealth of experience, to polish up an STCFF to an acceptable level of reliability and then stay ahead of the game. Aside from weaknesses in the business's systems and processes, the biggest obstacles are typically political and cultural.

If the CFO and/or the senior finance people are reluctant to relinquish control to experienced outsiders, there is a danger that forecasting quality will be compromised. And if staff at the coalface do not take their new cash forecasting responsibilities as seriously as the situation requires, the danger only increases.

This can have grave consequences in view of the heavy reliance placed on the STCFF by the board, the lenders and a variety of other stakeholders. It is a vital prop for the board's credibility and the lenders' confidence; the directors of a business in crisis should, therefore, be prepared to rock the boat and cause the senior executives discomfort if it appears that personal interests and insecurities are jeopardising the interests of the business.

It is vital that those relying on the STCFF of a business in crisis, in which liquidity is scarce, appreciate its true nature and limitations. Because in such circumstances until someone experienced starts using it as a tool to mitigate cash, its best use is as an increasingly accurate prediction of when the Titanic is going to hit the iceberg.

The forecasts

A three-year, three-way integrated financial forecast is a complicated beast. It comprises the forecast P&L, balance sheet and cash flow (top-down, not receipts and payments). The reference to integrated means that a change in one part of the forecast model will automatically be reflected in the others.

I have never found a business that routinely used such a forecast in normal times, although I understand that certain packages used by large corporates claim to have that capability.

They are complex to build and the construction process will unearth all kinds of technical issues that need to be resolved if the outputs are to be reliable. Given its vital importance in the later stages of the restructuring, and also the future need – after the restructuring – to compare monthly actual figures against the forecast for between one and three years at the same level of detail, it should be a no-brainer that specialist, experienced resources need to be engaged to start building the integrated forecast without delay.

A key technical challenge is that the model needs to produce granular information about cash. Corporate forecasting models tend to be very weak on this: they prioritise the P&L, roughly forecast the closing balance sheets and then use high-level metrics, such as debtor days, to mechanically produce the cash flows and the closing cash balances.

If an existing corporate forecasting model is adapted, a

major vulnerability in the forecasts produced will be the delta in cash versus the real-time and near-term cash positions reflected in the STCFF. Most people understand well enough that top-down and bottom-up cash forecasts are prepared on different bases and will, therefore, never give precisely the same answers. But it is reasonable to expect that over time they will converge.

Whichever model is used, the age of the starting balance sheet will be a key factor in its reliability, because cash and working capital movements will need to be retrofitted to approximate the real-time cash position reflected in the STCFF. The older the starting point, therefore, the higher the risk that the exercise will end up being entirely artificial and so of no use for forecasting future movements.

Even with a purpose-built model, if the existing corporate forecasting structure and process are used, and if the people at various levels in the business responsible for providing P&L inputs do not also have control of the corresponding cash and working capital, the forecast produced may still not provide the specific cash-related information needed for a restructuring. If the cash and working capital are controlled at higher points in the structure, a way needs to be found to aggregate the P&Ls and the balance sheets at the various levels at which cash and working capital are being managed. But this brings further challenges, because a way has to be found to recognise internal flows between those 'units', which may be artificial, and it becomes necessary to achieve consistency of definitions and timings. If that is done artificially, then in future the model will be of no use when trying to compare actual cash movements to those forecast.

If the forecasting exercise is done by way of separate spreadsheets, the risk of errors will increase and the model is likely to become cumbersome, quickly making the whole process very resource-heavy.

Unfortunately, at the early stages of managing a crisis and financial restructuring, it is common for the senior executives and the finance team to claim that the way the business already does its forecasts is absolutely fine and only a few tweaks are necessary. In my experience, this will almost certainly prove to be a massive, potentially fatal, error that may not become discernible for some time. But if, at a critical juncture down the line, numbers that the business has produced swing wildly from one version of the forecast to the next each time they are prodded in response to queries from those sitting around the table, it will be too late to do anything about it. The problem will be even worse if all parties are working to a tight deadline, possibly against the backdrop of worsening liquidity, and each update takes a day or more to process because the model has been constructed as a series of linked spreadsheets.

Such a situation can cause lenders and other stakeholders to simply run out of confidence and any remaining runway to rapidly disappear. The risks of this are higher if there is an information vacuum for a much longer period than was anticipated when the forecasting exercise started, all the more so if the board has not been keeping the existing corporate forecasting model refreshed in parallel to provide near-term visibility. In such a situation, when the answer finally pops out of the opaque forecast-building process, the outlook might be so bleak that a funeral is the only feasible answer.

If the board does not grasp the nettle at the outset, as the restructuring progresses and shortcomings in the existing forecasts become obvious, there will be no easy fixes. Either the business will belatedly start doing what it should have done months earlier or attempts will be made to retrofit enhancements to the existing forecasts. If the business has made a series of acquisitions but never properly integrated them, the task will be much more difficult.

To compound the problem, the work involved in any remedy attempted at that stage will necessarily swamp key finance people because the option to bring in specialist interim executives will no longer be feasible, as there would be insufficient time available for them to get up the learning curve and run an orderly process. Taking these key people away from important business-as-usual tasks when the finance team will be under enormous pressure risks both a breakdown in the finance function and the loss of valuable employees to illness and resignations. Moreover, the key operational people on whom the raw inputs will be dependent will lose much of the bandwidth that is critical to keeping the business functioning.

Eventually some outputs will be produced, but if the technical challenges prove to be insurmountable in such pressurised circumstances the information that is critical to the board and the stakeholders will be of questionable reliability.

Bringing in an army of young advisers at that point will seem to the board like a good way to repair its credibility. But the situation will need doers, not analysers who have never worked in the finance team of a business.

Advisers for all the stakeholders will be relying on the

forecast to be able to do their work, and with the business responsible for their costs, all the errors and inefficiencies will quickly start to cause material increases in restructuring costs. Inevitably, these will far outstrip what it would have cost to hire a team of specialists at the outset to do the job properly!

17

ACHIEVING STABILITY

The management presentation to lenders

It is important to realise that the relationship bankers with whom the business has dealt with until recently – who always seem to be in sales mode and who may have been very amenable to requests for additional credit – will have been replaced by their workout colleagues, who will take all of the credit decisions and will be in a very different mindset. Some CFOs find this very difficult to adjust to.

When designing a presentation to lenders, it is easy to think that you are speaking to the decision-makers. In reality, they will have to make their own presentations to their credit committees, with their recommendations.

So the prospects of the lenders agreeing to the business's requests will be improved if the presentation and the accompanying reports and forecasts can be easily adapted for the unseen next part of the process and cover most of the bases.

It is common for lenders' advisers to be in the dialogue with the credit committees and if, at the planning stage, there are below-the-radar conversations about key issues then they can also be enormously helpful.

Lenders will expect the presentation to cover all of the following: the cause(s) of the crisis; the board's emerging plans to remedy them; the liquidity position and outlook; actions to mitigate liquidity; the likely impact on trading and covenants; the restructuring roadmap; the support the business is seeking; and the contributions that other stakeholders will be asked to make to create stability.

As well as additional short-term liquidity, support required by the business is likely to include covenant relief (deferring the testing of and/or resetting the financial covenants) and waivers of past or anticipated future breaches.

At the risk of stating the blindingly obvious, it is critically important to make a big enough request at the first time of asking. That will help to shore up credibility and confidence from one end of the chain to the other: from the executive team through the board, the lenders' workout people and the credit committees to the advisers on both sides.

The presentation should be led by the leader appointed by the board. Lenders will expect to hear from the most senior executives about the business and its trading, its balance sheet, and so forth, as well as from those members of the board with direct responsibility for the restructuring. The lenders will expect them all to be in the room unless there are compelling reasons for them not to be.

Obviously, the advisers to the business will be in attendance, but it will dent the lenders' confidence in the board if it appears that they have outsourced leadership responsibility to the advisers.

Achieving stability

The process essentially involves the negotiation of commercial terms that, once implemented, will provide a stable platform for a longer-term resolution to be agreed and implemented. Usually within a few months.

If the business is publicly listed and its board and advisers are confident that a rights issue is feasible, it is likely that the platform will be needed for a relatively short period. The same applies if the shareholders of a privately owned business are going to fund a capital injection. But without a liquidity cure provided by equity, it is difficult to know how long the platform will be needed for.

It is not unreasonable for the board to seek waivers of existing and past breaches while stability is negotiated. Lenders will have the option of putting the company on a short leash by extending month to month. This provides the board with an incentive to move the process along at pace.

In principle, the most senior lenders provide the financial support needed for stability by way of additional facilities while other financial stakeholders stand still and make concessions, typically by varying the terms on which they will pay or be paid. Less senior lenders are likely to have to agree to defer any cash paid interest.

As mentioned in Chapter 3, lenders may take the opportunity to introduce conditions that are designed to keep the board focused on realistic outcomes and discourage them from wasting time or risking value by pursuing unfeasible solutions. These might include milestones expressed as days within which the unlikely solutions must be either delivered or abandoned and the delegation of the oversight of strategic options to a new board subcommittee, the workings of which are transparent to the lenders.

The business will have to agree to a variety of terms, typically preventing cash leakage and giving additional security. Lenders are likely to use the opportunity to address weaknesses in the borrower's personnel, if their attempts to date have been rebuffed by the board. This could involve adding a non-executive with restructuring experience to the board – possibly in conjunction with the new board committee – shoring up the management and the finance team with experienced resources and even swapping out advisers whose performance has so far not inspired confidence.

It is common for the negotiations to be focused on a single document that summarises the principal commercial terms, known as the term sheet. This is batted back and forth between the business and the stakeholders and once it is finally agreed, then the legal advisers commence drafting the documentation.

Depending on who and what type the lenders are, there may be a credit approval step in the process before the documentation starts.

18

THE FINANCIAL RESTRUCTURING PROCESS

As this book is about financial crises, the scope of this chapter will not include situations in which an approaching debt maturity has lit a long fuse – in other words, it is a core assumption that there will be an urgent need for new money, some of which is likely to have been provided as part of the stabilisation.

The backbone of the financial restructuring process will be a series of calculations, based on the refreshed business plan and the integrated forecasts that support it: a valuation of the business; its current and future debt capacity; how much new money is needed; and excess debt in the current structure.

For capital providers embarking on a restructuring process, there are two pieces of critical information: where does 'the value break', in other words, is the enterprise value greater than the debt or vice versa? And does the business need new money?

The most manageable scenario for a borrower would be:

enterprise value exceeding debt; new money being provided by a party junior to the incumbent lenders; and leverage going forward at a tolerable level. The lenders would be likely to be comfortable supporting the current equity owners, board and management team.

Lenders' tolerance for risk

The current economic and lending environments and the near-term outlook can be very influential on the likelihood or otherwise of lenders supporting financial restructuring proposals.

For example, in a market in which there is excess liquidity, there may be competitive pressures on bank lenders to protect their own P&L. Credit funds might prefer not to receive repayment because the terms on which the funds could be re-lent might well be inferior. This, coupled with opportunity costs in the meantime, would affect the fund manager's earnings.

Sometimes there are systemic reasons for the lending industry not crystallising losses, for example, when property prices are depressed, since lower market prices would affect the recoverability of a sizeable part of their lending books.

At the same time, lenders may have internal reasons for not wanting to recognise immediate economic reality, perhaps because there are plausible reasons that support a higher valuation in the future. Or because they do not have the room in the current financial year's bad debt provision to accommodate the loss that would be crystallised. This is referred to as 'kicking the can down the road', via an 'amend and extend' that typically involves loosening the covenants and pushing out the maturity date.

On the other hand, the amount of new money needed in a restructuring may simply be considered excessive for the situation, in the context of the valuation, existing debt and risks. It is unlikely that a need for new money would be partially funded, as that would increase the incumbent capital providers' losses if the business ran out of money at some future date. The exception being the provision of funding as a bridge to an outcome – in which case the present restructuring might only be a precursor to one or more future restructuring.

The importance of forecasting

Incumbent and potential new lenders will scrutinise the integrated forecasts. Credit funds tend to do their own analysis but if the lenders are banks, their individual credit committees will usually require the lenders' financial adviser to conduct an Independent Business Review (IBR). This can take weeks or even months.

Hence the availability of forecasts is essential to progress. As producing them sits squarely on the critical path, it is advisable to start preparing them as early as possible after the financial crisis has been triggered. If they are to prove fit for purpose at the critical time high standards need to be set, with shortcuts taken only when pragmatic or expedient. If expectations and confidence suddenly drop later in the process, it will be too late to go back and fix earlier shortcomings.

As has been detailed in earlier chapters, throughout the stabilisation and restructuring processes the senior lenders will want to keep all of their options open and will be doing work on them in parallel, albeit with the most favoured outcome receiving the most attention. And they will expect the business to be doing the same.

The lenders' expectations will be underpinned by the integrated forecasts and if these prove unreliable or unrealistic, it will be difficult to sustain the optimistic assumptions underlying the most favourable outcome.

Numerous factors can cause a switch from one option to another, less favourable option late in the process. In my experience, the most common causes for this are a material drop in expectations and running out of runway, sometimes in a combination that is toxic and very difficult to recover from.

If the forecasts are poorly constructed, unresponsive or require time-consuming workarounds to produce key data, that can cause the board and the lenders to lose confidence that the business will have sufficient liquidity. It may also be the case that liquidity has deviated materially from the forecasts for reasons unrelated to the quality of management and forecasting.

Replacement of capital providers

At the end of the process, there may be new equity owners and new lenders.

There are numerous permutations for this. Incumbent lenders may acquire equity by swapping some of their debt. Bank lenders are generally very reluctant to own equity so if this is the only option they would be likely to sell out at a discount to non-bank lenders. These might include credit funds with a 'loan-to-own' strategy.

If a full refinancing is viable, incumbent lenders may be replaced by new lenders with similar criteria and objectives.

In recent years, high yield bonds have been a very popular source of refinancing debt for larger situations. These typically have a flexible borrowing base, which can increase but not reduce, that gives a borrower the ability to raise capital from new lenders on identical terms.

In the liquid markets that have developed following the end of the global financial crisis, there are high-risk lenders with an appetite to fund the gap between senior debt and equity. At the time of writing, their ceiling is typically 6x leverage. The cost of borrowing is eye-wateringly expensive and the terms include a transfer of the equity if the sponsor fails to meet performance targets, which can be aggressive.

Asset-based lending is suitable for certain situations, particularly those in which the borrower's profitability is limited. The debt is secured against inventory and receivables, with availability fluctuating on a daily basis.

In a crowded and very liquid debt market, firms offering debt advisory services will have a credible offering based on their current knowledge of, and relationships with, the proliferation of lenders, covering a wide variety of products and risk appetites.

At the option of the sponsor or the borrower, this may involve setting up a competitive process and inviting various lenders to submit their proposed commercial terms.

Restructuring alternatives

There are fundamentally three directions that a financial restructuring can take: a recapitalisation or refinancing of the business, possibly in combination; a sale of the business to repay debt; or an insolvency process that enables lenders to realise the value of their collateral.

There can be hybrids, for example, a business sale via a pre-packaged insolvency process. And a business can use a CVA process to gain a one-time cost or liquidity benefit, generally as a part of an operational restructuring that is launched after the terms of a financial restructuring have been agreed.

People in restructuring situations sometimes talk about the lenders 'taking a haircut'. In my experience, any lender that is being forced to take a loss will be most reluctant to see the incumbent board and management benefit from that situation. They would thus be more likely to support a different outcome, even an economically irrational one, unless the individuals involved were being jettisoned.

Recapitalisation and refinancing

Recapitalisation and refinancing are usually, but not always, done in combination. An outcome that leaves the senior lenders on tolerable leverage will be sought and there will be a balance to be struck between achieving an acceptable (although not necessarily prudent) debt-to-equity ratio, interest cost and cash outflow on debt service.

In situations with only one or, perhaps, a few lenders and vanilla private debt in a simple structure, the options will be limited to: new equity or junior debt; partial repayment of the senior debt; or partial equitisation by the lenders – or a combination or permutation of the options.

New equity is funded by way of a cash injection, possibly alongside the conversion of a portion of existing debt into equity. If existing equity has lost all or most of its value, it is often dealt with by conversion into worthless, non-voting deferred shares. To tidy up the balance sheet, it is common for the share premium account, if there is one, to be set off against accumulated losses.

If senior lenders are willing to hold equity, publicly listed lenders will be sensitive to owning more than a modest proportion, because beyond a fairly low threshold the lender would need to account for the borrower entity as a subsidiary.

In a capital structure with a high proportion of expensive junior debt, one way to limit the cash outflow on debt service is to roll the interest into the capital at the end of each interest period. These typically range between one and six months and the length of each new interest period is selected by the borrower, in advance. Debt with interest paid in this way is referred to referred to as PIK (Payment in Kind) and its real interest cost is higher than the face value, owing to the effect of continuous periodic compounding over the life of the loan.

The process of creating a three-way match between the debt capacity of the business, the availability of lending products in the market and retaining the support of the incumbent lenders will be led by the borrower. The Ringmaster – or the stakeholder management point person, or firm – will manage the process on a day-to-day basis. Quite possibly supported by a debt advisory firm.

If new or replacement debt is being sought, in a liquid market with a proliferation of funds all competing to get money out of the door, a tender process may produce the best terms for the borrower.

The focus of the process will be a term sheet, authored by the borrower and haggled over by various incumbent and potential new financial stakeholders, including non-lenders such as pension fund trustees.

Once the terms have been thrashed out, bank lenders will seek the approval of their credit committees and if there are differences to be reconciled within a lending syndicate the firm or institution in the role of co-ordinator will do that before forwarding the 'credit-approved term sheet' to the borrower's board for acceptance.

The process will then enter its legal documentation phase. It is usual for this process to bring to the surface detailed terms that need to be negotiated. This can seriously jeopardise timing.

The term sheet will list all of the conditions precedent to the financial restructuring. The fulfilment of these can create onerous workstreams that have to be run at pace and under pressure to avoid delaying completion.

In an international situation, involving multiple jurisdictions, the time, effort and cost of repaying incumbent lenders and simultaneously releasing security should not be underestimated.

A sale of the business

If the option of selling the business is identified upfront as a less-favoured option, it may be elevated as a consequence of an adverse IBR.

Lenders might provide funding as a bridge to a sale. Without such funding, there is likely to be a burning platform that will require an accelerated M&A process, involving investors with an appetite for higher risks and an ability to do deals quickly. They may insist on transacting via a pre-packaged insolvency process, if runway is fast running out, indemnities and warranties are unavailable or considered to be of little value and the probability of skeletons subsequently emerging from the cupboard is considered to be high.

The lenders' main activity will be the monitoring of the process and the borrower will be responsible for running it with the help of corporate finance advisers and possibly a variety of others as well, depending on whether the business is publicly listed or is in a sector that involves specialist knowledge. Tax, regulatory and competition issues could also require specialist advice.

The process will involve preparing an information memorandum, setting up a data room and conducting a competitive process to identify a potential buyer on the basis of an offer subject to due diligence. Proof of funding may be required at that stage. Typically, the party selected will be granted a period of exclusivity during which its advisers will have access to the business. If an acceptable offer results, there will be a period of negotiation followed by documentation and completion.

When a business is being sold, the integrated forecasts may recede in importance. Vanilla buyers will generally be content with the P&L-focused forecasts that are typically produced by businesses in normal circumstances. In contrast, distressed buyers will be very focused on bottom-up cash flow, particularly in the early stages. Moreover, if the process involves leaving behind suppliers there might need to be granular assumptions around issues such as dealing with ransom creditors; only the bidder is in a position to make such assumptions.

Formal proceedings

In the UK, both a CVA and a scheme of arrangement require creditor and shareholder approval before they can proceed.

A CVA cannot bind secured creditors but a scheme of arrangement can. The latter can be used to 'cram down' creditors that are 'out of the money' – in other words, limit their claims or render them worthless.

Both processes offer creditors advantages, including certainty, and because neither is currently available elsewhere in the European Union (EU), some companies incorporated in other EU jurisdictions can be artificially 'brought to the UK' to enable them to be used.

Under EU regulations, courts in all of its member jurisdictions are bound to recognise formal insolvency proceedings that are main proceedings approved by a court in any other EU jurisdiction. But a court can only approve them if a company has a 'centre of main interest' (COMI) in that jurisdiction. A non-trading company's COMI can be shifted relatively easily, by making some straightforward changes to the company's registered office, domicile of directors, place of business and so forth.

Completion and the aftermath

Even small deals can generate a surprising amount of paperwork. What usually happens is that all of the papers that need to be signed are laid out in the offices of a lawyer for one of the parties, almost certainly the one that has 'held the pen', and the various signatories have a window in which to call in and sign them. Usually by midnight.

Funds transfers are managed by the various parties' lawyers and those making payments have to be satisfied that security has been released by the recipients.

The aftermath can be an eerie experience: months of frenetic activity involving emails, calls and meetings, and usually a big push to get the deal over the line, are followed by complete silence!

Usually there will be a number of conditions subsequent that the borrower will be obliged to fulfil, typically within 30 to 120 days after completion.

PART IV

The director's dilemmas

19

GAINING ACCESS TO ESTABLISH THE CAUSES

A board established conventionally in compliance with contemporary corporate codes will have a majority of non-executive directors. Their typical time commitments will range from 10 to 25 days a year, to accommodate regular monthly meetings of the board and any committees in addition to one-off events such as strategy away-days.

Thus their routine contact with executives who are not also directors will necessarily be limited. And their access to information will be controlled by the executive directors, who may restrict, filter or misrepresent facts, for a range of motives. Given the sway that the executive directors hold, it is natural for the people in the ranks below to be reticent about speaking openly.

If the triggering of a financial crisis causes the accuracy and reliability of the information provided by the executive directors to be challenged or mistrusted, then the non-executives' trust in their colleagues has to be reappraised. This requires the reasons for the doubts to be established and the executives' motivations to be evaluated.

If the onset of the crisis was followed by revelation after revelation that came as one surprise after another to the non-executive directors, then perhaps the scales need to fall from their eyes, particularly those who, having gained their executive experience in the professions or in well-run businesses, are not inherently 'street wise' to the ways of business.

The non-executives thus face the major challenge of gaining direct access to meaningful information. They need a clearer view and they need to have confidence in the information that will be used to manage the financial crisis and restructuring. If the crisis has caused the executive directors to feel more insecure, or they have developed sinister agendas, then this task will be even more challenging.

Judging the character of the senior team

This will be critical to determining the size of the challenge and the angle of approach. One can never discount the possibility that the business is run by a team of rogues. The opportunities nowadays to earn life-changing rewards can distort even honest and decent individuals' moral compasses. Before long, there could be a whole team of rogues at the top: setting the exam questions, sitting the paper themselves, and then marking it too.

Perhaps the business is run by honest incompetents who lack the ability to manage but who present convincingly. One possible reason may be that they excelled in a lesser job but the people who promoted them failed to take into account that the personal qualities that served them well in that more junior role are not the same as the leadership and organisational qualities that are needed in senior positions.

Alternatively, the CEO may be a competent salesman whose laser-like vision on top-line growth served the business well, and who is beloved by investors and believed by lenders, but who, in the top job, has too little respect for, and pays too little attention to, the other parts of the operation.

The senior team might be hubristic deal junkies, whose expertise lies in M&A and not in running the businesses they already have. Or, even worse, perhaps the CEO is the driving force behind a roll-up strategy and the gravity-defying share price growth has made him or her a dangerous and untouchable Midas who squashes every challenge and quickly silences or eases out anyone foolhardy enough to make one.

Whatever their character, if they have been living on Planet Junket or if they do not have a reverse gear when the going gets tough, the challenges will be even greater.

The risk of administrative rot

The common problem with all of these different types of leader is that they are likely to have presided over worsening administrative rot that may run layers deep. This, in turn, provides a fertile breeding ground for all the factors that underlie unreliable numbers, as outlined in Chapter 20 – and not just because of incompetence or ignorance. Opacity and weak back offices allow rogues to keep their jobs, they stop inconvenient facts getting in the way of salesmen, they do not embarrass the incompetents and they are not considered by the deal junkies, and especially by Midas, to be as relevant as the share price as a measure of performance.

In the worst situations, key positions will be occupied by weak and underqualified people who have discovered the attractions of being paid and promoted beyond their capabilities and expectations, simply on account of their loyalty. Hence they will serve any rotten, incompetent or overbearing master and in the face of any threat they will fiercely cling to their jobs out of a fear of how difficult it would be to find another one that pays so well and in which they will also be able to get away with performing so woefully – all the more so if bonuses for the second and third tiers are being misused to reward loyalty rather than good performance.

Finding employees who will speak the truth

Good people recruited by accident into such situations tend to run a mile as soon as they have worked out what is going on. Fortunately, it is common to find competent, hard-working employees loyal to the business who have hung on grimly by keeping their heads down. However, do not expect them to identify themselves or to speak out in a public forum, because they are overseen by people who blindly support the regime, with whom they share a bent common cause. They are surrounded by informants who have their own agendas and motivations.

There are techniques for finding such people and getting them to open up.

Turning the tide

Unfortunately, lifting the lid on reality is not enough. The damage has been done, the survival of the business is in jeopardy and the buck stops with the non-executives. That requires all the key people in the ranks to start becoming a part of the solution and to weed out those who cannot or will not cooperate.

But the rot will have been building over a long period and there is no time to lose. If the situation is to be remedied, diktats from the top will be of little use. Key staff in the ranks will need to be convinced that change for the better is permanent and that they need have no fear of the regime.

This quote from Machiavelli's *The Prince* sums up the situation very well:

"And it ought to be remembered that there is nothing more difficult to take in hand, more perilous to conduct, or more uncertain in its success, than to take the lead in the introduction of a new order of things. Because the innovator has for enemies all those who have done well under the old conditions, and lukewarm defenders in those who may do well under the new. This coolness arises partly from fear of the opponents, who have the laws on their side, and partly from the incredulity of men, who do not readily believe in new things until they have had a long experience of them. Thus it happens that whenever those who are hostile have the opportunity to attack they do it like partisans, whilst the others defend lukewarmly, in such wise that the prince is endangered along with them."

Thus, the minimum requirement is a firm and very visible commitment from the non-executives, which is seen and understood further down the business, to address and remedy the situation, driven by very visible leadership and a clear and sensible finance change programme in which all the key people are involved.

The audit committee is an effective platform from which to drive such change.

To terminate or scaffold the executives?

This is one of the most difficult judgements for the non-executives to make and there may be strong arguments on both sides. On the one hand, the non-executives need to bear in mind that the value of the business will be reliant on many more factors than just the reliability of information, for example, customer and supplier relationships and commercial and domain knowledge. Terminating senior executives who have built those relationships and have that knowledge may do more harm than good.

On the other hand, the administrative rot needs to be addressed and the very presence of the regime could retard the effectiveness of the finance change programme. Putting people back behind the wheel of the bus that they have just crashed could seriously undermine confidence in the board, from the top to the bottom of the business.

An alternative to termination is 'scaffolding', a term used to mean reducing the scope of an executive's responsibilities so that they are focused on the core value factors that their departure would jeopardise. Other responsibilities can be transferred to incumbents or individuals brought in, until a permanent solution can be implemented.

If the non-executives make effective use of the audit committee as their platform, this can help to distance the 'scaffolded' executives from the change programme.

To cocoon the executives?

It is also tempting to 'cocoon' the executives, wrapping them in a safety blanket of expensive advisers. This can give the illusion that the non-executives have grasped the nettle. However, this is unlikely to be more than putting lipstick on a pig, a largely meaningless gesture designed just to get through the process. It will neither treat the rot nor result in any lasting remedy. And if there is a successful outcome to the financial restructuring, the advisers will depart, leaving the problem executives in place, along with the original causes of the problems.

Sharing information about the causes

The stakeholders, particularly the lenders, will have an interest in the board's discoveries and in its plans to remedy them. But sharing should be restricted to significant issues, which of course is a matter of judgement. Moreover, omitting to mention a cause upfront could be embarrassing and confidence-sapping if it subsequently becomes significant.

The lenders are likely to put much more store in the information provided by a board, as they will expect executives to downplay the seriousness of the causes and over-simplify the remedies. In fact, executives might prefer not to disclose some key issues at all, issues which, if uncovered late in the process by the lenders, could derail the planned restructuring and result in a suboptimal outcome.

The lenders will understand that discovering the problems in a business and putting remedial action into effect is an evolutionary process – no one will expect everything to be known in the immediate aftermath of the crisis.

20

UNRELIABLE NUMBERS: NO HIDING PLACE

One element crucial to establishing the causes is confidence in the numbers produced by the business. In their normal state, many businesses survive, and some even thrive, despite routinely generating numbers that are unreliable. In many cases, those at the top of the business are aware of the shortcomings and while frustrated or concerned, remain largely indifferent, believing, in a calculated gamble, that the unreliability will never have serious consequences. And as we have seen, the opacity that unreliable numbers sustain is compatible with the agendas of rogues and incompetents.

The heightened importance of reliable numbers

Once a financial crisis has been triggered, the risks that unreliable numbers pose increase significantly, because the issue is likely to become a critical factor in whether a board will succeed in managing a financial crisis and restructuring.

The numbers will be used in the liquidity forecasts,

updated every week.. As we have seen, those forecasts underpin the confidence of the board, lenders and other financial stakeholders that there will be a comfortable cushion of cash right up until the financial restructuring has been completed.

They will also be used in the forecasts that underpin the business plan which will be the basis for negotiating the reconfiguration of the capital structure and, if required, the raising of additional capital.

They will be used by all stakeholders and their advisers to scrutinise the performance of the business every time the monthly management accounts are produced.

And if the financial restructuring will be completed only after the external reporting deadline for the year-end or, in the case of a publicly listed company, the half-year, then they will be used by the board and the auditors to sign off 'going concern'.

Hence, numbers that prove to be unreliable can cause a rescue plan that everyone has been working on to have to be abandoned, usually late in the restructuring process, in favour of a suboptimal outcome, possibly even insolvency.

Directors have to grasp the nettle

Experienced business people would expect the directors of a business that has suffered a financial crisis to assume that it has routinely produced unreliable numbers. Especially if the unreliability of numbers was itself a root cause of the crisis. It will fall to them to rectify the issue and the stakeholders will presume that they will use the powers that they have to do so.

Directors ignore this responsibility at their peril. If they allow the crisis stabilisation and financial restructuring processes to progress without taking meaningful action to deal with unreliable numbers they are risking unnecessary value destruction and reputational damage, not to mention potential personal liability. Hence, turning a blind eye or making token gestures, in an attempt to be seen to be doing something about the problem, imperils the whole process.

Can't the audit be relied upon?

It is futile to equate a clean audit opinion with confirmation that a business routinely produces reliable numbers. The primary purpose of an audit is to opine on whether the representations of management in highly specific external reports provide a true and fair view. An auditor has a duty to report, if at all possible, rather than disclaim an opinion.

Therefore even the most unreliable numbers produced contemporaneously can be kicked into shape months after the balance sheet date. Hindsight is an enormous help. That is a very different proposition from the business being good at routinely producing reliable numbers that support the executives in managing the business and keep the board well informed on a continuing basis.

The sample testing of transactions that auditors carry out ahead of each year-end will provide an opportunity for some outsiders to lift the bonnet. But unless their findings are so serious as to risk stopping the audit, their significance is likely to become diffused by the time the auditor's report has passed through the audit committee up to the main board, where the concerns raised will be treated as compliance issues.

The strategy

In most circumstances, curing the unreliability of numbers will be an inseparable part of remedying the causes of the crisis, the causes will be deep-rooted and the fix will involve time and possibly significant cost. If undertaken seriously, the cure will necessarily be feared by some employees in the support and central functions of the business. But it will be welcomed and supported by many more across the entire business.

In approaching the issue, the board faces a spectrum of possible decisions that need to be based on judgements that, as far as practically possible, account for the realities and the risks faced.

At one end of that spectrum is a decision that a fix is simply not viable and so the business should be sold, leaving the buyer to deal with the problems. At the other end is a comprehensive self-help programme, using specialist resources engaged directly by the business.

A response somewhere along the spectrum risks a symbolic but futile effort that places an additional burden on a business just as it is facing a challenging situation. If that burden proves to be too much for the business, the directors will find themselves trying to change the wheel of a car while it is still moving.

An important principle to bear in mind is that 'best is the enemy of good'.

The nuts and bolts of the challenge

The starting point is to rapidly gather and assess key

information, as the basis for designing a solution that can be presented to the board.

The reliability of numbers is a product of four elements in a business: its back office, bookkeeping, accounting and finance. These are distinct but interdependent disciplines.

Think of numbers reported as business apparel, say, a suit. The back office sources the wool, bookkeeping is the weaving process that produces the raw fabric, accounting finishes the fabric and finance is the tailoring operation.

Plainly, it would be a miracle if low-grade wool, substandard weaving, inferior fabric finishing and inept tailoring produced a high quality business suit. But a person looking to buy such a suit might not find it easy to tell that just by looking at it in a shop.

Capable resources

The more deep-rooted the causes, the more likely it is that experienced and independent outsiders will need to be brought in to do the job. Hence the issue of remedying unreliable numbers should be pervasive in the board's early decision-making, most particularly the choice of Ringmaster, the number and type of interim finance resources to be engaged and the inputs needed from financial advisers.

In parallel with diagnosing the causes, such specialists can rapidly effect running repairs so that the crucial reports and forecasts that support the crisis mitigation and financial restructuring are fit made for purpose, by 'inspecting quality in'. The same people can prescribe a durable solution in the longer term, provide costs and timings for the operational restructuring plan and stay on for a period after the financial restructuring has been completed, to recruit, induct and hand over to new or upskilled permanent employees.

However, many directors would instinctively think about hiring a brand name firm. And of course those firms would be very happy to help out. But there are limitations and horses for courses. Continuing the suit manufacturing analogy will help to explain this.

If the problem was good quality fabric ineptly tailored (finance), accountancy firm employees with finance skills could reasonably be expected to diagnose the problem. And if the problem arose earlier in the process, in the finishing of the fabric (accounting), senior accountants employed by an accountancy firm could be expected to have the right skills.

But if the problems existed even earlier in the 'supply chain', in the back office (wool sourcing) and the bookkeeping (fabric weaving), then, in my experience, advisers' employees who had never before worked in a business would possess very little relevant experience to enable them to diagnose the problems, let alone fix them.

So employees of restructuring advisory firms are unlikely to be able to help a board to diagnose or fix problems in such areas. And it would be unrealistic to expect them to provide leadership. .

The auditors might make a limited contribution if their senior staff have relevant skills and experience or additional specialisms. But it should be borne in mind that their employees' skills mostly cover the sphere of accounting, in particular examining the amounts at which the assets and liabilities on the balance sheet are stated.

Belated efforts to remedy poor decision-making

If the board's failure to recognise and remedy problems with the back office and bookkeeping comes home to roost late in the day, it is usually impossible to recover the situation.

It will be too late to bring in specialist interim executives. They need some runway to get up to speed and if all the senior people are unavailable to show them the ropes, either because they have left or are working crazy hours to stop the ship from sinking, then they are unlikely to be effective.

It commonly happens that, very late in the day, the board throws an army of advisory firm employees with accounting and finance skills at the problem, all on expensive day-rates. In my view, that risks the board's interest in a successful outcome and the advisory firm's vested interest in maximising its fees to begin to diverge.

Given the veil that falls over failed restructurings in the absence of a bespoke inquiry, I believe an advisory firm will be free to enjoy its fees while the directors suffer reputational damage, possible financial losses and years of stress. You have been warned!

Sharing details with stakeholders

The issues surrounding unreliable numbers are very important and require delicate handling when it comes to sharing details with stakeholders. For a start, it may well reflect badly on the lenders who failed to spot the problems when doing the original deal. What is more, it could undermine the confidence of the people working on a solution.

Soul-baring confessions are to be avoided. But thoughtful explanations and reassurances that problems have been identified and reliably assessed and that deliverable solutions are either in planning or already under way, and that the board is committed to the process, will be well received.

·

21

DECIDING WHETHER TO STAY OR RESIGN

When a financial crisis has been triggered, a director may instinctively decide that staying on the board would be the most responsible thing to do. A director might also been keen to avoid a loss of income or the social stigma of a resignation being seen as desertion.

However, my view is that staying on without a sound reason to do so can damage the interests of the business, perhaps fatally. Resignation could, therefore, be in the best interests of all concerned. One type of individual I have in mind is the one who stays for the wrong reasons and becomes a deadweight or, worse, feels like a hostage who can only be freed from a nightmare existence if the business is euthanised. I have seen such people become adviser fodder and contribute to the destruction of enormous value.

The financial restructuring will be only a part of the picture

Every situation will have its unique facts, but it is likely to be the case that if the business is to survive, the ensuing financial restructuring will only be a subset of the work that the board has to manage in the short term.

Put another way, if the crisis is a manifestation of the symptoms and the financial restructuring is the cure, to protect value in the short-term and maximise it in the future the directors will also need to cure unreliable numbers, address the causes in order to prevent the crisis recurring, and deliver the benefits of the subsequent operational restructuring,.

A longer-term commitment

Hence, while the focus of the lenders, other stakeholders and advisers will be on the financial restructuring and the planning of the operational restructuring, the directors will in addition have to bring about change in other areas, including the senior team, the finance function and possibly also the board. This will inevitably require effort and commitment over a much longer period.

A more direct involvement in the changes

It would not reflect well on anyone involved if it transpired that the board was managing an artificial situation that ended badly when the truth came to light. This is a real risk because, as we established in Chapter 19, the non-executives rely almost exclusively on the executives for their information and therefore they need to gain considerably more access than they have in normal times, in part because the executives on whom they rely may be a significant element of the problems that the changes are intended to remedy.

Some of the necessary changes could be urgent, particularly if unreliable numbers are a problem. Others will take time to assess and decide upon. And without more reliable numbers it can be difficult to make proper assessments.

The process of gathering information, diagnosing what is broken, designing solutions and putting up remedial plans needs to be managed directly by the board. Personnel changes might result and the non-executives might need to temporarily fill gaps to mitigate the loss of knowledge in the short term. Or to provide leadership.

Timing

If a director decides to resign, the timing of the announcement is a sensitive issue. Inappropriate timing could send harmful signals that would risk damaging the business, the restructuring and the individual's reputation. I believe there are two junctures at which those risks are lowest: ahead of the formal management presentation to lenders; and when the financial restructuring has been completed.

There is, therefore, little time available for the directors, both individually and collectively, to assess the situation after the crisis has been triggered. They need to act quickly and decisively.

Personal assessment

Key issues that an incumbent director may have to assess personally are outlined below.

Are you staying out of *fear*? Standard legal advice – that resigning upfront will not lessen your responsibility for what has happened so far – requires further analysis. It may be that your risks will only increase in the future. Interpreting the legal advice to mean that remaining on the board would be less risky than leaving, because then you would retain some influence over future events, could be a flawed assessment if you are unable to make a meaningful contribution.

Can you be realistic about the *personal risks* or will you be a rabbit in the headlights, unwilling to do much without legal advice?

Will you be able to make available the *additional time* required? Overseeing the management of a financial crisis and restructuring can consume enormous amounts of time. You might need to get more directly involved, particularly in relation to the changes needed, which might run on well after the financial restructuring has completed. How long will it be before the commitment reverts to what you originally signed up for?

Will your *remuneration* increase to recognise the changed circumstances? Often, an emotional argument is used to shame directors into doing much more work and assuming more risk for the same fees, on the grounds that the crisis happened on their watch. Frankly, that is water under the bridge. If the stakeholders are going to be relying on individuals who they expect to make a meaningful contribution with increased personal risk to oversee a difficult process that, if successful, will protect their interests, then it is unrealistic to expect those individuals to do so without adequate and fair remuneration.

Could you *master the complexities* involved in the restructuring? If you were hired for your expertise in widget making, can you realistically acquire the expertise, rapidly, to enable you to make a meaningful contribution? Would your experience be of any use if the non-executives need to get more directly involved? Could you provide leadership, if the circumstances require this from the non-executives?

Do you have a *personal conviction* that there is a valuable business underneath the current mess?

Are your board colleagues *in denial*? If so, will they embrace reality quickly enough? How likely is it you will be a *lone voice in the wilderness*, hopelessly outnumbered?

Do you have *faith in the equity owners*? Since you joined the board, have they retained credibility? Have they shown the board respect? Having regard to the issues outlined in Chapter 7, on being a director of a private equity business, do you consider they will act responsibly? Will you simply be along for the ride, with no influence?

Do you have *confidence in the chairman*? Is he or she a good leader? Or a patsy of the equity owners or the CEO? Are you comfortable that conflicts will be identified and properly managed?

Will the *standard of governance* improve? When comparing the way the board has been operating with the good governance guidance given in Part VII, how serious are its shortcomings? Was the business simply an accident waiting to happen?

Will you find *allies* among the non-executives to join you as an advocate for making the necessary changes? Conversely, are there board colleagues who you think will make a difficult situation worse, or even impossible?

Would your answers to the five preceding questions change if a *competent independent individual* with suitable situational experience joined the board?

Are you up for *changing your style*? If you have always kept your head down and avoided rocking the boat, you may need to start acting robustly if you are going to make a meaningful contribution.

Do you have the *stomach* for the politics, conflict and confrontation that lie ahead which will almost certainly cost you personal relationships?

Will your *contribution be valued* and will it provide you with an ongoing role? Many people who help a business through a difficult time find that newcomers brought in afterwards to take the business forward have little interest in the history and regard all the people who were involved in the same, negative light.

Group assessment

Unless your personal assessment of the situation has resulted in an unequivocal decision to resign, sharing the bulk of your personal assessment with your non-executive colleagues, or at the very least the chairman, would be a responsible course to take.

If you are minded to stay, bilateral contact with non-executive colleagues will provide opportunities to explore beneficial alliances and assess whether a consensus could be built.

You might be pleasantly surprised to discover that there is a weight of support for your views. Perhaps none of the others will have approached the issues so thoughtfully.

It is essential that the non-executives should be able to meet without the executive directors present. If the board has not done that before, and the chairman has to ask the permission of the executive directors, or if they object, that in itself could be a strong reason to resign.

The context for the meeting is that the board is now front and centre of the situation; and acting in the best interests of the business is likely to mean something quite different from what it was before, particularly if under UK law the directors' primary duties have switched from the shareholders to the creditors.

The optimal outcome is a setting of a tone that reinforces or restores the board's authority. Ideally, this will be done by means of a three-part action plan: to remedy governance shortcomings that are impairing the board's effectiveness; to put the board on a war footing to oversee management of the financial crisis and restructuring; and to set about diagnosing and addressing the causes, including remedying unreliable numbers.

The attitude of the group and the alignment of their views with your own should be a significant factor in a decision to stay or resign. If they recognise the board's past shortcomings and appear sincere about wanting the problem to be solved, providing you think there is a good prospect of building alliances and achieving strong consensus, that should be a boost to your confidence in your fellow travellers.

On the other hand, if you consider that a majority of your colleagues seem happy to tolerate suboptimal performance and prefer not to rock the boat, if you feel that they are simply paying lip service to the need to act more effectively in the future, or if you think they will start promisingly but probably backslide before long, then you seriously have to consider whether you want to be part of a flawed group and leave your reputation in their hands. This dilemma may be particularly acute if the chairman is weak and the CEO is strong and some of the non-executives are in the CEO's pocket, or if a group of them constitutes an axis with a potentially sinister agenda, that sees the crisis as an opportunity to advance or achieve it!

Mission impossible or Pyrrhic victory?

If, following the meeting, you conclude that the board is likely to fail in its leadership role in the financial crisis and restructuring, there would need to be strong extenuating circumstances for you to decide to stay.

It is all very well having honourable intentions, but boards have collective responsibility and if you consider you are being set up to fail, you should not have to continue to be exposed to the heightened reputational and financial risks when you are in the minority. And it may be that the best way to serve the interests of stakeholders would be to resign and thereby send a helpful signal.

Perhaps the harder decision is whether to stay because you believe that you and the allies that you have identified have good prospects of prevailing by being smarter and more dogged in standing up to incompetence, mediocrity, indifference, and vested or perhaps even sinister interests.

Bear in mind that the battle might be toxic and the victory Pyrrhic. Moreover, there is the risk that the obvious conflict would make incumbent and potential new lenders uncomfortable. Or they may act irrationally in any event, possibly because they are blind to the virtuous cause that you and your colleagues are fighting.

Altering course instead?

Managing the financial crisis and restructuring will be difficult, but at least there will (or ought to) be a strong mutual interest in a successful outcome. If the organisation is in a state of disrepair, it is likely that the most arduous battles around the boardroom table will be about what the causes are and how to remedy them in a way that is sustainable.

If so, the answer may lie not in going head-to-head but instead in promoting an outcome for which majority support can be garnered and that avoids the need to transform from within.

A sale of the business would be such an outcome. It would likely involve presenting to the market a flourishing business with adequate funding that potential buyers would covet and compete with each other to buy. On the basis of *caveat emptor*, the issues would be the bidders' to discover and the buyers' to fix.

A conditional conclusion?

You might conclude that staying on the board would only be feasible if certain serious concerns that you have could be suitably allayed. This should be part of a discussion with the chairman, or the equity owners if the business is privately owned. It does not have to be a negative conversation. It might be that you are pushing at an open door. Perhaps they will have arrived at a similar conclusion.

One of your conditions might be an assurance that the board will treat the situation with the seriousness it deserves, get onto a proper footing and commit to doing the best possible job in the circumstances, no matter how much discomfort that might cause to individuals.

Managing the message

If you decide to resign, then, whatever your grounds, you clearly have an obligation to avoid harming the interests of the business either deliberately, or by omission in not thinking carefully enough about the reasons you will give or by giving mixed messages to different audiences. The grown-up way to do this is to agree a text with the chairman or the equity owners that is anodyne. 'Personal reasons' is often an acceptable fig leaf that no one believes anyway! If 'being unable to commit the time required by the situation' is a genuine reason, it would be difficult to criticise someone.

If you consider that your reputation in the lending community is of significance, a discreet call, perhaps to the lenders' adviser, to add flesh to the bones would probably be advisable. However, for the sake of everyone it would be best for the details to align with the reason given publicly and for any damaging or pejorative comments to be avoided. And be mindful that many of the possible reasons you could give, although candid, may not reflect well on your contribution to date!

PART V

The Ringmaster's art

22

EARLY ACTIONS

The Ringmaster's early actions are a function of the agreed scope. Actions common to any scope are dealt with in this chapter. Those actions that relate directly to the specific elements within the scope – governance, stakeholder management and operations – are dealt with separately in the following chapters.

Assuming the scope does not simply involve being a pure non-executive on the board, with a limited time commitment, the Ringmaster has to work quickly from the outset to set up the various plates that will have to be kept spinning for some considerable time.

The right Ringmaster will have experience of responding effectively to the onset of a crisis in a focused way, and will therefore make a valuable contribution to helping the board consider and decide the priorities that are outlined in Chapter 8 – judgements, organisation and modification of the modus operandi – as well as possibly offering some bandwidth to assist the senior team at a challenging time.

Creating order

The first six to eight weeks are likely to be pandemonium, with the Ringmaster working very long days, travelling a lot, being constantly pulled in several directions at once, alternately zooming in on detail and then zooming out to a high level again, several times in the course of a single day, and having conversations and meetings about an eclectic range of topics.

The Ringmaster's overriding short-term objective is to create order from chaos, by moving everyone involved to a more orderly state. Yes, the atmosphere will still be intense and people will still be working very long hours, but there will be fewer unknowns and a focus on key issues will be developing, with milestones becoming discernible and the workstreams taking shape.

Strategic assessment

Soon after the crisis was triggered, when preparing to engage initially with the lenders, the board will have made a snap assessment without the benefit of much information.

That assessment needs to be updated and the Ringmaster, with the benefit of years of experience, will bring a fresh pair of eyes and a new focus. If the Ringmaster had an initial off-the-record dialogue with the lenders before committing to the role, that might also provide valuable information.

Debating the key issues with the board and senior team will identify the need for specific legal and financial analysis. Usually, the big fundamental questions are: what is the liquidity outlook? Is there a need for new money? What impact could an adverse reaction in the marketplace have on liquidity? Will covenant and other breaches threaten the available headroom? Where on the spectrum of valuable to valueless is the business now? Does the value break in the debt? If so, is lender value shrinking rapidly? What options will the lenders perceive?

There are three ballparks.

At the one end of the spectrum, there is no alternative to a corporate funeral. The board's priority becomes maximising value for creditors and options are rapidly developed for lenders. If one option is new equity, investor appetite could be tested in a small window, while other options are being developed in parallel.

At the other end, the board is confident that the crisis has created neither solvency nor liquidity issues for the business: the balance sheet is strong, adequate funding facilities are in place and there are no covenant issues.

In both of those scenarios, there is little need for the services of the Ringmaster. But, very obviously, a board needs to be cautious in the extreme about delivering either of these messages on the basis of a flawed assessment.

Between those two bookends, however, some form of lender support will be required in response to some or all of performance, valuation, liquidity and solvency issues.

It will help lender confidence enormously if their expectations are managed competently. As one senior banker put it to me quite early in my restructuring career: 'We do not mind being told we are on a journey to Glasgow and the train breaks down at Carlisle, because we understand that these are difficult situations and often, by the time you are called in, it is too late. But we will be very annoyed to discover that the train has taken us to Bristol!'

Legal analysis

The appointed restructuring lawyers will rapidly get to grips with the documentation for all of the debt facilities, hedging agreements, security documents and so forth and provide a high-level analysis of the key issues, including maturity dates, tripwires, triggers, events of default, cross-defaults, covenants and key dates. They will also identify the various baskets that will be defined in the facilities documentation that principally limit indebtedness that can be incurred from, and made available to, third parties.

If there is still an opportunity to manage a potential drawstop, as detailed earlier, that must be a priority.

Crucially, the lawyers need to identify all breaches and potential breaches and to advise on options and tactics for procuring waivers.

Working with the finance team, the actual definitions in the facility documents that feed into the covenants need to be clearly established from scratch and the calculations underlying past covenant certificates need to be validated. A similar exercise will be necessary in relation to the various baskets, to enable available headroom – and perhaps any breaches – to be identified.

If there have been misrepresentations, these need to be detailed.

The lawyers also need to schedule all of the dates upon which information is required to be delivered to lenders, under the terms of the facilities. These dates need to be dropped into the timetable that the Ringmaster will develop. If more time is needed, requests for extensions should be added to the waiver requests.

Selecting financial and other advisers

A business that engages a Ringmaster acquires instant access to a specialist network along with valuable insider insights into the strengths and weaknesses of the various financial advisory firms, in some cases based on recent, first-hand experience, as well as to the restructuring community and its grapevine.

Based on the initial conversations, analyses and assessments to date, the Ringmaster will rapidly develop a view of the types of financial and other advice and consultancy that are likely to be most valuable in assisting the board in managing the financial crisis and restructuring.

After considering the various options and outcomes, as well as the possible courses that the associated processes may take, the different types of advisory service likely to be needed are identified, if necessary by brainstorming, and a skeleton scope is developed for each. This will typically lead to a competitive pitch process being established for each type of service, for which an objective evaluation methodology can be created.

For example, a sale of a business will need corporate finance and possibly vendor due diligence services; raising additional debt will need debt advisory services; while the core restructuring will need expertise in developing capital structures and experience in negotiating commercial terms.

Having rapidly established which firms the lenders are considering, the Ringmaster can assist the board in developing shortlists for each pitch process. The Ringmaster will then lead those processes and provide recommendations to the board.

People in the restructuring industry move very quickly and this can all be done, end-to-end, in a compressed timescale.

Resourcing

A Ringmaster will be aware that a financial crisis will cause employees to feel insecure, at the very time they will be needed to give greater attention and an increased commitment to the day-to-day management of the business, in a more challenging environment.

Hence, to mitigate the risks that their performance will dip or that they will leave, one aim should be to minimise their direct involvement in the management of the financial crisis and restructuring by engaging additional external resources in the form of specialist interim executives and, exceptionally, advisory staff. The nuts and bolts of this are covered in earlier chapters.

The direct involvement of the Ringmaster should ensure that the resourcing job is done effectively. The Ringmaster will have the network to find specialist interim executives of a high calibre and might have worked with some of them previously. Unless the board requests otherwise, they will be engaged directly by the business, rather than via the Ringmaster.

Resourcing will take up considerable time, particularly as the specs for unfilled roles could mutate as each firm or person is confirmed and their scope nailed down.

Time also has to be spent on inducting and setting up every

new resource, to ensure that they get off to a flying start and can quickly operate under their own steam, thus maximising their productivity.

The finance team

The finance team will come under enormous strain after a financial crisis has been triggered and the success of the restructuring effort will be heavily reliant on it. Therefore, unless it is a top quartile team – which by definition a business in crisis is unlikely to have! – it is inevitable that it will need to be bolstered.

In early conversations at various levels, a Ringmaster with operational capabilities will rapidly assess what gaps need to be filled.

A restructuring would be the worst possible time to be embarking on a conventional HR-led recruitment process that involves long timescales while candidates are interviewed, made offers and then work their notice periods, before taking months to settle in, work out the internal politics and eventually make their mark.

Besides, good calibre candidates are not going to join an organisation in crisis, and if they do so with their eyes closed, they will quickly head for the exit. Hires with vanilla skillsets may well flounder when faced with shortcomings in processes and systems. To adopt a farming analogy, a candidate skilled in hosing down the yard every morning may be required to shovel out lots of manure before settling down into a routine of daily hosing – and they may never get there!

As covered more fully in Chapter 6, drafting in battle-hardened interim executives with situational experience will almost always be by far the best solution. They will identify the problems, help design the solutions and then implement them, before handing over to their permanent replacements. That is the time for the conventional recruitment process – and, of course, by then there may be many more suitable internal candidates who have benefited from working under the interim executives.

Depending on the circumstances, the interim executives drafted in may be the same ones who will cover the urgent restructuring workstreams. If not, then more will need to be hired.

If the senior finance people buy into this philosophy from the outset, that is a bonus. If not, persuasive efforts need to be made to sell it to them. If that does not work, the board and the senior team need to back the Ringmaster's judgement or they will risk undermining the restructuring and jeopardising the survival of the business. As General George S. Patton is credited with saying, 'Lead, follow or get out of the way!'

For this and other reasons, it is important that the Ringmaster manages the relationship with the finance team proactively but sensitively from the outset.

In the circumstances, the senior finance people are likely to feel a mix of negative emotions: alienated by all the new people brought in; marginalised if in their inexperience they feel they could be doing the restructuring-related work themselves; threatened if they fear the new people brought in are going to replace them or take their jobs; frustrated if they believe the financial crisis was triggered because their repeated warnings had fallen on deaf ears; and perhaps even vilified if the rest of the business blames them for the financial crisis, all the more so if the finance team had already become the whipping boy of a dysfunctional senior team, in an environment of administrative rot.

If the Ringmaster has a deep background in finance, the common finance language and the Ringmaster's obvious experience should provide an instant platform from which to build a collegiate and collaborative relationship. The prospects of achieving that will be increased by the Ringmaster taking the time to explain what is happening and why, keeping the team informed with regular updates and seeking their input on issues where they have relevant knowledge and experience.

There is another angle that should not be ignored. Because finance employees are at the hub of a business-wide informal information network, and the information they impart is more sought after at times of widespread employee insecurity and mistrust of management, keeping the senior finance people onside creates good ambassadors within the business for the restructuring process and thus helps breed confidence among employees and, to an extent, the external people with whom they interact.

But this same internal network creates a risk that junior finance employees who are routinely privy to sensitive matters will very quickly broadcast information through their own networks to colleagues in other parts of the business about the costs of the restructuring. Such conversations, between people who lack a proper understanding of the situation, will feed the rumour mill with destructive and possibly even malicious consequences.

From this it should be clear that the processing and payment of invoices in relation to the restructuring need to be done in a confidential manner by senior and trustworthy finance staff.

I find the best way to do this is to have the restructuring resources who are responsible for cash also being given responsibility for managing all of the restructuring-related invoices until they are approved and ready to be paid. This has the additional benefit of facilitating tight control and accurate forecasting of the costs.

As these people will interact frequently with less senior finance employees, they have a valuable role to play in managing the relationship with the finance team at another level and it is important to brief them about the sensitivities and to encourage them to share with the Ringmaster the feedback and intelligence that they glean.

Planning for the management presentation to lenders

The management presentation to lenders is a key early milestone and a very important task for the Ringmaster, the financial advisers and, if appointed, the stakeholder management point person.

It needs to be pulled together as soon as practically possible and will have to cover numerous critical issues that will remain visible throughout the process. It is important not to omit something that might later become significant. It also needs to set expectations realistically.

The restructuring strategy is the cornerstone. Assuming the latest assessment is not at the extremes of the spectrum described above and also that the board has not concluded that the business should be sold, the optimum strategy is likely to be one that seeks: first to protect value for lenders; second, to restore it; and third, to create value for equity.

In terms of tactics, the board needs to be clear about a roadmap to get to a balance sheet fix. There may be voices on the board making a case for jumping into a transformation of the business. Perhaps the individuals will have had experience of this approach working well in a subsidiary or a division of a large corporate with a big balance sheet. But under conditions of scarce liquidity and time it would be risky in the extreme.

The fact is, when support is needed from stakeholders external to the business, the process of securing that support will be complex and will take time. Much bespoke information will need to be generated – and subjected to due diligence – before terms can be agreed, approved and documented.

A good Ringmaster, with the support of financial advisers, will make clear what preconditions those onerous requirements create before the leadership can embark on transformation: first, stability will have to be achieved; then, a detailed case for an operational restructuring will have to be worked up and costed; and, finally, the additional liquidity required will have to be secured.

Obviously, triage that is demonstrably cash-generative in the short term should be started without delay. However, it would be dangerous to treat liquidity that is expected to flow from triage as a dead cert, by baking it into forecasts. Disposals, cost cutting and better liquidity management are all fine on paper, but a business in crisis will find execution challenging if suitably experienced senior employees are not already in place and, in that crisis, have bandwidth to spare and can remain sufficiently motivated. Moreover, a seller in crisis will find it hard to achieve pre-crisis prices;

smelling an opportunity for a discount, savvy bidders will be in no hurry to conclude a deal, and if the overall process is perceived to not be going well there will be genuine concern about the value of warranties offered by the seller.

Lenders will be alert to the danger of inexperienced management being over-optimistic and possibly even in denial.

To secure their support for the board's strategy and tactics, the borrower's plan needs to cover the key factors that would underpin lender confidence. This will include: the requisite situational experience on the board and in the senior team; the calibre of the Ringmaster and advisers engaged by the board; the reliability of the liquidity analysis; the proposed roadmap, timetable and action plan; the proposal to win support from other financial stakeholders; realism about perceived threats and the credibility of contingency plans to deal with any that materialise; enhanced focus on business performance; plans to manage non-financial stakeholders and marketplace concerns; execution capabilities, particularly in relation to triage; and, if numbers produced by the business are unreliable, whether the issue has been acknowledged and there is a credible commitment to address it urgently and convincingly.

The overarching concern of lenders will be that the board and management acknowledge that protecting and, if necessary, restoring lender value is the priority, and there is no implicit assumption that their balance sheets will continue to be available while the shareholders and management focus their energies on trying to improve their own positions.

The lenders may be prepared to support the aspirational, possibly even audacious, goals of the board to restore equity value in due course. However, they will expect the board to develop and work on fallback plans that provide options for protecting financial stakeholders' value.

If, however, they lack the requisite confidence that equity value will be restored, they may favour instead a sale or break-up of the business. Or they may decide to sell their debt.

In preparing the presentation, the board needs to thoroughly explore and debate all of these issues, recognising the valuable contributions that the Ringmaster and financial advisers will be able to make.

The liquidity ask

If liquidity support is going to be requested, it will be necessary to formulate a definite ask, that will be scrutinised by the lenders' advisers.

If the board has engaged an advisory firm very early on to provide support in the area of cash management, some rudimentary measures will already be in place. But, as detailed earlier, initial forecasting is only the first step in a long journey, and the board's confidence in such early forecasts should, therefore, be low.

An important part of the Ringmaster's work will be to probe the forecasts. The parameters here are that, on the one hand, the business does not want to ask for an increase in facilities to be made available that is so big that it makes the lenders so uncomfortable that they instead provide nothing. On the other hand, there should not be a second ask.

It is likely that the Ringmaster's recommendation will come as an unpleasant surprise to the board, more so if the earlier forecasts on which their expectations were based were prepared without external help.

However, the directors can take comfort from the skin that the Ringmaster will have in the game: endorsing a flawed liquidity forecast carries immense reputational downside risks for an independent restructuring professional. Whatever the Ringmaster's agreed scope, the lenders will always assume it includes responsibility for liquidity!

It is likely that there will be possible mitigations, such as the benefits of internal initiatives, asset sales and using lease finance to fund capital expenditure. But, for the reasons outlined earlier, it would be inadvisable to bake these into the forecasts at an early stage.

23

GOVERNANCE OF THE PROCESS

Setting up the leadership platform

As managing the financial crisis and restructuring is something new within the organisation, – and is not expected to be needed for a long period of time– the Ringmaster needs to establish a platform that in due course will become redundant.

If the board has constituted a committee that the Ringmaster is to chair, its terms of reference have to be developed with inputs from legal advisers. If this concept has originated from lenders' conditions or requests, the terms agreed with them should be reflected.

A budget for the restructuring, for which the Ringmaster will be responsible, will need to be retrofitted to the existing corporate budget, and finance will need to create the ability for the Ringmaster to commit to the necessary expenditure, subject to bard oversight, which may require the established approval authority policy to be updated.

Restructuring cost control

Given how expensive restructuring can be and the potential for avoidable material overruns if controls are lax, an effective Ringmaster should exercise tight control of the costs of advisers to all parties. I have been involved in situations in which the benefits of this approach have covered the costs of the Ringmaster and all the interim executives several times over.

These costs will be visible as a separate line in the liquidity forecast and there should be a detailed forecast that sits behind the numbers, which is maintained by those resources running liquidity management. If done properly, it is hard work.

Every adviser to the borrower should have a time and costs budget that reflects the scope agreed in its engagement letter. If fees are time-based, then each week the time incurred and that planned for the following week should be reported promptly for the Ringmaster's review and approval.

As the borrower is responsible for the fees of the stakeholders' advisers, it is reasonable to expect that a representative of each stakeholder or group will exercise similar control and provide transparency. It is up to the Ringmaster to establish a protocol and to maintain regular communications. If there are increases to budgets or additional types of work needed, there should be governance around these changes, involving the borrower and the stakeholder representatives.

Inevitably, budgets agreed upfront will come under pressure and the Ringmaster should be responsible for staying on top of this and formalising any increases that are agreed as well as for updating the various engagement letters for all variations.

It is reasonable to expect all advisers, to all parties, to only bill for work that has been budgeted for, in a manner that aligns with the detail underlying the budget, with any variations being agreed in advance. Usually that means each adviser creating a charging code for each stream of work, to enable it to provide the detail in its reporting and billing. And to provide explanations for any variations before they are accepted.

The arrangements I typically set up are for details of proposed monthly charges to be submitted to the borrower by the first Friday of the following month, for any queries to be raised by the second Friday, for the bill reflecting the agreed charges to be received by the third Friday and for payment to be made by the fourth Friday.

One costly and avoidable practice is sending unnecessary emails and needlessly copying in individuals who do not need to be on the chain. Law firms have software that recognises which matters incoming emails relate to and automatically creates a time charge for each one. If there is an email to, say, 30 people of whom 10 are lawyers, someone innocently hitting 'Reply All' just to say 'Thanks' might unwittingly incur a charge of 10 x 6 minutes at an average hourly rate of, say, £1,000!

Project management

With the resources in place and a plan and timetable agreed with the stakeholders, the process can be broken down into a series of workstreams, for which specified people and firms have been allocated responsibility. This, in turn, is reflected in their letters of engagement and their agreed fee budgets.

As the leader, the Ringmaster has responsibility for monitoring all of the various workstreams, and this is usually done by way of regular updates, involving reporting, meetings and calls.

This involves co-ordinating a lot of external firms and people and providing the right information at the right time. In my experience, employees of firms that mainly advise lenders can provide very useful assistance to the Ringmaster, if they have the situational experience. This reflects their experience walking in the shoes of some of their opposite numbers as they not only understand the domain but can also be adept at handling the politics and tactics. And those with sector experience can be helpful to management in hosting an IBR by a lender's financial adviser.

In addition, there is usually a series of internal updates that feed into the board committee, followed by a stakeholder update and a confirmation of priorities for the following week. There will invariably be many variations to the plan along the way, that will require decisions to be made about how to keep things on track. As in any project, the variables are time, quality and cost.

It is good practice for the board committee to update the full board at least once a week and if decisions are required between such updates, calls or additional meetings can be convened at short notice.

From a distance, a well-run process may appear to be like a

swan gliding gracefully across a pond, while under the water its feet are paddling away like mad!

Even with the best project management, there is always the risk that the process will go off the rails. In that event, the Ringmaster needs to lead from the front, developing and agreeing alternative plans and timings in order to maintain confidence in the board, to keep relationships civil and to prevent the mood from becoming confrontational.

Board oversight

Notwithstanding its delegation of the day-to-day management to a committee led by the Ringmaster, the board still retains responsibility for managing the financial crisis and restructuring. Moreover, in the course of the process, the board will face some big decisions in relation to it.

This will include consideration of commercial terms and conditions, and the monitoring of delivery against deadlines and targets, including disposals. From time to time, circumstances will necessitate tactical debates.

Just as a driver on a long journey needs to keep an eye on the dashboard instruments, so too the board needs to monitor a dashboard of the survival KPIs. At a minimum, these will include liquidity and covenants.

Liquidity updates will be available weekly and while it is important for the board to digest these and to remain engaged and curious, it is even more important that the senior executives recognise the high priority that the work of the restructuring people in this area deserves.

The covenants – including valid definitions and the true history – should have been clearly established at the outset, as detailed in the earlier chapter, and they should be projected as part of the forecasts that are updated regularly throughout the process. If the projections start to show uncomfortable tightening, or even a breach, it will be necessary to request relief – or even for testing to be suspended.

If the restructuring strategy has to be reviewed, that can create difficulties for the board. It will mean that its original goals are not going to be met and if those were the basis for restoring equity value, a change could well mean abandoning them in favour of protecting lender value.

24

GOVERNANCE OF THE BUSINESS

The experience of the Ringmaster

As a seasoned veteran, the Ringmaster is likely to be an expert in the matters dealt with in Part VII, in which I provide my views on the fundamentals of effective governance, and will, therefore, be well qualified to evaluate quickly where on the good–bad spectrum of effectiveness a board lies.

Doing so will involve no great effort on the part of the Ringmaster; rather, it will be a judgement largely based on instinct. It is likely that some of the incumbent directors, if they have a relevant depth of experience, will be willing and valuable sources of information.

This matters a great deal because a board that is already functioning effectively will be better positioned to adapt to changed circumstances once a financial crisis has been triggered, and it should therefore have greater prospects of delivering a better outcome.

As I articulate in Part VII, I believe the factors that are most relevant to whether a business will enter a crisis in a fit state are: a clear strategy; robust plans that are owned by the second tier of management; the capabilities of the senior team that a CEO has built; whether the CFO is independent-minded and of high calibre; rigorous performance monitoring; respect for the authority of the non-executive directors; and a chairman and CEO who are both good leaders.

Such a board should find it easier to adapt and its more reliable financial information will give it a firmer foundation for the highly specific forecasting that will be essential to survival.

Improving board effectiveness

Whatever the Ringmaster's recommendations, it is up to the non-executives – under the leadership of the chairman – and possibly also the shareholders to use structured discussions as a platform for constructive change, rather than to put up barriers on the basis of 'not invented here'.

Clearly, in a financial crisis and restructuring, a complex and time-consuming change programme aiming to achieve gold standards would be inappropriate. However, the benefits of adopting many of the elements outlined in Part VII, in order to enhance governance at a critical time and thereby improve the prospects of a successful outcome, are likely to far outweigh the costs, if any.

Adapting to the changed circumstances

The fact that a board functions effectively prior to a crisis is a helpful starting point. But this alone in no way guarantees that its decision-making will continue to be sound. The better use it makes at the outset of the time, headroom and symbiotic goodwill of its most important stakeholders, the more viable will be the runway it creates for managing the crisis.

After a financial crisis has been triggered, a board will need to change the way it operates, in order to place itself front and centre in managing the crisis. To achieve that, some or all of the directors will need to commit significant additional time.

I have outlined elsewhere in this book what that is likely to involve, most notably in:

- Chapter 8 on the immediate response
- Chapter 13 on personal risks
- Chapter 19 on gaining access to establish the causes of the crisis
- Chapter 20 on unreliable numbers
- Chapter 21 on deciding whether to stay on as a director.

Division of responsibilities

Broadly, my recommendation is to implement a three-way division of responsibilities: running the business; managing the financial crisis and restructuring; and dealing with the meaty issues. The board will have considered some of these issues soon after the crisis was triggered, as outlined in Chapter 8.

Firstly, the board needs to up its game in terms of overseeing the performance of the operating business, given that conditions will be more challenging and that trading performance will come under more external scrutiny than usual.

Secondly, the chairman and the senior team will need to be more engaged than in normal times with the business, the market and the key non-financial stakeholders including customers, suppliers, regulators and the unions.

Thirdly, its agenda should be de-cluttered, with non-essential issues put on the back burner.

Fourthly, as outlined in Chapter 2, the board will need to oversee the management of the financial crisis and restructuring and, in so doing, mitigate the directors' personal risks by holding meetings and taking advice, as necessary.

Fifthly, meaty issues that the crisis has brought to light or caused – such as the need to replace the senior team, the need to investigate accounting irregularities or executive misconduct, the need to confront the poor calibre of administration, litigation and a disenfranchisement of the equity owners – may all need to be dealt with.

Adding new directors to the board

It goes without saying that the board needs to be realistic in its assessment of where the business is. This links to the strategic evaluation that is the cornerstone of the management presentation to lenders.

It follows that if the incumbent directors lack the bandwidth, the skills and the situational experience, adding new directors becomes both important and urgent. These are unlikely to be conventional appointments managed through headhunters. The candidate backgrounds are likely to be atypical and the timescales will be compressed.

A board may be hesitant to add new directors. If one

concern is that the appointment of people with Red Adair-type backgrounds will spook the market, then a quote that Mr Adair himself is credited with is germane, 'If you think it's expensive to hire a professional to do the job, wait until you hire an amateur.'

In public company situations, short selling often indicates that the market is already aware, in which case the board going into laager (an Afrikaans word meaning to arrange a column of wagons in a circular formation for defence) and putting out upbeat and optimistic announcements only risks making the situation worse.

Clearly, there will be situations in which the storm will soon pass and there is no need to alter the composition of the board, on the basis that 'Before long, things will be back to the way they were'. But thinking that is going to happen when it is not would be a costly and possibly fatal misjudgement for a board to make.

Monitoring of business performance

If EBITDA or similar measures are key to the value of the business, it will be vital for the executive team to be focused on driving trading performance and for the board to give monthly results even more attention than they would in normal times, despite the demands of managing the financial crisis and restructuring.

Focusing attention on the monthly results for the duration of the process reflects the fact that the lenders – and, if the business is for sale, any potential buyers – will be subjecting the management accounts, particularly the P&L, to rigorous scrutiny. It happens that sale processes are aborted because trading disappoints.

The key to managing expectations is a realistic forecast. As mentioned earlier, the existing corporate forecasting model should be refreshed and the board needs to be involved in sensitising a version that is then adopted. This dovetails with the workstreams to manage liquidity and produce three-way integrated forecasts for the financial restructuring.

Despite the high-level nature of the exercise, the key assumptions do need to be articulated by management and the final agreed versions should be documented carefully. Providing no lilies have been gilded, this approach should facilitate robust variance analysis and maintain high confidence through the process that the board and management are competent.

In parallel, the board needs to ensure that the effectiveness of the established monthly executive review processes is maximised.

25

STAKEHOLDER MANAGEMENT

The framework

The management presentation to lenders will provide the initial framework for managing stakeholders. It will reflect the board's updated assessment of the starting position, the proposed destination, the roadmap, a plan and a timetable. If appropriate, it should also include fallback plans and associated options.

Although there is unlikely to be much in the way of granular forecasts, the assumptions and other information underlying the various issues will need to be articulated for the lenders.

As such, the management presentation will be a request to the lenders to buy into the board's proposals to give them back either their money (by selling the business) or their confidence (by fixing the balance sheet).

Having received the presentation, the lenders will need to go away and consider the board's proposals. Then come back with a strategy of their own, as a framework for their response. By that stage, they ought to have the benefit of other work done by their advisers, in particular, a review of their security, liquidity and the identification and initial valuation of possible options. They will also have made preliminary assessments of the directors and senior executives and have started to gauge the position of the shareholders and the capabilities of the borrower's advisers.

The lenders' response will fall somewhere on the spectrum between 'largely agree' and 'largely disagree', and it will be accompanied by a set of proposed conditions.

Some conditions will be beyond the control of the board, particularly those that relate to other financial stakeholders. If the board disagrees, on logical grounds that are politely rationalised, the lenders can be expected to drop or ameliorate specific conditions. But if the board is simply disagreeable, that is likely to create positions some distance apart, which could lead to disharmony and even discord.

At that early stage, it is possible that the lenders will lack sufficient confidence in the shareholders, board and management, in which case their options will include insolvency and making the process lender-led.

A timetable to create stability and agree a financial restructuring

The timetable incorporated in the management presentation to lenders needs to be pragmatic, rather than wishful, in relation to the ability of the business to produce a credible new business plan that is fit for purpose. It is likely to be both the longest activity on the critical path and present the biggest risk, because the time needed will impact directly on the liquidity support required until the financial restructuring has been completed.

The development of the business plan should not be taken lightly, for two reasons: firstly, an inability to produce a document and underlying forecasts that are both credible and sensible in the timescale agreed could fatally deplete lender confidence and bring the restructuring process to a value-destructive end; and secondly, because a failure by the management to deliver the business plan after the restructuring could have dire consequences. Falling significantly short of the plan could be much more serious than, say, missing a budget, because it may not be capable of being reconciled away. Creditors' losses would be crystallised, people might lose their jobs, and reputations could be trashed.

So the plan to create stability and agree a financial restructuring needs to be set with a very high chance of success to ensure, if possible, that the business is always ahead of the game in terms of board and stakeholder confidence, throughout the process.

Achieving this requires a great deal of thought and rigour on the part of a Ringmaster who comes with considerable situational experience and has credibility with the lenders and their advisers and who, based on the initial diagnostic, has taken a realistic view on what the causes of the crisis are, how much of a risk unreliable numbers pose, and how difficult it is going to be for the finance team to cope with all of the demands on it.

The Ringmaster leads the process to create the timetable, with strong support from financial advisers. Juggling the roadmap and the proposals that the board is planning to present to the lenders, and working with the company secretary and the senior finance people, the Ringmaster starts to feed dates already in the diary for the key organs of the business into the emerging timetable: board meetings, strategy away-days, the budgeting cycle, half-year, year-end, the audit, results announcements, the AGM, report and accounts, investor away-days, and so forth.

In publicly listed businesses, results announcements constitute red-letter restructuring milestones and possibly deadlines, because going concern sign off by the board and the auditors will be essential, and that can only be achieved if forecasts show that there will be sufficient liquidity for at least the next 12 months. This requires not just sufficient cash and available headroom on revolving facilities, but also assurances that there is no forecast of a covenant breach that could result in headroom being taken away or debts becoming immediately due for repayment.

Thus, the plan needs to provide for forecasting, that is both credible and fit for purpose, that will be essential to support the necessary assessment, to be in place in good time and available for scrutiny by the financial stakeholders' advisers. If their support is going to be requested, a longer runway will be needed.

If it is expected that additional facilities or covenant relief will be required from the lenders, the board will have the tactical choice of seeking sufficient support to achieve stability and then seeking more at a later date, when the going concern assessment is made. That will be a big call to make when setting the timetable: a single process or two in a series?

Here, the board's credibility could be at risk: stability is not a completed financial restructuring and going concern needs a sign off that covers at least the next 12 months, so securing additional facilities twice in a short period could give rise to the perception that it is not handling the situation well.

It would, therefore, be ideal to kill two birds with one stone and announce that, while sufficient funding has been secured for the next 12 months, the longer-term funding needs of the business require a financial restructuring in the near term and a stable platform has been created to enable that to commence.

That may require a longer runway or a shorter timescale to prepare forecasts of the quality needed. And, in turn, it will require some tough planning decisions to be made, involving priorities, resources with the requisite experience and incremental cost.

With those decisions made, the first draft of restructuring timings, including key milestones, are laid on top of the rudimentary corporate timetable. In building the timetable, it is necessary to bear in mind a few features of how the restructuring community operates: deals or stages of deals are almost always completed just ahead of the Easter, summer or Christmas breaks; not much will happen, in terms of stakeholder interactions, over those breaks or during the three school half-term weeks each year; and early in each new year, workout bankers might be distracted by their involvement in finalising their institutions' December year-ends.

Next, the workstreams for which the finance team will be responsible are tested against the provisional timings. They will still have all of their internal and external customers to serve and it will be more important than ever that they support the senior team in monitoring ongoing business performance. So there are going to be certain times of the month when the bandwidth that can be made available to the restructuring effort will be very limited. It should also be recognised that in certain phases of the restructuring effort, dealing with requests for information from stakeholders' advisers will take up a lot of time. That all has to be factored into the plan.

Because the pressure on the finance team will be relentless, and key people getting sick or resigning could put the whole process at risk, it is important to build short breaks into the timetable so that they can reconnect with their families and recharge their batteries.

At this stage, therefore, the plan and timetable are provisional and based on internal timings; they need to be tested with the lenders' advisers. That necessarily means that the key assumptions and the associated workstreams are going to have to be discussed and debated with them.

And the lenders have to confirm that they can deliver to a tight timescale and, if necessary, commit to keeping their credit committees sufficiently warm. Their advisers will also need to commit the bandwidth, with regard to their other client commitments.

Ideally, the necessary conversations will be conducted informally, because this is not a negotiation. Off the record, the Ringmaster and the financial advisers can share candid early observations and this necessarily leads to a high-level discussion of potential obstacles and headwinds.

Clearly, if there is professional respect among the

Ringmaster and the advisers, these exploratory conversations below the radar will be considerably more valuable than an inexperienced Ringmaster, with colleagues and their advisers, formally facing off against the lenders and their advisers and shadow-boxing around the key issues. A discussion conducted in that manner would be of even less value if egos come into play and executives who lack restructuring experience insist that they can deliver quality outputs to aggressive timescales.

Once the advisers give their feedback from discussions with lenders, the first draft of a plan can be circulated among the board and senior executive team, which gives an opportunity for individuals' planned absences to be factored in. If key people have plans to be absent at critical times, that also needs to be recognised in the plan.

26

OPERATIONAL: LIQUIDITY MANAGEMENT

Liquidity management is the one area in which an independent restructuring professional can make a decisive difference: both to liquidity and to lender confidence and thus by extension to the outcome of the financial crisis and restructuring. Such a role can be filled either by the Ringmaster or by the Ringmaster's point person to whom responsibility has been delegated.

The fundamental problem with liquidity management is that people assume it is straightforward. In reality, it is anything but.

From that flawed starting point, managers in businesses then take all sorts of decisions that unwittingly make it harder to manage liquidity, overlooking the impact from policies, people, systems, processes and management information right across the business.

The triggering of a financial crisis can obviously put the very survival of a business at risk. A crisis can have a variety of causes and it is a matter of extreme urgency that all of the past mistakes and current shortcomings are identified and remedied starting with the most critical. Many people within the business don't know what they don't know; some will be well aware of some of the issues and have their own ideas for improvement. But these usually represent only a few pieces of a much larger puzzle.

Group situations present problems of a different order of magnitude. At all times, every division and subsidiary will need to have sufficient cash available to run its operations. In normal times, this can be achieved with less cash overall and relatively little effort by using treasury arrangements such as pooling and netting to manage all bank accounts in a country, or across a continent within a global limit, from the centre.

When the triggering of a financial crisis results in these arrangements being restricted – or in the worst case terminated overnight – emergency measures will buy some time. But if the accumulated in-built flaws are not dealt with promptly, the liquidity will be drained out of the system and the Titanic will be on a collision course with the iceberg.

Below, I provide examples of inherent difficulties commonly encountered and I highlight complexities and give examples of flaws. I then go on to explore the craft of the effective liquidity manager.

To rapidly identify the flaws in the business and to design and implement solutions, there is simply no substitute for an individual who brings expertise and a well-developed sense of what good looks like, amassed from years spent working in a wide variety of businesses with cash and working capital challenges. Someone with executive authority who can quickly win staff buy-in and then provide the leadership to collaboratively implement the necessary changes.

Earlier chapters have touched on liquidity management at a high level. In some cases, shortly after the financial crisis is triggered, brand-name advisers are brought in to provide a cash management offering that is an advisory commodity. In my experience, that is a positive move that covers some essential ground and should produce early benefits. However, it should not be confused with the work that an experienced independent restructuring professional has to do. So, in terms of effectiveness, early efforts are likely to hit a glass ceiling fairly soon.

Hence it is vital that those relying on the STCFF of a business in crisis should appreciate its true nature and limitations, specifically, that until someone with the requisite experience is brought in, its best use is as an increasingly accurate prediction of when the Titanic is going to hit the iceberg. In my view, that would likely present some of the advisers involved with opportunities to increase their involvement and earn more fees.

Amateurish efforts can be counterproductive

On numerous occasions I have entered situations to find that well-intentioned but naïve attempts to manage liquidity in response to a crisis have actually made matters worse.

A common example is suppressing payments to all suppliers of overheads. If these represent a relatively small proportion of total expenditure, for example, in a business with significant payroll and property costs, then suddenly stopping payments to all of those overhead suppliers is like throwing fuel on the fire. The problems it will cause far outweigh the modest one-off benefit it will achieve, which will anyway dissipate quickly as suppliers put the business on stop, increase prices or shorten payment terms. It also needlessly impacts on the morale of operational staff who are disrupted by having to arrange settlement of suppliers' accounts or cash payments and to find new sources of supply. The same goes for the accounts payable team, who experience an increase in workload to deal with calls and emails from suppliers and have to juggle payments.

All this occurs at a time when the employees, customers and suppliers of the business are sensitive to any indications that the crisis is worse than management is letting on.

A far better way to mitigate liquidity is to look at the front end of the transactions and suppress the purchases, through various initiatives, and to seek improved prices and payment terms by working collaboratively with suppliers. Another way to create a positive impact on all concerned is to pay all overdue accounts of a low value and thereafter keep them to terms.

Senior management failing to engage

It is not uncommon to encounter boards and senior teams that, while paying lip service to liquidity, pigeonhole it as a technical subject and leave it to the CFO and the finance team to sort out. (Incentives based on profitability rather than liquidity might be a factor.) But this lack of engagement undoubtedly increases the risks that the business will not survive the financial crisis. It is a powerful reason for the Ringmaster to be on the board.

At the level of subsidiaries and divisions, if the management teams believe that providing capital is the parent's responsibility – and if it is needed, it must be made available – that may be a stumbling block.

This lack of engagement can frustrate efforts at the centre to implement group-wide forecasting and it often shows up in the early stages in the form of sloppy forecast submissions to the centre. In turn, this becomes an obstacle to improving liquidity. Often, the requisite level of engagement will only happen once the Ringmaster has taken direct control.

A lack of trust in the centre

A common occurrence in the early stages of a crisis is requests for business units – divisions or subsidiaries – to send spare cash to the centre as very short-term loans. Often, the centre undertakes to repay the cash but then fails to do so. That leads to a breakdown in trust, especially if it causes business unit managers to worry that there will be insufficient funds to make their own critical payments, particularly payroll.

In certain jurisdictions, this can additionally create a fear of personal liability for the directors of subsidiaries, under local insolvency laws, which can in turn lead them to take legal advice which will sometimes be that no more cash should be loaned to the centre. This is understandable and the solution lies in the restoration of trust, which is not always possible after a rocky start.

I have seen heavy-handed executives at the centre seek to lay down the law, without success, because business units have responded by managing their cash in such a way that there is none to spare intra-month, for example by arranging for customers to pay just before paydays and by paying suppliers on shorter terms.

'Invisible credit'

Banks provide credit to businesses in ways that are not obviously visible. When a crisis has been triggered this will almost inevitably affect available liquidity.

It is typical for businesses to have the use of 'ancillary facilities'. These vary according to the needs of the business and might include, for example, letters of credit for the supply chain and rental guarantees to landlords. It will also include businesses' use of their banks' electronic payment systems – for example, BACS in the UK – which exposes the paying banks at the intra-bank level for the time between initiating and settling each payment, typically three days.

Treasury services such as the pooling and netting arrangements outlined above and foreign exchange dealing require the provision of credit.

All of these business lines are important to banks' profitability, particularly when margins on term lending are slim in a liquid market. Therefore, when a new debt facility is being put together they will keenly vie for a lead arranger role, partly in order to gain a share of such business.

However, once a financial crisis has been triggered the credit exposure provided at the outset creates extra, bilateral risks for individual banks in the lending group. This in turn introduces additional dynamics into the negotiations. If a bank with such exposure is considering selling its debt it would have to weigh up how to mitigate losing the benefit of the security that it has.

Hence, once a business is in a financial crisis it may find that some arrangements are cancelled and others become limited or restricted, which is likely to have a direct impact on its liquidity.

For example, cash may have to be lodged as collateral for guarantees and letters of credit, foreign exchange transactions may need to be funded upfront and a reduction of the BACS limit might need supplier payment runs to be spread across days or to be made more frequently.

Cash that is not actually available

In the absence of treasury arrangements such as pooling and netting, cash forecasts that aggregate the accounts of all of the business units can be misleading.

As already mentioned, each and every business unit will need to have sufficient cash available to run its operations, at all times, and this creates a requirement for them all to operate an individual cash buffer.

Even when some parts of the group have surplus cash intra-month, it may not be practical to make it available to other parts. Moving cash from one country to another can take several days and there will be cost implications of moving funds in and out of different currencies and then back again within a short period.

The net effect is that not all of the cash shown as available will in fact be usable because: a portion will be needed as a buffer; amounts that exceed the various buffers may be difficult and costly to move around the group; and cash being moved may be unavailable to both counterparties while it is in transit.

Once in crisis, however, it may be possible to ease the situation by reinstating limited treasury arrangements that would involve the banks having no credit exposure.

The need to centralise cash

One of the ambiguities involved in cash management is that a group can be reporting net inflows on an aggregated basis, yet still need to be drawing down on facilities at the centre. This will be exacerbated by the outflows on restructuring costs.

Clearly, such a situation will not be conducive to lender confidence. So underlying analyses need to be performed to better understand which parts of the group are absorbing cash and why. Once that is done, measures should be put in place to maximise the centralisation of cash, where it will be under more direct lender control.

This is explored further below.

Suppliers' credit insurance

There are three major credit insurers in the UK. If a company buys credit insurance from one of them, it will be insuring its entire sales ledger and the credit insurer will continuously receive data that will enable it to create a factual record of how good or bad individual customers are at paying to the agreed terms. They also routinely monitor the public filings of those customers and in response to any bad publicity, such as the triggering of a financial crisis, they will zoom in on that business.

They will not disclose which of a business's suppliers they insure and the insured suppliers will be contractually restricted from sharing certain information with their customers for as long as cover is in place.

If a credit insurer withdraws or reduces cover in relation to an individual customer, all of the cover, over the whole of the supplier's sales ledger, will be in jeopardy if that supplier makes new supplies or exceeds the revised credit limit, as the case may be. And if cover has been withdrawn, it will not be possible for that supplier to make supplies on 'cash on delivery' terms, because the insurer would prefer any cash received to reduce its outstanding exposure, not to have that in effect frozen.

So a business may suddenly find that it cannot source supplies from specific suppliers. If all three insurers withdraw cover, the problem would be compounded. Conversely, it may be that one insurer has reacted by reducing rather than withdrawing cover and the threat can be mitigated by paying down the amount owed.

A credit insurer is unlikely to take unilateral action without first engaging with the business, typically by requesting non-public information and then following up with a list of queries. That initial engagement and the regular updates that follow can be labour intensive.

In my experience, once a restructuring is under way it is very difficult to sweet-talk a credit insurer into taking an optimistic view and the most effective actions are preventative: stay close to key suppliers, ensure they are paid to terms, research alternative sources of supply, and, of course, manage liquidity in a manner that enables key stakeholders to maintain high confidence.

If adverse reactions from credit insurers could be material, the likely impact should be quantified and included in the downside case of all liquidity analyses and forecasting.

Adverse reaction in the marketplace

The downside case should also recognise reactions in the marketplace to the triggering of a financial crisis. Some reactions will be obvious: a reduction in new or existing business volumes; account losses if customers source their supplies elsewhere; and suppliers reducing their payment terms and being more aggressive in chasing overdue invoices.

Other reactions will be less obvious, for example, the unwinding of negative working capital if overall business activity reduces, and the exaggerated impact that declining sales will have if invoice financing facilities are used.

Invoice financing facilities

Invoice financing facilities operate like an overdraft, but with a flexible limit based on the value of outstanding receivables, at an agreed advance rate. Usually, not all receivables are eligible, most commonly because they are old, the customers are in particular foreign jurisdictions or the amounts owed by individual customers exceed set concentration limits.

The beauty of such facilities is that when turnover is growing, the amount of funding available increases. Unfortunately, the opposite is the case when turnover reduces. So if adverse market reaction causes a drop in turnover, the borrowing base will shrink over time and this could worsen liquidity.

However, liquidity can improve if there is an adverse

differential between the margin that the business earns on sales and the advance rate on the facility, and if customers' payment terms are longer than suppliers'. In these situations, turnover growth would absorb capital and a reduction releases it again. One solution that would provide rapid relief would be to sell or transfer customer relationships and blocks of receivables to a competitor.

If it is feasible to convert an overdraft or other revolving facility into an invoice finance facility, that can be attractive to both the borrower and its lenders. However, because systems and processes need to be of a minimum quality, some operational shortcomings can present obstacles to the conversion or delay it.

One of the most serious is an in-built lag between making a sale and raising an invoice: the forecasts will show a sale, but there will be a delay before the underlying invoices are available to add to the borrowing base. This would need to be remedied before converting.

Unprofessional loan management

Term loan facilities impose a variety of mechanical obligations on a borrower, typically involving drawdowns, interest rate selection, provision of information and limits on financial indebtedness. More importantly, the definitions involved in covenant reporting can be more complex than is reflected in the models used by borrowers.

Although it should not be difficult for a senior finance professional to work out from first principles what needs to be done, if necessary with some assistance from legal advisers, on numerous occasions I have entered a situation to discover that loans have been managed unprofessionally.

Validating the calculation of covenants, and dealing with any past errors, is high on the list of the Ringmaster's priorities and this is dealt with in the earlier chapter on early actions.

Strictly speaking, failures in relation to other obligations can also constitute breaches of facility terms. In normal circumstances they are usually regarded by the facility agent as a recurring irritant that causes unnecessary work. But once a crisis has been triggered, they have the potential to erode lender confidence in the borrower's senior team.

It is, therefore, always a good idea to seek out the syndicate agent's loan operations person early on and to have an introductory call to ensure that there will be regular communications in the future. This should highlight shortcomings, which can be useful as a basis for identifying what needs to be done to professionalise the borrower's loan management.

Ill-considered operational changes

I have come across many examples of operational changes that have thoughtlessly locked up cash in working capital. One was an initiative to in-source specialist work in a services business – in the final stage of every project, each of which typically ran for years. This resulted in in-house expertise being aggregated under the management control of a remote subsidiary that did such work for external customers. Assumptions in relation to liquidity were naïve.

The outcome was that the overall owner of each project relinquished responsibility for completing the whole process and so lost sight of cash collection following completion. Within months, a material value of cash became locked up in working capital, leading to crisis talks with lenders.

Using the cash forecast as an action plan

A cash forecast is a very important tool for enabling a Ringmaster to discover both the complexities involved in a particular business's cash and working capital management and the flaws that create obstacles and pose risks.

In experienced hands, every line on a cash forecast is a gateway to a unique story. To discover what that is, it is necessary to meet the characters involved and learn about the systems, processes and information that they use. Once done, those involved will need some leadership to help them identify better ways of working, ways to break down obstacles and to put some routines, disciplines and reporting in place. Above all, they need to understand and appreciate that the cash impact of what they are doing is going to be measured and monitored.

Most people respond very positively to this approach. In fact, this effort can be pushing on an open door, because many of those involved do think about cash, already have lots of ideas of their own for how to improve things and are pleased to be empowered to make a positive impact, with the support of the senior ranks. The Ringmaster provides the missing ingredient, pulling together all of the individual contributions and adding vital experience of what good looks like and designing the remedies that reflect the art of the possible.

To illustrate this, I will use the straightforward example of cash inflows from the sales of a trading business that offers its customers credit.

This is typically represented by the top two lines on the cash flow forecast: receivables, which are sales made in the past that are expected to turn into cash in the future; and future sales which, if made, will become receivables before turning into cash.

The receivables are managed by a credit control team. When you meet them, you discover that leadership is weak, management information is poor and the credit control module of the accounting software is not used because no one knows how to use it (the training budget was slashed as a cost saving measure, before any of the current staff joined!).

The CFO focuses the team on frequent 'collection drives' that target only the largest outstanding invoices, in response to repeated demands from the CEO to reduce receivables.

Thus, the team never has the chance to be proactive or methodical in managing all unpaid invoices as they become overdue and consequently there is a material value locked up in a large volume of smaller value outstanding invoices. When you investigate a sample, many have valid reasons for not paying as a result of the same errors repeatedly made by colleagues in other parts of the business that are never rectified.

Other invoices remain outstanding because customers' own accounts payable operations are not well run. But there is no possibility of the two sides sitting down and methodically working through the list because the sales team have convinced the CEO that the business relationship and sales volumes will be jeopardised if credit control does anything that would risk annoying the customer.

For all these reasons, the credit control team has a bad reputation in the marketplace and no skilled professionals will work there. Not surprisingly, most new hires are of poor calibre, morale is low and staff turnover is high.

With the sponsorship of the Ringmaster, a good interim credit control manager can fix the problems within months, unlock a material amount of cash from receivables and leave behind a clean sales ledger and a well-led, skilled, trained and motivated team to do a professional job going forward.

As for the sales team, changing their commission scheme to exclude unpaid invoices will quickly eradicate errors made in other parts of the business. The credit controllers will become their new best friends.

When looking at future sales, it is found that the reliability of forecasting can be significantly improved by establishing mutually beneficial relationships with major customers' planning teams and regularly exchanging information. This revised approach has the additional benefit of allowing cash to be unlocked from the supply chain, as inventory levels are based on forecasts that have always proved overly optimistic.

If every line on the cash forecast is worked through methodically, under the leadership of the Ringmaster, then within months, cash will be mitigated by unlocking it from working capital, increasing incomings and reducing outgoings. The effects should begin to be felt within weeks. And more reliable forecasting will give the Ringmaster effective levers to pull and more runway to manage pinch points.

Group situations

Liquidity management in group situations can be very challenging because the pre-crisis treasury arrangements need to be very different post-crisis. Suddenly the flaws that have been papered over pose serious risks and have to be remedied.

However, if managed by experienced people, such situations also offer enormous potential for delivering stunningly good and unexpected results.

When different business units in a group transact with each other, the failure to invoice and settle those transactions on a timely basis creates a huge disconnect between each business unit's profitability and its cash generation. Moreover, because some business units that have liquidity are able to provide it to other business units that do not, each business unit management's ownership of liquidity is diluted and the only people with any interest in the subject are in the centre.

In essence, what is needed is for the management of the divisions to develop a very strong interest in liquidity. That can only happen if they collaborate with the centre and for that to happen they need to be motivated, have the tools and buy into the rules.

There are several steps to achieving this:

- Outlaw bilateral balance sheet lending and route all intra-group cash transactions via the centre
- Identify all cash spent by business units that is for transactions that will be reported in the P&Ls of other business units or the centre
- Identify all non-cash intra-group transactions that

are, and ought to be, reflected in the P&Ls of other business units or the centre
- Identify all central costs, including those that will be charged inwards by business units, exclude those that relate to ownership and agree logical and tax-compliant bases for recovering those from business units
- Set up protocols for invoicing intra-group charges and reconciling and agreeing month end balances
- Create the ability in the centre to settle all month end balances by means of a single payment to or from each business unit, in the currency of each.

With those changes made, the P&Ls and cash flows of each business unit will be capable of being directly related to each other.

The *pièce de résistance* is agreeing a monthly cash target with each divisional management team, in effect a dividend that is calculated by reference to the division's forecast profitability and delivered by sending cash to the centre each month.

A simple report can then be created, if possible on a single page, that details the division, the cash target, the amount received in the month and a green/amber/red colour code to indicate whether the target was met fully, partially or not at all.

This page should be included in the board pack. It provides a very powerful report that ought to have an electrifying effect on the importance that management attaches to cash, both in the business units and at the centre.

Putting such arrangements in place provides an enormous

boost to lender confidence: cash is centralised and drawdowns on facilities are reduced.

When I have implemented this way of managing cash in a group, there have been numerous additional benefits that have all helped to create a positive liquidity position, one that over time has created an ever-growing positive variance from the early forecasts and with it a confidence-boosting buffer as the financial restructuring progressed.

Those business units that are a cash drain come under the microscope and actionable plans can be put in place either to transform them into cash generators, sell them or shut them down.

Business unit management teams start to care about costs in the group even though they do not impact on their P&L-based incentives. They ensure they are recharged. The recipients of the recharges take an interest in them and that sometimes leads to the costs being reduced or eliminated.

As business unit management teams have in effect become paying customers of the centre, they start to give candid feedback about some of the central costs, as well as service levels. As a result, the central owners can be made more accountable for them. This provides a basis for cutting central costs, eliminating waste, strengthening ownership and improving quality – and possibly outsourcing as well!

Perhaps most importantly, if they are to generate the funds to meet the cash targets, business unit management teams have to develop a much stronger focus on working capital management in their own business units. In other words, if cash generated is less than profits reported, then delivering the profits to the centre is going to create a burning platform, and they have to discover why and take remedial action.

Being on the ground and running their own business units, they will have much better prospects of succeeding than would people in the centre issuing diktats. If their relationship with the Ringmaster and the cash management resources is collaborative, technical assistance can be provided to help the management unlock cash from working capital.

Such collaboration typically takes the form of agreeing a top-five list of working capital improvements, developing targets for each and measuring progress monthly. This material is then used to develop an agenda for regular updates involving the group CEO and the CFO and the individual business unit management teams. It underpins the delivery of the monthly cash targets, which people on both sides should be thinking about from the start of every month.

One example of a successful working capital initiative is the business unit of a group that invoiced its government customers annually in advance, on 1st April, for a total amount that constituted a material proportion of the business unit's annual revenue. The established routine was to send the invoices during April, and every year a large proportion of them were disputed because they did not reflect the adjusted commercial terms agreed with the sales team. This resulted in the bulk of the cash only being received in July and August. To improve working capital management, the business unit management changed the system so that pro forma invoices were sent in February and the sales team's commission calculation was amended to exclude invoices until they had been paid, with progressive reductions of the proportion eligible for inclusion for cash received after 60 days. Not surprisingly, that year a large proportion of the invoices were paid by the end of May!

I have also found that this gives some management teams a whole new perspective on cash locked up in legacy situations, for example, old disputes that no one has been motivated to resolve for years.

The routines

One of the most important routines to establish and maintain for the duration of a financial crisis and restructuring is the weekly cash cycle. The focal point will be a report provided by the borrower that lenders – and other financial stakeholders – will have the opportunity to scrutinise ahead of a call. The Ringmaster or the operations point person should always be visible, in a leadership role.

In practice, once stakeholders' confidence in the management of liquidity has been built up and sustained over a reasonable period, lender anxiety will wane and they may be happy for calls to be held less frequently.

In the London market, there are some cash report staples, including a revised 13-week forecast, one- and 12-week variances by reference to the previous week's report, commentary and an executive summary. Detailing cash mitigation plans and targets and reporting on progress is good for confidence.

Internally, the larger business units will each have smaller versions of the forecasts for the whole business and it is important to have internal weekly cash calls with them as well. In time, it would be expected that each business unit would become self-sufficient and, rather than relying on the centre to provide cash, will start delivering it against agreed targets.

Operational control

Operational control of liquidity should start straight away. Focusing first on bank accounts, the urgent tasks are to identify all banks and accounts and to find out who controls them and what they are used for. Then list who is on each mandate and who has the ability to operate the accounts online. This is so much harder than a layman would imagine because, although the banks appear willing and helpful, the exercise involves a host of different staff members and nothing moves very quickly.

It is important to reduce the number of accounts used to the bare minimum and refresh all mandates and authority limits so that a limited number of accountable individuals can be in control. Call for all online bank cards lying around on desks and in drawers to be handed in. I kid you not!

Investigate the standards to which the ledgers are updated for bank account transactions and, in particular, how long it takes for customer receipts and supplier payments to be allocated against open invoices on the sales and purchase ledgers, respectively. To be effective, credit controllers need to work with up-to-date sales ledgers every day. In the purchase ledger, unallocated payments on supplier accounts risk duplicated payments and settlement of invoices that ought to be queried.

It is also important to check the standard to which the credit control and accounts payable teams perform account reconciliations, how frequently they exchange the information with counterparties and the length of time that reconciling items remain unresolved.

Responsibility and accountability for all of the different types of expenditure should be reviewed along with how this links into the operation and approval of purchase orders. One of the very serious loopholes in modern corporate organisations is 'purchase to pay' systems, which satisfactorily control who can authorise which purchases, but never subject the purchase invoices received to additional scrutiny by the authoriser. This means that, providing there is a basic match, an invoice can be paid even if the goods or services as invoiced were not satisfactorily supplied.

It is important also to identify who can initiate or authorise cash payments or payments of invoices ahead of their due dates. At times of crisis, employees can act to protect the interests of suppliers with whom they have good relationships and there may be loopholes that need to be closed.

The knowledge gained through this process should be used to improve the quality of forecasting, to smooth the cash outflows and to flatten pinch points.

Shared services

If the business has centralised some of its services and this involves the centre paying, for example, payroll and suppliers, then it is important to ensure that every business unit on whose behalf payments are being made sends the cash in advance to settle its share.

27

OPERATIONAL: OTHER

The work that the Ringmaster's team does on liquidity and forecasting will generate a long list of opportunities for improving both profitability and liquidity, which can be tackled by means of separate initiatives. In many situations, the remedial work will start addressing unreliable numbers at the same time.

Rather than draft in a team of expensive and inexperienced brand-name consultants, my favoured approach is to work collaboratively with staff and interim executives, providing sponsorship and leadership, which not only assures their ownership but also enables durable benefits to be delivered. If required, consultants with analytical skills and tools can be engaged in support on a narrow scope, for only as long as is necessary.

Examples of low hanging fruit identified by liquidity work

In the sales function, there may be opportunities to invoice earlier and also to reduce customer payment terms.

In the sphere of managing customer relationships, there

may be a political imbalance between the sales and credit control teams which is limiting or preventing credit control from having adequate access to the relationships.

Does the credit control function need to be overhauled? Is there a backlog exercise to be done on the sales ledger, to resolve queries, bring all reconciliations up to date, validate reconciliations with counterparties, issue outstanding credit notes and collect or write off old invoices?

Can receivables forecasting be improved by linking it to credit control collection targets?

Has all VAT on debts written off in the past six years been claimed?

Do existing sales commission structures and calculations operate to the benefit of the business?

Who holds the payroll budgets and is this ownership aligned with who can authorise changes, for example, new hires, overtime and bonuses? Is there a report produced for each budget holder, ahead of each payroll being run, that highlights changes and variances?

Is cost control at the centre sufficiently robust? Is the reporting of the costs in each central function effective? Are monthly reviews conducted with the budget holders? Is all expenditure covered?

Is purchase activity sufficiently transparent to budget holders? What check is there that another budget holder has not been allocating purchases to their budgets?

Is accounts payable well organised and efficiently run? Is the functionality of the software fully utilised? Are all suppliers' details and terms accurately loaded? Is there scope for negotiating more favourable terms, for example, by moving from 30 days from invoice to 30 days from month end? On what basis are invoices selected for inclusion in payment runs? Are all such invoices checked against underlying documentation?

Is there scope to ask landlords to replace quarterly rental payments in advance with three monthly payments in arrears each quarter?

Are there opportunities to reduce or postpone corporation tax liabilities?

Has all R&D tax credit been claimed?

Would there be benefits in selecting longer or shorter interest rate periods on the term debt?

Can planned capital expenditure be funded with third party finance?

Is there cash trapped in legacy situations?

Reforecasting

If the situation allows, I always favour a business undertaking a comprehensive reforecast at the earliest opportunity.

In any event, the board will need the corporate forecast already in place to be updated as soon as possible after the crisis has been triggered. It will be the basis for setting stakeholder and possibly market expectations and projecting covenants in the near future. And it will be an essential component of short-term cash forecasting.

If a team of specialist interim executives has been engaged to start work on a three-way integrated forecast, on which it is envisaged the financial restructuring will be based, then as it takes shape the two will need to become aligned.

Participating in the in-depth review of the reforecast with selected business unit management teams provides a Ringmaster with the valuable opportunity to rapidly get down into some important details, to gauge the calibre of the business unit management teams and to establish the basis for building a trusting relationship. In parallel, it enables a Ringmaster to evaluate the standard of existing forecasting.

It is not uncommon to find, when visiting a business unit early on, that the centre's view of performance differs from that held on the ground. This can reflect the fact that the forecast submissions from the business units have routinely been altered at the centre.

Cost cutting opportunities

I find that all of the liquidity and forecasting work generates a list of obvious cost cutting candidates, for both triage and the longer-term operational restructuring. In my experience, the individuals at business unit level who actually make or direct hiring and purchasing decisions are very important to the process, more so if the framework of robust forecasting, meaningful reporting and effective oversight is enhanced by the Ringmaster.

Additionally, there will be costs that are controlled centrally, including property, various shared services and consultancy costs. These are usually the responsibility of central function heads.

If it is anticipated that the cost cutting exercise is going to be large and complex, it will usually be sensible for the

Ringmaster to hire a specific point person to set up and operate a Project Management Office (PMO). In my experience consultancy firms can provide value for money in supporting roles, particularly in terms of analysis, operating the PMO from day to day and compiling reports.

Baking planned operational restructurings into forecasts

In relation to changes to existing operations – as distinct from new ones – baking the planned operational restructuring into the forecasts can be both technically challenging and difficult to achieve within forecasting and reporting.

This is mainly because P&L forecasts and reports of actuals are two dimensional: in each, there should be a directly comparable category of income or expense, a period and an amount. For example, for payroll costs in June a variance will have been calculated by mid-July by comparing the forecast with the actual.

A planned operational restructuring introduces a third dimension. Each affected figure in the forecast can be built up in two parts: existing payroll and the saving from a headcount reduction. But, come July, there will still only be one report of the actual.

An additional issue is that it is far easier to calculate cost savings than revenue and margin benefits. Using the example above, there will be termination costs to reduce the headcount and the benefit will be a lower payroll cost and both of these are capable of being tracked. But if, say, the headcount reductions are possible because productivity benefits are expected to result from two offices being combined, how are those going to be discerned in the reporting of actuals?

To compound these difficulties, it is fashionable to approach operational restructurings by producing a 'target operating model', in other words, a forecast based on a vision of the business post-transformation. The model itself is usually driven by high-level metrics that are specific to the business.

For boards, all of these difficulties present challenges and risks. A vision of a fantastic future business can be sold to stakeholders on the basis of some high-level work. But tracking progress will be difficult if implementation costs cannot be tracked through regular reporting, and the forecasting and reporting of actuals is not modified in granular detail that shows whether benefits are being produced.

This may fall within the scope of the Ringmaster. In my experience, it can involve tough politics, particularly if the whizzy consultants who sell these types of transformations – who often stay involved for ages, talk a good game and build empires, but deliver little in the way of tangible benefits – find the actual tracking, and the accountability that tracking facilitates, inconvenient and therefore do little to support it and much to undermine it.

KPIs

I first introduced KPIs into some SMEs in the mid-1990s, before the term had become fashionable. As group CEO of a mini-conglomerate, I was interested in a subset of those KPIs that were reported every day on-site to the respective general managers. In my weekly update meetings and calls with them, a one-page weekly update formed the bulk of the agenda.

I found the use of KPIs exceedingly powerful. Firstly, the general manager could take remedial action on a daily basis. Secondly, it gave me a fact-based idea of what was happening in the business. Thirdly, the KPIs reported to me were incorporated into forecasting and reporting. This meant that the performance drivers underlying the forecasts prepared by the general managers were directly comparable with those in the actuals reported and that the monthly reports contained no surprises. After that happened, forecasts were seldom missed because preparing and owning these numbers in the knowledge that they would be scrutinised rigorously required the general managers to demonstrate that they understood their businesses.

Unfortunately, the proliferation of data held by IT systems nowadays tends to undermine the usefulness of KPI reporting within businesses. Typically, a long list of financial values and statistics, some with limited credibility, are sent out on a daily email to a long list of people, most of whom hardly bother to read them.

For a Ringmaster, such a situation is an opportunity. Delving into KPIs and the way they are reported, by reviewing them with people in the business, can produce a wealth of information about the drivers of the business and its systems and possibly also highlight factors relevant to underperformance and the triggering of the crisis. It can also provide a very useful starting point for improving the quality of forecasting.

Management information

Most efforts to bring about durable improvements in performance, processes and systems will rely on key people at various levels having access to up-to-date, credible and relevant management information. The information will be different at various levels; nevertheless, it needs to be derived from the same base. Think of different sections of a pyramid: the top section for the board, the middle section for the senior team and the bottom section for the second- and third-tier managers.

I commonly find that in businesses that produce unreliable information, employees hold management information in low regard. This suits the agendas of those who would rather not be measured and monitored. Over the years, I have often introduced one particular independent consultant, who has an enormous amount of experience and expertise and a great love for his work, to provide an evaluation in layman's terms after spending only a few days in the business.

Usually, the story is the same: for very little money, management information could be made vastly more relevant and therefore more valuable. He frequently finds that people who mistrust management information have produced their own workarounds, which are labour-intensive to produce.

Working with a few such people, he can quickly develop prototype reports, source the data from the correct databases and make the various reports accessible using desktop menus. Where helpful, snapshots of those reports can be emailed to customised lists of people at set intervals.

28

OPERATIONAL: FIXING THE FINANCE FUNCTION

Given the correlation between unreliable numbers and financial crises, coupled with the need for a board to address the deeper causes of the crisis rather than just seek to cure the immediate symptoms, fixing the finance function can be an important part of the Ringmaster's scope.

This has to be confronted at a very early stage and if doing so causes reality to collide with fantasy then some relationships might not get off to a great start. Accepting the assurances of the senior executives that the finance team is in great shape and that it will be able to cope easily with the extra workload is a road to disaster. Especially if the second-tier finance people are wheeled into the room and made to nod like dogs on the back shelf of a car!

It is, therefore, critical for the Ringmaster to develop *from the coalface* a realistic view of the finance team's capabilities. If the Ringmaster does not have solid functional leadership experience, gained from actually working in finance teams, being a senior executive and sitting on a board, this task should be delegated to someone who has – logically, the Ringmaster's operations point person.

It is unlikely that outside firms will be able to get to the heart of the matter. Inevitably, if an organisation has had underperformance issues over a period, the finance team will have had to host all manner of consultants and advisers and will have developed tactics to successfully deflect them and fob them off. This will compound an outsider's shortcomings.

In my experience, the diagnostic is best conducted by the Ringmaster in face-to-face conversations set up with an agenda that facilitates fact-finding and makes it clear that there is no element of appraisal involved. Clerical-level staff will quickly recognise that this is someone with deep and varied experience to whom they can speak candidly – a person of action, on a serious mission. A list of all the basics that do not work will start to take shape which will form the agenda for the next round of conversations, first with team leaders and then with the second-tier finance people. A decaying finance team will be the whipping boy of the organisation, a soft target for operational colleagues to scapegoat. If that is the case, a lot of unhappiness will bubble to the surface.

If the conversation is shaped around finance having internal and external customers, the levels of service those customers have a right to expect and how current service levels compare, then a dam may well burst as a long list of problems comes gushing out. The people who care will have been thinking about and discussing these issues for some considerable time and there will be enormous frustration that the board has remained oblivious to the reality.

The Ringmaster's art is in working out which issues are critical to resolve in the short term and in deciding the standard to which they need to be fixed because, as stated earlier, 'good is the enemy of best'. Ideally what should happen is that a self-help finance project is established under the sponsorship of the Ringmaster or the operations point person.

This provides a sensible and reliable platform for candid conversations about the restructuring-related additional work that the finance team is about to be loaded up with. The starting point is a timetable, constructed as an excerpt of the main timetable and populated with more detail that is specific to finance, such as month end timings.

Key dates and absences can then be overlaid and assumptions made about which restructuring work will need to be done by experienced permanent members of staff and how to compensate for their reduced availability for 'business as usual' activities.

In parallel, conversations can start with board members about the quality of material they receive and the room that they see for improvement. The feedback will be much more candid if the Ringmaster is on the board, because then the directors will be talking to a colleague about a matter of mutual importance, not to a 'consultant'.

While it is to be expected that some directors will trot out the party line, either through inexperience or anxiety to avoid rocking the boat, others will be anxious to share their burden and this should quickly introduce other issues into the conversation, such as the history of board decision-making in relation to finance and IT, the shortcomings of the leadership and the causes underlying the crisis.

The Ringmaster has to tread carefully, so as not to undermine the CFO, and to avoid creating a febrile atmosphere that could mislead the finance team into thinking that a saviour has arrived and a revolution is imminent.

The output from this work is three-fold: realistic timings for the completion of the forecasting work; a finance resourcing plan; and the means to perform triage on critical systems and processes.

PART VI

Carillion plc: a case study

29

INTRODUCTION

CARILLION PLC, A £5BN PUBLICLY LISTED UK business, collapsed into liquidation on 15th January 2018.

Nine days later, two parliamentary committees – the Business, Energy and Industrial Strategy Committee and the Work and Pensions Committee – of the House of Commons launched a joint inquiry. Their report (the Report) was published on 16th May 2018.

This is an excerpt from the Report's summary:

'Carillion was an important company. Its collapse will have significant and as yet uncertain consequences, not least for public service provision:

- *It had around 43,000 employees, including 19,000 in the UK. Many more people were employed in its*

extensive supply chains. So far, over 2,000 people have lost their jobs.
- *Carillion left a pension liability of around £2.6 billion. The 27,000 members of its defined benefit pension schemes will now be paid reduced pensions by the Pension Protection Fund, which faces its largest ever hit.*
- *It also owed around £2 billion to its 30,000 suppliers, sub-contractors and other short-term creditors, of whom it was a notorious late payer. Like the pension schemes, they will get little back from the liquidation.*
- *Carillion was a major strategic supplier to the UK public sector, its work spanning from building roads and hospitals to providing school meals and defence accommodation. The Government has already committed £150 million of taxpayers' money to keeping essential services running.*
- *Carillion's collapse was sudden and from a publicly-stated position of strength. The company's 2016 accounts, published on 1 March 2017, presented a rosy picture. On the back of those results, it paid a record dividend of £79 million—£55 million of which was paid on 10 June 2017. It also awarded large performance bonuses to senior executives. On 10 July 2017, just four months after the accounts were published, the company announced a reduction of £845 million in the value of its contracts in a profit warning. This was increased to £1,045 million in September 2017, the company's previous seven years' profits combined. Carillion went into liquidation in January 2018*

with liabilities of nearly £7 billion and just £29 million in cash.'

For the public, the evidence accumulated by the parliamentary inquiry offers a rare insight into how the board of a company managed a financial crisis and restructuring.

The analysis of that evidence and of the company's public announcements enables me to include in this book a case study that, at the time of writing, is high-profile and topical. My purpose in doing so is to aid readers' understanding of the guidance I have offered, by providing a real-life illustration of the principles involved.

I want to be clear about the limitations of this analysis and to explain what it is not.

The parliamentary inquiry covered a much larger window than the company's final six months such that the board's management of the financial crisis and restructuring was not a major focus. In fact, very little was said about this aspect in the Report. Consequently, the evidence available for my analysis is piecemeal and incomplete. The analysis is not, therefore, in the nature of an inquiry and it is not by any means complete.

. . .

The business plan it presented in early January 2018 provides clear evidence of how enormous and sprawling a group Carillion was. So my analysis could not possibly take into account the many and varied complexities that would necessarily have to be dealt with by the board.

Only minimal evidence was provided by Carillion's senior lenders, so there is little that can be included in any analysis about how the most important financial stakeholders were managed.

If individuals involved in the situation were to publish their own accounts, perhaps then the analysis could be expanded.

I also want to emphasise that I have avoided criticising any of the directors individually. It would be unfair of me to do so, particularly as they must have suffered a world of pain since January 2018 and I certainly do not wish to add to that.

As anyone will know from reading the relevant chapter, I believe that the current expectation that individuals hired for business as usual situations should find it difficult to leave a board once a business gets into a crisis and financial distress, is unbalanced and unfair. Moreover, it is seldom in the interests of stakeholders, who would be much better served by situational experts supplementing or replacing inexperienced incumbents.

. . .

All the evidence accumulated by the parliamentary inquiry can be found at: https://www.parliament.uk/business/committees/committees-a-z/commons-select/work-and-pensions-committee/inquiries/parliament-2017/carillion-inquiry-17-19/publications/

There are links to specific documents within that evidence that are referred to in my analysis in the Appendix.

I hope that an incidental benefit of this case study will be to add depth to the work of the parliamentary inquiry. As one of its chairs, Rachel Reeves MP, said, 'We will certainly channel our inner Agatha Christie to try to solve the mystery of what happened at Carillion.'

30

THE BACKGROUND

Although this case study focuses on the final six months of the life of Carillion, it is useful to briefly consider the background.

The bulk of the evidence provided here comes from two significant institutional investors in the company's shares, in the form of excerpts from their letters to the parliamentary inquiry and the oral evidence that their representatives provided. Given that it was their business to study information made available by the company and to meet its management, they are a valuable source of information.

Standard Life

We had been significant investors in Carillion, owning more than 12% of the shares at one point, and it did take quite a while for us to sell down the whole stake, which is why we started in late 2015 and finished that process during 2017 ... We got down to virtually zero active holding in the first quarter of 2017.

There were growing concerns from late 2015 on a number

of fronts, including the company's strategy, its vulnerability to worsening market conditions and financial management, including the strength of its balance sheet. As a consequence, our investment position on Carillion moved from a 'hold' to a 'sell' from December 2015 onwards.

... issues were raised with the management through our ongoing engagement. However, it was felt the management was not giving sufficient weight to the probability that trading may deteriorate further or to the downside risk from this scenario given the high level of debt. The board showed no inclination to drive the management to change.

What became clear to us was that the company was going to continue on its strategy despite our questioning of that. That strategy ... was leading to higher debt levels, a higher risk profile and greater complexity within the group, which also was a warning signal to us. It was clear, even through our engagement with the non-executive chairman, that that was not going to alter in any way.

There was a gloss to the presentations that we felt did not reflect the true business circumstances. When we looked at the 2016 results ... the picture that was painted on perhaps the first couple of pages of those results was not supported by the information that lay deeper into the accounts.

Our dealings with the company suggested a confidence in their approach that was not necessarily supported by the facts as we identified them.

Aberdeen Standard Investments

Took the decision to start selling on 3 August 2017 ... sold down ... over a matter of months and the final sale took place on 3 January 2018.

Our approach is very much to spend a lot of time in the audited financials ... The two issues we were not aware of and were not evident from the financials were first the poor operational performance, in terms of contract management and so on, bidding for contracts at low prices, and, secondly and critically in this case, the aggressive accounting that has come to light ... There must have been prior issues that were not presented to investors that then caused that quite calamitous collapse. The scale here is extraordinary ... their profits warning ... was a big red flag. The evidence the Committee has produced—notably the FTI Consulting report—is very strong evidence that the issues here were pre-existing over a number of reporting periods.

In fact, again, going through the minutes that have been produced—it is not often we get to see these—the minutes from the board on 22 August make it quite clear that these were pre-existing issues. You had a company with a culture of meeting the numbers and, whenever you have a 'meeting the numbers' type culture, then people will tend to push the accounting and push the cash flow management to hit short-term targets.

I put on record again my frustration with the fact that: yes, we knew there were issues with the balance sheet. Yes, we knew there were issues with short-term cash flow but they were placed in the context of a longer term history of quite attractive margins and apparently secure cash-generative contracts and a relatively small construction book. It was less than 20% of profit for that going back over two or three years.

What was brought to the table in July last year was evidence of misstatement of profits over a prolonged period of time, evidence of aggressive accounting and evidence of extremely poor operational management, which was completely at odds with the way the business was presented to the marketplace. Periodically that happens and that is why we run diversified portfolios. You cannot put all your eggs in one or two baskets.

Press reports

In the session in which representatives of these two institutions gave oral evidence to the parliamentary inquiry, Rachel Reeves MP, one of the chairs, referenced a view from the ground, 'There was an interview in the Guardian ... with a former executive at Carillion, and he told the Guardian that "the supply chain wasn't being paid, money was getting transferred [between different parts of the group] to pay salaries, loans were coming in from the UK to the whole of the Middle East. By mid-2016 we were already seeing these problems." He then goes on to say, "For them [directors] to say it all happened in April and May 2017 when the world changed ... it's absolute nonsense. [The write-downs] were all lurking and developing, they had even crystallised, but nobody was accepting it. There was no cash."'

The Carillion business plan

The board presented a fresh business plan to financial stakeholders days before filing for liquidation. In it, the board was candid about some of the underlying causes.

'The Group had become too complex with an overly short-term focus, weak operational risk management and too many distractions outside of our "core".'

In a section headed 'Key themes and issues', it detailed fundamental failings:

- Increasing size and complexity of services contracts, compounded by growth, not matched by our capability
- Contracts taken on with high degree of uncertainty around key assumptions
- Success on construction contracts dependent on performance of others not under our control
- Insufficient understanding of, and adherence to, contract requirements
- No focus on contract demobilisations, leading to cost overruns
- Lack of effective handover from bid to mobilisation to delivery, leading to lack of knowledge transfer
- Risk transfer
- Claims not managed or pursued in a timely and effective manner
- Portfolio not balanced in terms of cash generation
- Ineffective change control – e.g. design changes on construction contracts agreed without agreeing incremental costs
- Poor planning and lack of effective contract controls and monitoring leading to inconsistent operational performance management
- Lack of ownership of issues
- Geographic risk.

An insider's view

Gazelle, adviser to Carillion's pension trustee, had access to the company's forecasts. In its May 2017 covenant report, it raised some red flags:

'The overall impression gained is of a group, dependent on accurate management of a very complex set of financial inter-relationships, which is close to becoming capital constrained but still able to opportunistically exploit pockets of additional or replacement finance from capital markets.

'Gazelle assessment would be that Carillion is currently capital constrained because it is approaching maximum debt capacity and access to equity markets is also currently debilitated by short-term trading of its shares.

'Management actions to improve business performance and place the group on a much better longer-term footing have not delivered sufficient net operating cash flows to prevent a trend of increasing average net debt.

'As a result we are not currently wholly confident that the business could withstand a material financial shock. Our confidence reflects not a lack of management ability to find additional short-term financing, at which it is adept, but that a material shock could quickly impact the debt market confidence on which Carillion is currently very reliant because it is currently so close to maximum committed facilities.'

31

WHAT WE SEE

The profits warnings

In the final six months of the life of Carillion, its board issued three profits warnings.

The first, on 10th July 2017, totalled £845m. The second, on 29th September 2017, comprised an 'additional £200m provision'. (A further £60m was identified subsequently and confirmed in the business plan, but had not been announced by the time the company went into liquidation.)

Of the total of £1,105m – all provisions against contracts – £634m related to receivables and £299m to future losses (FTI Consulting's analysis, in its IBR).

The third profits warning, in November 2017, was an update that profits would be materially lower than current market expectations.

The cash impact of the profits warnings

When announcing the first profits warning, the board said that the contracts provided against represented '£927m of receivables on the Group's balance sheet at 31 May 2017'. They went on, 'The expected provision includes £599m against [those] receivables and the remainder is for future costs, with the estimated future net cash outflows for these contracts of between £100m and £150m mainly in 2017 and 2018, based on estimated receivables of £328m net of estimated payables of £443m.'

In its IBR, FTI Consulting explained that the receivables that had been provided against 'represented claims against customers and subcontractors that the Group had previously recognised as revenue and profit. The review identified significant risk that these balances would not be collected.'

In other words, by making these provisions, the business no longer expected that £599m (ultimately £634m) of specific future cash inflows would be received. These had previously been posted to the balance sheet when the revenue and profits had been booked. And in the following 18 months, it also expected to have to pay out £443m on specific loss-making contracts in order to receive back £328m (a net outflow of £115m, ultimately increased to £299m).

However, in his evidence to the parliamentary inquiry, the former interim CEO Keith Cochrane said, 'If you look at the bulk of the provision that we recognised, it was non-cash. The reality is that the cash had been spent already, and it was all around how quickly we could collect the cash.' He added, 'The cash flow forecasts on 10 July suggested that this was a problem linked to specific contracts.'

It appears that the board, on the one hand, provided against contract receivables because it no longer expected they would turn into cash but, on the other hand, still included the receipt of the receivables in its cash flow forecasts. Evidence given by former CFO Emma Mercer implies that the board considered this doable:

'The drive of getting those receivables back from organisations was, for me, on an operational level in a division, the key to trying to make a success of this business in terms of cash flow. We talked about Qatar. Huge amounts of money were owed there on one particular contract, and there was a huge amount of effort to try to drive and collect that cash. Actually, that was viewed at that point in time as one of the easiest things to do: to get the receivables that we were due from our clients.

'From my perspective, the way of getting the debt down was two-fold. First, there were the routes of other mechanisms like debt for equity, for example, or even raising additional equity, but, more importantly, it was collecting the debt that we were due from our customers. That was all around the world.'

In his evidence, Keith Cochrane said, 'As I came into the business, there was a lot of focus on reported debt across the business. Was there the same focus on collecting cash, day in, day out, with the relentless attention that we applied post 10 July? Did that appear to be the case before 10 July? No ... When I came in ... we appointed EY. We initiated weekly cash flow forecasts. We revamped the cash flow forecasting process to ensure that it was robust.'

There was also the indirect impact that the profits warning would have on cash. In his evidence, KPMG audit partner Peter Meehan referred to this:

'It is key to note that the £845 million is not all about the small number of contracts with the adverse change. It is also about management's decision to exit territories, which will obviously have a negative effect on sentiment in those territories. The supply base knows that you are not going to give them any work anymore. They will get tough. The customer knows you are not going to be there in 12 months to fix retentions and so forth. There are various reasons why that will have an impact.

'Once they had posted that announcement on 10 July, they knew two things. First, sentiment was going to be against them, obviously from the crash in the share price but also, operationally, customers and suppliers, understandably, were going to be nervous about dealing with them. There would be fewer new contract awards. Subcontractors would perhaps not want to go to site until they are paid in advance and that sort of thing. Also, the company knew that they were going to be in a position where they were going to need cash and would potentially sacrifice cash for a higher-profit settlement on some of these claims that they had. It was because they needed cash; customers will take advantage of that, but the company would not be keen on entering into longer mitigation.'

The role of EY

Within a week of the first profits warning, the board announced the appointment of EY, 'to support its strategic review with a particular focus upon cost reduction and cash collection'.

In September 2017, it announced that EY partner Lee Watson had been appointed on secondment to the Group

Executive (leadership team) as Chief Transformation Officer.

In a letter to the parliamentary inquiry on 2nd February 2018, EY detailed the work that it had done, between July 2017 and January 2018. This can be summarised as:

- Liquidity and working capital: identifying areas to improve; recommendations to improve the cash forecasting processes; support to identify and deliver opportunities to improve cash and working capital, assisting management with liquidity reporting
- Assessments of priority contracts: review of the process, scope and information
- Cost reduction: support to deliver immediate opportunities
- M&A work: support
- Five-year business plan and integrated forecasts: support to deliver it
- Tax: advice and support
- Future operating model: support defining it
- Entity priority model: options and modelling
- Restructuring: ad hoc advice to the board; assisting with restructuring discussions with the financial creditors, the pension scheme trustee, the pensions regulatory authorities and the government
- Contingency planning
- A partner on secondment (Lee Watson) focused on assisting the Interim CEO and the client's CFO with matters relating to the restructuring, including interaction with stakeholders.

Approximately 190 members of EY's staff (including support staff) were involved. £13.1m was billed for the work, of which £2.3m was unpaid at the time Carillion entered liquidation.

The parliamentary inquiry criticised EY, saying it was 'paid £10.8 million for its six months of failed turnaround advice as Carillion moved inexorably towards collapse'.

In its response on 12th July 2018, EY wrote that its 'role at Carillion was to support the company's management in reorganising the business and reducing its costs; to identify ways of improving the company's cash flow; and to assist in preparing a detailed financial model which [was] then used by the company's management to develop a five-year business plan to present to its creditors'. They added, 'We also supported the company's lead advisor in liaising with creditors and other stakeholders.'

Three EY restructuring partners – Alan Bloom, Lee Watson and Andrew Wollaston – gave oral evidence to the parliamentary inquiry.

The role of Lazard

Lazard was financial adviser to Carillion. The work that Lazard and EY did in combination is referred to in EY's 12th July 2018 letter.

In its letter to the parliamentary inquiry, Lazard said that its engagement had commenced during June 2017, 'given the financial difficulties that it was apparent were being faced' by Carillion. In the 5th July 2017 board minutes, reference was made to a disposals paper that Lazard had prepared for the board.

On 5th September 2017, Lazard's engagement to provide financial advisory services in connection with disposals, various means of repairing the balance sheet and the sale of the whole company was formalised. Over the following months, Lazard provided the assistance to the extent requested by the board. It was also appointed sponsor in connection with proposed and potential disposals.

Lazard listed the three key factors that were critical to success: a credible business plan; a credible restructuring and implementation plan; and a stable platform with sufficient liquidity to provide the necessary time.

Lazard's team included four Managing Directors and nine other bankers. The firm's fees were structured to include a significant proportion that would only be payable on the successful completion of a transaction or event. Such fees did not become payable. £2m was paid by way of monthly retainers for eight months, with a further £250,000 on the announcement of a disposal and £500,000 in relation to the provision of sponsor services.

Lazard's letter also provides some insights into the most problematic contracts. It mentions the UK government in its role as counterparty on some of those contracts. And it confirms that the board was aware that potential new money investors were unlikely to fund losses on such contracts.

Legal advisers

Slaughter & May's letter to the parliamentary inquiry is brief and contains no surprises.

However, in an appendix, it does provide some insights into

some of the options that the board was considering behind the scenes:

- Project Gold, 12th April 2017 (the date the matter was opened): Possible equity investment by third party or strategic relationship
- Project Mumbai, 11th May 2017: Possible takeover of Carillion
- Project Swordfish, 9th October 2017: Possible takeover bid by a third party.

In the last eight months of Carillion's life, the firm was paid fees of £5.5m. At the time the company filed for liquidation, bills of £1.4m remained unpaid and a further £1.2m had yet to be billed.

The 5th July board meeting

At the board meeting on 5th July 2017, the profits warning that the board would deliver a few days later was not on the agenda per se. It was mentioned only in passing, in relation to its expected adverse impact on the share price and therefore on the reduced prospects for the success of an impending rights issue.

The company's two joint corporate brokers, Morgan Stanley and Stifel, attended the meeting to inform the board that they could neither recommend nor underwrite a rights issue at that time as they did not believe it would succeed.

The board had no questions and endorsed 'Plan B', namely that the announcement of the first profits warning should exclude any reference to the proposed rights issue. 'Self-help' and 'maximising value for shareholders' were discussed as potential mitigating factors.

The next agenda item was the 2018–2020 business plan, which the board approved following some discussion that included two mentions of cash, both very high level.

The 22nd August board meeting

At the board meeting on 22nd August, the minutes of the meetings of 5th, 6th, 9th, 12th, and 20th July 2017 were approved, together with the minutes of the committee meeting of 9th July. The Notes of the Board Calls of 19th and 26th July were also 'noted'.

Under an agenda item entitled 'Strategy', for which Lee Watson of EY joined the meeting, there was a wide-ranging discussion. Cash and working capital were mentioned in passing and there was an oblique reference to the consequences of failure 'within' the business.

It was noted that 'there were three remaining action areas under the strategic review – of strategy, disposals and the business plan'.

Three further EY representatives then joined the meeting for the next agenda item, which was an update on 'Project Ray'.

After the EY people had left the meeting, the board continued with the agenda. A non-executive asked 'whether an equity issue would, or would not, be required'. The board's conclusion is not clear.

This was in response to an update provided by HSBC, appointed on 14th July 2017 as joint financial adviser and joint corporate broker, which had been prepared in consultation with the two incumbent brokers. An excerpt titled 'Equity Process Consideration' was subsequently provided to the parliamentary inquiry.

On a page headed 'Investor Feedback – Key Themes' the update highlighted major concerns that investors had expressed, in particular about: the adverse impact of the profits warning on investor confidence; the damage potentially caused to customer and supplier relationships, working capital and the prospects of winning new work; uncertainties surrounding the value of the business; the clarity needed around leverage, liquidity and the use to which fresh equity would be put; the timing of appointing a new senior team and potential future changes to strategy; existing equity value, potential dilution and the paucity of potential buyers of the whole business.

The company was in dialogue with two new banks about 'funding streams' and would be required to conclude steps before such funding might be available. The chairman asked that the position be pinned down as a matter of urgency.

Under the agenda item, 'Chief Executive's Report', the interim CEO spoke to his report, noting 'the current position with the banking groups, and discussions with the pensions trustees and the regulator'.

Some additional detail was provided under the CFO's agenda item, 'A 13-week forecast had been submitted to the banks earlier in the week, and ... discussions continued with the four key banks who were acting as a lead for the [Revolving Credit Facility] banks.' The CFO noted the key assumptions in the forecast provided to the banks and further commented that 'the current pinch point was in mid-November, where there was committed headroom of £103m'.

The prospects of a rights issue

In a letter to the parliamentary inquiry, Morgan Stanley said that in mid-April 2017 it had 'advised Carillion that in addition to measures that it was already contemplating, it should consider a potential equity raise by way of a rights issue'.

The letter also supplemented the information given in the board minutes: ahead of 5th July 2017 it had increasingly believed that Carillion's senior management could neither produce nor deliver an investment proposition that would convince shareholders and new investors to support the potential rights issue; and that, at the 22nd August 2017 meeting, the board had been advised that there was very limited ability for Carillion to announce an equity offering alongside its interim results in late September 2017. The 'key gating items' listed in the letter included a liquidity review, a revised business plan and confirmation of management changes.

The board's 'restructuring strategy'

In the trading update of 10th July 2017, the board announced that, as a response to the profits warning, it would be 'undertaking a comprehensive review of the business and the capital structure, with all options to optimise value for the benefit of shareholders under consideration'.

A week later, the board announced that creating 'a balance sheet that will support Carillion going forward' was a priority of the strategic review, and that EY would 'support its strategic review with a particular focus upon cost reduction and cash collection'. The announcement also mentioned achieving 'cost efficiencies, an increased focus on managing working capital and on recoveries and cash collection'.

In a subsequent announcement on 29th September 2017, the board explained that one of the focuses of the strategic review was 'balance sheet and cash – strengthening the balance sheet and reducing net debt through a range of self-help measures'.

Kiltearn Partners LLP, another significant investor in Carillion's shares, told the parliamentary inquiry that a member of its investment team had met with interim CEO Keith Cochrane on 13th October 2017. 'Mr. Cochrane noted that the additional GBP140 million in secured liquidity given by Carillion's lenders should avert any immediate covenant concern ... stated that the disposal target [of] GBP300 million ... needed to be achieved to get Carillion's net debt to management's target level ... [and said] there would be little point trying to raise significant debt or issue equity until: (i) cost reductions and disposals had been delivered; (ii) Carillion had shifted its focus to its core business, namely UK support services; and (iii) a permanent CEO had been recruited, as potential investors would need a clear idea of what they would be investing in.'

The operational restructuring

Pursuant to the board's stated 'restructuring strategy', the senior team set about planning an operational restructuring: reorganising and transforming the business, reducing costs, making disposals and strengthening the balance sheet through self-help measures.

About half of the minutes of the board meeting on 22nd August 2017 were devoted to the early stages of planning the operational restructuring. Unsurprisingly, EY had been very active since being appointed just over a month earlier.

One EY workstream had focused on the strategic review and a draft strategy presentation had been circulated to the board. A number of strengths and weaknesses had been observed and consideration of this surfaced some of the non-executives' frustrations. A three-page excerpt of an EY report has been made available by the parliamentary inquiry. It identifies priorities under the headings of, 'Simplification, Selectivity, Efficiency, Culture and Capability'.

The proposition would focus on 'fewer bigger things, with better people', the achievement of which would require a radical reshaping of the business. A reorganisation into 'four sectors – Building, Infrastructure, Central Government and Regions & Corporate' was considered.

Another EY team had been working on 'Project Ray'. Based on contract data requests, interviews and how a sample of people spent their time, they had drafted a 150-page report. It 'covered the overall opportunity; the operating model, proposed headcount reduction, third party spend opportunity, immediate cost saving opportunities, indicative phasing and implementation costs, and early views in relation to the Middle East and Canada'.

The board was 'supportive of the work which had been done to date and on the continued work now envisaged to develop a structure and strategy'.

Some six weeks later, in its announcement on 29th

September 2017, in a page and a half, the board detailed the finalisation of the operational restructuring plan and the early stages of its implementation: the business had been 'refocused on its core strengths and market'; there was a 'new leadership team and operating model – creating a simpler, more cost-effective operating model'; and 'proceeds from non-core business disposals [identified had] increased to £300m from £125m'.

In his evidence to the parliamentary inquiry, EY partner Andrew Wollaston provided some insights into the approach taken, 'Clearly there were very tight margins in this business. As our own work showed, there were a lot of costs that had built up that could have been taken out. Those two factors led to losses. Those losses were funded by an increase in debt and obviously pressure on cash flow. When we arrived in July those were observations that we made. Our work was to come up with a restructuring plan, an operational plan ... which we started to implement with the company in September, and also to identify cash improvement opportunities.'

Lender engagement

In the documents made available by the parliamentary inquiry, there is little information about lender engagement.

The first public reference that the board made to its lenders was in the interim results on 29th September 2017 when it announced an 'agreed further £140m committed facility with a number of banks'. Completion was announced on 24th October 2017.

It appears that the new money need came as a surprise. The FTI Consulting IBR refers to it as 'emergency funding'.

And in his evidence to the parliamentary inquiry, EY partner Lee Watson confirmed that it had become 'clear in early September that new funding was needed [and] the company approached a range of different creditors for support'.

He added that, 'given the capital structure of the group, security was not available for any of the lenders apart from £40 million'.

From the oral evidence given by PwC partner Gavin Stoner, we know that the process to negotiate terms was challenging: his firm had been engaged only a week ahead of the finalisation deadline and much of the information needed to perform the work was not available because the company had still been working on its business plan.

He also outlined the scale of the challenge posed by the very high levels of leverage. At that stage, he said, projected EBITDA was less than £200m with balance sheet debt of £1.4 billion and off-balance sheet debt of £400m (the early payment facility) plus the debt of the pension scheme.

It would be an enormous surprise if, in combination, all of these factors – shock/emergency, unavailability of security, high-risk fundamentals, compressed timescale, state of unpreparedness – did not corrode lender confidence.

On one level, they had no choice but to provide new money, because the alternative would have been an inability by the company to announce its half-year results in the absence of going concern sign off by the board and the auditors.

On a different level, the company's situation appears to have been precarious and the need for liquidity support immediate. EY partner Lee Watson confirmed to the parliamentary inquiry that what his colleague Alan Bloom described as the 'reasonable prospects test [which] tends to be applied by the lawyers to the board: is it reasonable for us to continue in business and not to call time by way of liquidation or administration, given the circumstances in which we find ourselves?' was being 'continuously applied ... from September'.

Having agreed to provide the emergency funding that the business needed to keep going, it appears that the best the lenders could do in the circumstances was to try and mitigate their downside risks.

The strongest mitigating factor appears to have been a partial de-levering within months, funded by the proceeds of disposals. A letter from the Santander UK Chief Risk Officer to the parliamentary inquiry confirms this: the 'new money facilities were part of a package designed as a bridge to Carillion completing certain disposals'.

The lenders also procured the company's agreement to three specific enhancements in its situational capabilities: the establishment of a common information platform that would be accessible by all of the financial creditors and the pensions trustee; a request that a non-executive director be appointed 'in order to strengthen the Board's restructuring experience'; and a request that THM Partners be engaged 'to provide assistance in the reporting and management of short-term liquidity'.

By Christmas, however, residual lender confidence had all but ebbed away and, over the Christmas break, the board and lenders were engaged in make-or-break discussions.

In its letter to the parliamentary inquiry, Santander

outlined that its own confidence in Carillion's position had deteriorated during December when 'the envisaged disposals did not take place [and] detailed business and restructuring plans ... were further delayed' and after the receipt of 'updated financial analysis' from the business.

Stabilisation

EY partner Lee Watson explained to the parliamentary inquiry that the support provided by the creditors in late September, in the form of new money and bridge finance, was a 'bridge into a restructuring in the first quarter of 2018' and that 'there was a very proactive and agreed process set out to allow time in order for ... the business planning process to be carried out'.

In addition to the £140m of new money provided by five lenders:

- The pensions trustee agreed to defer pension contributions worth £25.3 million, due between September 2017 and April 2018
- The private placement noteholders agreed to defer the repayment of £16m due in November 2017 and, if the new money was still outstanding, a further £49m due in September 2018
- The surety providers made available £80m of new committed bonding facilities.

Separately, in October 2017, HMRC (the UK tax authority) agreed to a £22m deferral of tax liabilities under a 'time to pay arrangement'.

Lee Watson further explained, that 'the approach to the pension trustees was made in parallel to certain banks and various other creditors. Both of those approaches became quite quickly intermeshed through the course of September, as it became clear – and it is common in these types of situations – that the support of one party is interdependent on the support of another.'

Liquidity management (and covenants)

Various announcements made by the board during 2017 provide evidence that liquidity and covenant forecasting was consistently subject to material adverse variances and was, therefore, highly unreliable:

- Announcement on 1st March 2017: 'Net borrowing of £218.9 million at 31 December 2016'; 'We will ... begin reducing average net borrowing.'
- Announcement on 10th July 2017: 'Net borrowing at 30 June 2017 expected to be £536m'; '... well within its 3.5 times net debt to EBITDA covenant'; 'We must take immediate action to accelerate the reduction in average net borrowing'; 'The Group expects net borrowing at 31 December 2017 to be slightly lower than at 30 June 2017.'
- Announcement on 29th September 2017: 'Net borrowing at 30 June 2017 increased substantially to £571m'; '... compliant with its covenants at 30 June 2017 and is forecast to be in compliance with covenants as at 31 December 2017'; '... has identified mitigating actions, which it could take if the forecasts are not achieved.'
- Announcement on 24th October 2017: 'There is

no change to 2017 guidance as set out in the interim results announcement on 29 September.'
- Announcement on 17th November 2017: The board 'now expects a covenant breach as at 31 December 2017'.

In its business plan, presented in January 2018, the board reported that net debt at 31 December 2017 had been 'higher than expected' at £1,100m. Whereas the expectation, announced six months earlier, had been 'slightly lower than £536m'.

This continuing unreliability was especially in evidence in the support negotiated with five lenders and other financial creditors ahead of the half-year results announcement. On 29th September 2017, the board announced that this support would improve committed headroom by between £170m and £190m over the course of 2018.

And in the accompanying interim results announcement, the board gave assurances that such support would be sufficient to enable the company to continue operating for at least 12 months. It said it had 'undertaken a rigorous assessment of the ... assumptions underlying the forecasts' ... including 'sensitivity analysis', which showed 'compliance with covenants as at 31 December 2017 and 30 June 2018, before accounting for the positive impact of the disposal of its Canadian operations'.

However, a little over three months later, an *incremental* funding need had been identified. The board assessed this as £360m. FTI Consulting calculated it at £495m.

The board's awareness

Evidence made available by the parliamentary inquiry provides several accounts that reference the board's awareness of the company's position.

One is from Gazelle, the firm that advised the pension trustee. Following the first profits warning, Gazelle was engaged to provide additional advice and assistance, but it was replaced by PwC on 20th September 2017, ostensibly after a disagreement on tactics. In the later stages of its engagement, Gazelle worked jointly with Short Partners, a specialist restructuring advisory firm.

In that period, Gazelle held weekly monitoring calls with Carillion. It reported:

'Time was wasted pursuing the existing management's view that they could recover the situation, whereas a reasonably experienced corporate finance and/or debt restructuring adviser (i) would have been aware of the material scale of Carillion plc's combined bank, surety and pension liabilities and (ii) would have been cognisant that Carillion plc as a contracting business depended on continuing multiple credit sources for its existence. Accordingly, Gazelle would have expected greater urgency to secure additional liquidity by whatever reasonable means.

'During the initial critical phase in July and August 2017 it was apparent that Carillion plc did not secure additional liquidity from its banks and Carillion plc did not draw down upon uncommitted bank facilities ... Gazelle would normally have expected, in this type of distressed situation, that the main creditors of Carillion plc would have at least started to consider restructuring their respective financial exposures by 20th September 2017 ... it was not explained why the bank creditors appeared to be inactive ... (based on

Carillion plc's account of developments on Gazelle's weekly monitoring calls).'

Throughout July and August 2017 Gazelle held the view that the situation was serious but proper evidence for this only emerged after certain 'EY disclosures' had been made.

Another account is provided by former interim CEO Keith Cochrane. In a letter to the parliamentary inquiry, he details how the board came to realise that liquidity ought to be a serious concern, some eight weeks after the first profits warning.

On a board call on 30th August 2017 to discuss a draft announcement about the proposed reorganisation of the business, former CFO Zafar Khan provided an update on liquidity that indicated no need for new funding. (Prima facie, this was consistent with the position reported by him at the board meeting eight days earlier, namely projected minimum headroom of £103m in the period to mid-November.)

Within days, a deterioration in the liquidity outlook was reported, based on revised figures produced in conjunction with EY, who at that stage were becoming closely involved in the cash management and forecasting process. A further revision being worked on indicated a materially higher funding need.

In EY's view, Carillion needed to consider obtaining additional liquidity from its banks. An urgent board call was arranged for four days later, a Sunday, ahead of a pre-arranged bank presentation two days after that. In a discussion with four key lenders at the end of the bank meeting, the possibility of providing an additional £150m of liquidity was raised. The board met again the following day and an update was given in relation to the bank meeting.

Yet another account is provided by former CFO Zafar Khan in a letter to the parliamentary inquiry. He expresses surprise at the board's apparent lack of awareness, 'My sense was that in the post 10 July 2017 period the board was becoming disappointed as to the direction of travel of Carillion's financial performance ... I was informed by Mr Cochrane, shortly following the [Sunday] 3 September 2017 board update, that my update had "spooked" the board ... [however] it should have been apparent to the board by then that the company was struggling to improve both its net debt and profit positions.'

In his oral evidence to the parliamentary inquiry, Keith Cochrane said, 'At that juncture, we were concerned at some of the revisions that were being made to our cash flow forecasts, which seemed to have come as a surprise.' Although he 'sacked' Zafar Khan shortly afterwards, he conceded in response to a question from Peter Kyle MP that 'it was an honest assessment'.

Financial restructuring

In his evidence, EY partner Lee Watson said that the additional support detailed in the half-year results announcement was based on an anticipated financial restructuring in the first quarter of 2018, allowing time in the interim for the business planning process to be carried out.

The board had signalled, in its announcement of 17th November 2017, that this would likely involve 'some form of recapitalisation, which could involve a restructuring of the balance sheet', to 'reduce net debt and repair and strengthen the Group's balance sheet'.

But this proved increasingly challenging. Firstly, the business planning timetable slipped. In its letter, Santander told the parliamentary inquiry that it had 'originally expected the detailed business and restructuring plans to be received by 8 December 2017'. And the FTI Consulting IBR confirmed that they were made available on 4th January 2018, but remained subject to finalisation until 11th January 2018.

Secondly, the liquidity outlook deteriorated. From the timeline provided in the Report, we know that in the 'first week of December, changed assumptions in weekly cash flow materially reduced the company's short-term cash flow forecasts'.

Thirdly, as explained in Santander's letter, 'The envisaged disposals did not take place.' In other words, the new money lenders' exposure was higher than had been anticipated.

The quest for government support

The Report tells us that the board 'formally approached the Government to ask for financial assistance on 31st December 2017, when it became clear that it was a prerequisite of discussions with existing lenders about further support'.

It adds that proposals for such further support, which involved the lenders swapping debt for equity, were presented to lenders on 12th January 2018.

In his letter to the Permanent Secretary for the Cabinet Office on 13th January 2018, the chairman said, 'There has been tremendous progress over the last few weeks with key stakeholders, and we have every reason to expect that it will be possible to agree the commercial terms of a deal before the end of January.'

The board anticipated that funds would be provided by 'potential new money providers in relation to longer-term funding to be injected as part of the restructuring'.

He continued that the board 'believes (and is seeking confirmation from FTI that it agrees with its analysis) that the quantum of the new money ask will be less than £300m for longer-term funding, which is an amount [it] is confident can be raised'.

However, in its IBR, released just two days later, FTI Consulting calculated the funding requirement would be materially higher, at up to £495m.

The letter to the government on 13th January 2018 and the accompanying funding proposal are in effect a request for the government to participate in achieving (the second attempt at) stability, while the terms of a financial restructuring are agreed, 'The requested support would be put in place alongside support from commercial banks ... the Group is simply asking for temporary support – not a permanent subsidy. The support would be cancelled and repaid in full upon completion of the restructuring.'

In summary, the government was asked to provide £160m directly, plus £63m of tax deferrals via HMRC, over four months, in addition to the £22m deferral agreed in October 2017. And to help find longer-term solutions on three projects, potentially involving the provision of funding. There was a suggested decision point at the end of January, when the government's exposure was projected at between £80m and £90m and HMRC's at £41m.

Other participants would be the banks, providing up to an additional £60m, and the surety providers, supplying a £10m advance payment bond.

In summary, the business was seeking incremental support of up to £293m over three months – three-quarters of it from the government – as a bridge to a longer-term solution that a financial restructuring would have provided.

From evidence provided by PwC partner David Kelly to the parliamentary inquiry, it is clear that the government had been tracking Carillion's situation closely for some months, 'The work that we were doing for the Cabinet Office from September [2017] was to help to support them as they were supporting the various Government Departments in relation to the contingency plans that those Government Departments were preparing. Our role in that phase was to provide the insolvency and the contingency planning experience to supplement what the Cabinet Office were doing ... to prepare their contingency plans to ensure that in the event of an insolvency of Carillion, they were able to ensure that there was continuity of those critical public services.'

In a session of the parliamentary inquiry on 7th March 2018, joint chair Rachel Reeves MP asked the institutional investors providing oral evidence, 'On 13 January [2018] Carillion wrote to the Government and asked them to essentially be the investor of last resort because they had run out of other options. Do you think that the Government were right to not provide that bailout to Carillion that they asked for and instead to go into liquidation? Do you think the Government had any other options?'

Murdo Murchison of Kiltearn Partners replied, 'I thought [the FTI Consulting] report was very interesting, a review of just the scale of the problem at one point. What was intriguing, in particular, was that management clearly required all of the banks to write off pretty much all of their debt and start afresh. There was a huge complex restructuring here. Looking at it, I am not convinced—even if the Government got involved for the space of providing short-term financing for a matter of weeks—that that was nothing other than a band aid. The structural issues were there. The liabilities relative to the cash flows were just so out of kilter, it is an extreme event. It would be quite reasonable in these circumstances to pass by on the other side. It was not a solution.'

Forecasting and business planning

At its meeting on 5th July 2017, the board approved the 2018–2020 business plan.

But within three months it had been discarded, to be replaced by what EY partner Alan Bloom described in his evidence as 'a ground-up business plan that would be credible to financial stakeholders, creditors, the Government, pensions'.

He explained, 'It clearly was necessary. We had recommended it back in August, and bear in mind we only got involved in July. We were uncomfortable with the level of financial forecasting and business planning, so we said to the company, 'You need a fully integrated cash flow forecast, profit and loss account, balance sheet, and an explanation of your business plan going forward. Without that you will not get the financial support that you need."

He added that EY had to 'help the company – which is unusual – help them to build a ground-up business plan that would be credible to financial stakeholders'.

In the FTI Consulting IBR, we read, 'Following the provision of £140m emergency funding at the end of September 2017, the Group commenced a bottom-up business planning process, supported by EY.' We know from the Santander letter that delivery was expected by 8th December 2017, that is, within 10 weeks.

The FTI Consulting IBR provides valuable insights into what a difficult undertaking this planning exercise proved to be: it comprised '211 contract templates ... [that] consolidate into 12 [business unit] models which are further consolidated into the Group forecast ... [with a] number of [central] adjustments'; challenges included 'individual business units [preparing forecasts] for the first time', 'consistency of treatment of some items across the [business units]', and the 'complexity of the ... contract and JV arrangements [which has] added to the size and complexity of the model'.

The IBR continues:

'The size of the model means contract templates, [business unit] consolidation models and the Group model are all separate Excel workbooks. As a result, tracing the source of numbers and making changes is time consuming.

'The model is based on a September 2017 opening balance sheet. Historical figures included in the model are incomplete and cannot be used as comparable for review purposes.

'The model cash flow is calculated on an indirect basis and inputting contract cash flow forecasts prepared on a direct basis by contract teams in the ordinary course has proved a challenge.'

A particular challenge proved to be the 'modelling of cash held in JVs and not available for set off in the Group's cash pooling arrangements until it can be released via dividends (non-set-off cash)'.

Although 'the first draft ... was provided on 17 December 2017 and the final model on ... 4 January 2018', it remained subject to finalisation until 11th January 2018.

Unreliable numbers

Carillion's inability to produce reliable numbers would have been a significant obstacle in delivering 'the business planning process'.

The minutes of the 22nd August 2017 board meeting record the directors' discussion of the issue, under the agenda item on strategy, 'A culture of "making the numbers" has been identified and there is "wilful blindness" among long-serving staff as to what was occurring in the business.' The board concluded that the culture of the organisation required 'radical change'.

A presentation by Keith Cochrane, the interim CEO, to the same board meeting identified 'continued challenges in quality, accessibility and integrity of data, particularly profitability at contract level'.

An EY report to the same board meeting noted:

1. There is a level of complexity that appears unwarranted
2. Despite many layers of management, there is limited visibility and transparency of performance at the appropriate level to make interventions
3. There is an abundance of data, however the complexity of systems, ways of reporting and processes make it difficult to have meaningful information
4. The value that the Group provides to the performance of the business is not clear.

The FTI Consulting IBR criticised the group's poor accounting information systems, lack of senior finance resource/bandwidth at group level and weak corporate knowledge in view of extensive management changes throughout the business.

In his evidence to the parliamentary inquiry, EY partner Andrew Wollaston provided some colour, 'This company had come together from a series of acquisitions, each with their own data centres, and in our view and in our experience companies that mature post ... acquisition ... integrate their data systems, often centralised data systems, in order to produce quality information that management can then rely on. In our view, Carillion had not invested sufficiently in data and data analytics and, therefore, in our view, there were areas where that should have been improved. [That integration had not taken place] ... not to the extent that we would have expected it to.'

Optionality

Behind the scenes, a limited range of alternative options were being considered.

Slaughter & May's letter to the parliamentary inquiry provides evidence of three of these: possible equity investment by a third party or a strategic relationship (Project Gold, April 2017); possible takeover of Carillion (Project Mumbai, May 2017); and a possible takeover bid by a third party (Project Swordfish, October 2017).

In his evidence, EY partner Alan Bloom disclosed that:

'In parallel with the work ... over the period October to December ... banks and other stakeholders said, "What if we don't support this rescue, what would happen, what are the alternatives? Could you, EY, please model for us what you think will happen if we don't support this."

'They asked us to model two options. The first one was a straight liquidation immediately, which would have yielded, according to the numbers that we produced, just under a penny in the pound for unsecured creditors. They then asked us to model ... a version of effectively an enhanced liquidation model.

'It still would have been a liquidation but would have provided roughly a two-week window. It would have required £20 million a week from some source or the other to fund it, but it would have provided a couple of weeks to do some distressed sales of property. A fire sale would be a pretty good description of that environment. That would have yielded around about 5 pence to 6 pence in the pound, still a very poor return to creditors and certainly not an attractive outcome for anyone.'

Execution

'Self-help' had been identified by the board as a means of reducing debt and thereby managing liquidity. Adviser Gazelle was critical of this.

The concept had been discussed at the board meeting on 5th July 2017, after the joint corporate brokers had advised that they could not support a rights issue. In its announcement on 17th November 2017, the board outlined self-help measures taken since July 2017 as a focus on 'reducing costs, collecting cash, executing its disposals programme and implementing its new operating model'. Yet in that period the board had fallen considerably short of its ambitions and targets.

Of the £300 million non-core disposals target announced as part of its strategic review, only one transaction was announced, the sale of a large part of its UK healthcare facilities management business, for expected net disposal proceeds of £41.4m. This deviation from plan clearly caused a problem in terms of lender confidence, as outlined in the Santander letter.

In terms of cost cutting, although EY had identified '£125 million worth of cost opportunities' in the early stages of its engagement in mid-2017, from the business plan delivered to stakeholders six months later it appears that little in the way of cost cutting had been delivered by then, because the 2018 target was £100m plus a further £25m in the following two years.

As for cash collections, the former CEO Richard Howson, in his letter to the parliamentary inquiry published on 12th July 2018, queried whether sufficient effort had been expended on cash collection in the last few months immediately preceding the liquidation, 'when 4 out of the 5 existing experienced Divisional Managing Directors were removed from their roles'. He added, 'I have had numerous concerns raised with me, from those there to the end, that amounts owed were not pursued by senior and executive management, and that they appeared to ignore the fact that those on the other side of the negotiating table expected executive management (given the seriousness of the situation) to be present to lead the collection of cash or conclusion of accounts.'

In the business plan provided to financial stakeholders in the company's final days, Carillion's board conceded numerous administrative weaknesses, which would have hampered execution.

'Addressing functional capability is critical – Finance, IT and Supply Chain.'

'External hires to bring fresh talent and perspectives to the Group, including in Supply Chain and IT. A Head of Shared Services is also to be appointed.'

'Finance transformation is a priority – the function is being strengthened through [three senior appointments] alongside the replacement of three out of five business unit finance directors.'

'Transformation will focus on strengthening separate towers of control, reporting and performance monitoring.'

'Robust commercial and financial risk management processes now in place.'

'Additional senior functional capability' would be provided by a recently appointed new interim Head of Business Improvement.

A 'Transformation Programme Management Office (TPMO)' had been created in late November 2017.

The board had embarked on a self-help mission, using an army of consultants but had not addressed administrative weaknesses after six months, by which time it was on the brink of liquidation.

The final piece of the jigsaw

In the Report, several references are made to the first witness statement of Keith Robertson Cochrane, dated 15th January 2018. This supported the application by the directors to the High Court to have Carillion placed in liquidation. It was not published by the parliamentary inquiry.

I have been advised that the statement is confidential and while a creditor would be able to obtain a copy, publishing anything about it would not be permitted.

32

WHAT WE DO NOT SEE

Leadership

According to the minutes made available by the parliamentary inquiry, the board meeting on 22nd August 2017 was the first time in almost four weeks that the directors had met or had a call. Perhaps not surprisingly, given that they were oblivious to the liquidity crisis that would blow up within ten days, responsibility for liquidity and lender engagement had been delegated to the interim CEO and the CFO, who each referred briefly to the issues. Instead, the meeting focused considerable attention on the planned transformation of the business, including the executive leadership team.

In the days following that meeting, work on the leadership team was finalised and on 30th August 2017, the board reviewed a draft market announcement that detailed the changes. These included the creation of a new post of Chief Transformation Officer or CTO. However, the announcement was delayed when concerns surfaced about the deteriorating liquidity outlook which, within days, would cost the CFO his job.

The business transformation plan survived that episode and when the leadership changes were announced on 11th September 2017 they included both the CTO appointment and the replacement of the CFO. From the evidence, it appears that this senior team, picked to execute a challenging operational restructuring that was fully detailed in the half-year results announced on 29th September 2017, was immediately sucked into leading the stabilisation of an emerging crisis that within weeks had evolved to become the early stages of a consensual financial restructuring, albeit one that could make only limited progress without a business plan, which had to be started from scratch.

Had the business transformation become a mission impossible for the new team? With hindsight, it would certainly seem so, particularly given that the business planning challenges were exacerbated by the reorganisation of reporting, implemented on 1st October 2017.

Beyond those reporting changes, it is not clear how much of the planned business transformation was actually implemented. Announcements made after the end of September 2017 make no mention of them. From the changes outlined in the business plan in mid-January 2018 it is obvious that, four months later, much still remained to be done.

Did the board's leadership decisions give the banks confidence? Apparently not, because relatively soon after the additional facilities became available, on 1st November 2017, Alan Lovell was appointed as a non-executive director, at the request of the creditors. His scope has not been made public, but given his wealth of executive, board and restructuring experience, it seems reasonable to assume he was in effect appointed as Ringmaster – which would be consistent with his visible involvement in the final negotiations with the government, as evidenced in the correspondence.

Would the board have appointed a suitably experienced individual to the role of Ringmaster at the outset, if its awareness of the liquidity outlook had been aligned with reality? Would such an individual have made different strategic decisions? All we have to go on is the evidence of Gazelle, 'Time was wasted pursuing the existing management's view that they could recover the situation ... Gazelle would have expected greater urgency to secure additional liquidity by whatever reasonable means.'

Given his considerable restructuring experience, Lee Watson of EY would seem prima facie a plausible stakeholder management point person to support a Ringmaster. From his evidence, he became immersed in managing the stabilisation workstream, which saw support provided by numerous creditors in a complex deal.

At the time Lee Watson was formally appointed, the board had the opportunity to bring in a battle-hardened interim CFO with deep restructuring experience as a replacement for Zafar Khan.

But it is not clear what restructuring experience the board wanted in its new CFO. Interim CEO Keith Cochrane told the parliamentary inquiry that one of the reasons that 'Mr Khan was not the right person to be Finance Director ... was that he did not have the confidence of the banks given the likely need for raising new funding or the experience and skills to facilitate a broader financial restructuring with multiple stakeholders'.

However, in making a replacement appointment he 'wanted someone in the CFO role ... to focus very much on the business units ... Emma, I felt, was best placed, given her knowledge of the UK construction business, to take on the role and to drive that cash generation'.

A situationally experienced CFO could have provided air cover for Emma Mercer while she got on with the inward-facing job. And bolstered the board with vitally important executive situational experience at a critical time. We do not know whether the board considered that option.

There is a wealth of evidence pointing to some deep-rooted causes of the financial crisis, notably in the board minutes of 22nd August 2017, in the testimony of EY partners Andrew Wollaston and Alan Bloom, in the business plan produced in mid-January 2018, and in the FTI Consulting IBR which highlighted 'poor accounting information systems, a lack of senior finance resource/bandwidth at Group level and weak corporate knowledge in view of extensive management changes throughout the business'.

In the situation in which Carillion found itself, such operational issues would themselves create very challenging obstacles to a successful restructuring: financial stakeholders and the board would be reliant upon critical data; and cash generation, cost cutting and other triage would have to be executed.

Yet we do not see evidence of the board recognising the need to: put itself front and centre of managing the crisis; appoint a highly experienced individual to the board as

Ringmaster with the sole responsibility of leading the company's management of the crisis; and strengthen both the board and the executive team with individuals possessing situational experience, in order to cope with the demands of the situation and to provide support for the Ringmaster.

And we do not know why the gaps in management existed, or why they were not filled.

All we see is a single senior battle-hardened independent restructuring professional appointed to an execution role, just weeks before the end, and aspirational plans to upgrade the capabilities of the finance organisation using permanent employees six months after the crisis had been triggered.

Liquidity

Although a contemporaneous analysis of liquidity has not been made publicly available, it seems reasonable to assume that a recently prepared long-term cash flow forecast existed at the time of the first profits warning, given the substantial work that the executive team, supported by external advisers, had very recently performed in connection with the potential rights issue.

There is, however, a proxy in the form of Gazelle's report for the trustee board meeting on 22nd May 2017 which shows total free cash flow of £478m in the three-year period 2017 to 2019 and notes mitigation opportunities of some £100 million.

As the contract provisions detailed in the first profits warning totalled a minimum of £699m, logically there would be a prima facie case for the board to conclude that the company was facing an existential financial crisis.

One significant investor thought so. Clients of Kiltearn Partners LLP owned in excess of 10% of Carillion's shares at the time of the first profits warning. In a letter to the parliamentary inquiry's chairs, dated 2nd February 2018, Kiltearn's CEO Murdoch Murchison wrote that, on the basis of its analysis, Kiltearn determined that 'Carillion had a significant funding deficit, in the region of GBP600 million, and it was unclear how Carillion would close this funding gap'.

The letter added that, at a meeting on 17th July 2017, 'Carillion's representatives acknowledged that the ~GBP600 million impairment to receivables was large, asserting that the company would do everything possible to recover its receivables – even suggesting that Mr. Howson may be retained to collect them.'

Their conclusion was, 'Kiltearn was of the opinion that the ~GBP845 million provision effectively destroyed Carillion's capital base ... Kiltearn determined that the higher level of debt, lower profits and minimal capital meant that a recovery in Carillion's fortunes was unlikely and a restructuring involving a debt for equity swap to raise at least ~GBP600 million on unknown terms had become highly probable.'

We do not know why, when it met on 22nd August 2017, liquidity was not the number one priority on the board's agenda.

Possible other options

We know from the Slaughter & May letter to the inquiry that throughout 2017 the board had been examining numerous other options out of the public eye. These included possible equity investments, takeovers and strategic relationships. It is plausible that the likelihood of potential transactions such as these influenced the board's thinking in the final six months of the company's life. But we simply do not know.

In terms of the board's financial restructuring options, the Guardian reported on 2nd March 2018 that a month before the company collapsed, EY had produced two scenarios:

- An unplanned insolvency that would see just £49.6m recovered from the business, including £12.6m for pensioners
- A break up that could have raised £364m by selling profitable assets prior to liquidation, securing £218m for a retirement scheme.

Presumably this refers to the work that EY partner Alan Bloom had outlined to the parliamentary inquiry.

On advice, the board opted to pursue a financial restructuring. Although restructuring professionals subsequently lamented that having to use the compulsory liquidation procedure highlighted shortcomings in the UK's rescue culture; it seems that the board simply had no other option once its requests for funding had been turned down.

Without government funding for three contracts, which was a condition of the lenders and potential new funders, liquidation was inevitable. We do not know how much funding was requested in relation to these contracts.

Legal experts have commented that the 'problem contracts' could not be ringfenced through the tactical use of an insolvency process because of 'ipso facto clauses'. These are commonly used in business contracts and they typically give counterparties termination rights in the event of insolvency.

After Carillion went into liquidation, its joint venture partners on one problem contract (Aberdeen) had to go it alone, work on the Midlands Metropolitan Hospital and Royal Liverpool Hospital projects was stopped, and the Qatar subsidiary responsible for the Mshiereb contract was itself put into insolvency.

The business plan forecast that, together, these four contracts would require £198m of funding in 2018 and 2019. Assertions in a letter sent subsequently by Mshiereb Properties in Qatar to the parliamentary inquiry indicate that the figure would almost certainly have been considerably higher.

33

SO WHERE DID IT ALL GO WRONG?

The immediate response

Within a week of the first profits warning in July 2017, a significant investor in the company met the management and concluded that a highly dilutive financial restructuring was inevitable because the company's capital base had been destroyed. However, it is impossible to discern that the board even registered that a crisis of any magnitude had been triggered.

As the country went into the summer holiday season, the board did not meet or have a call for nearly four weeks. When it did reconvene, in the seventh week of the crisis, much of the time was spent talking about how to transform the business. Liquidity only warranted a brief mention near the end of the meeting.

. . .

On the evidence, the management considered that in excess of £700m of contract provisions would not impact materially on the cash. By the eighth week, reality was catching up: the CFO flagged that liquidity was an issue and the board was spooked. A week after that, the board was in crisis, meeting regularly and frequently applying the reasonable prospects test.

The board's liquidity analysis

When announcing the first profits warning, the board said, 'Net borrowing at 30 June 2017 [is] expected to be £536m,' and 'The Group expects net borrowing at 31 December 2017 to be slightly lower than at 30 June 2017.'

The analysis used to support such a statement has not been made public. It was spectacularly wrong; on 31st December 2017, net borrowing was in fact c.£1,100m, some half a billion pounds greater than the board had projected.

In the two sets of minutes made available by the parliamentary inquiry, no director asked how bad the situation was, how long the business could survive, or what could be done to improve survival prospects and buy more time.

The closest any of them came was in the second meeting, seven weeks after the first, when a non-executive asked whether an equity issue would, or would not, be required. No clear answer to the question is recorded. Perhaps there was a strategic investor waiting in the wings – a bird in the bush?

And no curiosity was displayed about the knock-on effects of the profits warning in the marketplace. In his evidence, KPMG audit partner Peter Meehan had flagged this issue. And as FTI Consulting later confirmed in its IBR, the business 'struggled to win new contracts and some counterparties have become more cautious about supporting [its] working capital. As a result, the negative working capital position in the ... business is forecast to unwind resulting in additional cash outflows in addition to the contract losses.'

Logically, the provisions and the knock-on effects would have increased net debt. But when announcing the first profits warning, the board said, 'We must take immediate action to accelerate the reduction in average net borrowing.' The reality, as reported in the FTI Consulting IBR, was a 'build-up of uncollectable receivables ... being funded in part by short-term measures such as stretching trade payables (supported by use of the EPF), advance payments on contracts and over measure on contracts'.

The 'restructuring strategy'

Most likely as a result of its flawed liquidity analysis, the board professed faith at the outset in 'self-help' measures – which involved 'reducing costs, collecting cash, executing its disposals programme and implementing its new operating model'. In the words of Gazelle, 'Time was wasted pursuing the existing management's view that they could recover the situation.'

On the basis of those unsound assessments, the board then pursued a 'restructuring strategy' that would have been more appropriate for a business owned by a large and well-funded corporate parent.

It embarked on a strategic review to 'realise value for shareholders', which a realistic liquidity assessment would have revealed to be negative, or at best zero, because, at that stage the lenders' value was impaired by reason of the real liquidity outlook.

On that unsafe premise, the board in effect adopted a 'restructuring roadmap' that simply bypassed the critically important stopping points of 'crisis stabilisation' and 'financial restructuring'. Instead, it set course directly for destination 'operational restructuring' – without a reliable plan.

Although there is no evidence on this point, it does seem counterintuitive to embark on a wholesale restructuring of the operations ahead of the arrival of a replacement permanent CEO.

. . .

The absence of a reliable plan

As the three-year plan that the board had approved at its meeting on 5th July 2017 was jettisoned just two months later, the board was committing to an operational restructuring armed with a plan that was not fit for purpose.

The business plan that it eventually produced six months later, which itself was far from perfect despite months of intense effort and millions in advisory fees, showed just how much time (two years) and money (around £1 billion, half of it spent within the preceding six months) would be needed to execute an operational restructuring.

The state of the business

The minutes provide evidence that, seven weeks into the crisis, the directors were aware of problems at a high level. However, they were confident that retaining consultants would enable such issues to be remedied. In the following weeks, a detailed transformation plan was produced and the leadership team refreshed.

After the planning process had been completed six months into the crisis, the board was able, with the benefit of hindsight, to discern the true state of the business. It had grown too complex, taken too many risks and been weak in planning, managing performance, controlling costs and pursuing claims. But by then it was too late. And in any event, the harsh realities of the liquidity situation had overtaken the transformation plan.

Administrative weaknesses

Pervasive administrative weaknesses were a significant underlying factor. The business plan also outlined what changes would be essential, to strengthen the support functions and back office.

These included addressing Finance, IT and Supply Chain functional capability; making external hires who would bring fresh talent and perspectives to the Group; appointing a Head of Shared Services; and transforming finance as a priority, with a focus on strengthening control, reporting and performance monitoring.

When committing upfront to an operational restructuring, the board had made assumptions about such administrative weaknesses and the ability of consultants to surmount them. Both proved to be incorrect.

Management gaps

. . .

We know from the evidence that '4 out of the 5 existing experienced Divisional Managing Directors were removed from their roles' and that there was 'a lack of senior finance resource/bandwidth at Group level ... and weak corporate knowledge in view of extensive management changes throughout the business'.

A dearth of senior managers would have made it impossible to adequately mitigate the risks posed by the state of the business and its administrative weaknesses.

Execution capabilities

In the aftermath of the first profits warning, the board publicly made several announcements about the benefits that 'self-help' would deliver, principally through improved cash management, disposals and cost cutting.

Yet as we know, relatively little was delivered in six months and in the business plan, the bulk of these benefits remained aspirational.

Leadership

To the outsider, it appears that the dismissal of CEO Richard Howson in July 2017 was a direct result of its joint brokers concluding that Carillion's senior management could neither produce nor deliver an investment proposition that would convince shareholders and new investors to support the potential rights issue.

Yet the catch-22 was that a rights issue would be even more difficult to get away in the absence of a permanent CEO. It is not clear whether the board considered the option of keeping him in office, and if necessary scaffolding him, while a search for a successor was undertaken. It did, after all, demote him and keep him in the business for a period.

Failure to stay focused on a rights issue

When the company's joint brokers told the directors on 5th July 2017 that they could not support a rights issue, the board's minuted reaction was to rubbish the reasons given and, in effect, shoot the messenger.

Yet the appointment of a third joint broker did not provide the desired outcome. Seven weeks later the joint brokers fed back a litany of serious investor concerns. Notwithstanding those, a rights issue, to be announced alongside the company's interim results in late September 2017, was still considered feasible if a strategic investor or a group of institutional investors who were prepared to make a material investment in Carillion could be identified.

This was dependent upon on completing certain 'key gating items'. In subsequent months, the board did address most of those items, but critically it had not taken the opportunity to do so in the two months since early July. A clue as to the possible reason for this is given in the minutes, when, as noted above, a non-executive asked 'whether an equity issue would, or would not, be required'. But the board's conclusion is not clear.

The cumulative impact of early misjudgements

In the three months following the first profits warning, the board got all the big calls wrong: it did not realise that a liquidity crisis was inevitable and imminent; it did not, therefore, give immediate priority to working out how much headroom and time the company had; and it did not use that time to stay focused on exploiting the very limited opportunity to get a rights issue away.

Instead, it embarked on planning an operational restructuring. And it did so without a reliable plan, ignoring the reality of what state the business was in and making optimistic assumptions about cash, cost savings and disposals.

These misjudgements can only be attributed to inexperience. Director profiles in the company's last annual report indicate that no one on the board had experience of a restructuring of a comparable size or complexity. And the board did not appoint anyone with such experience for several months.

False stability

Reality caught up with the board in early September. The financial stakeholders were suddenly faced with Hobson's choice and there was a scramble to put in place sufficient headroom to satisfy the going concern requirements in the half-year results, announced weeks later. Within a few weeks, the company had secured additional headroom of between £170m and £190m.

Yet, with the board's focus on transformation, the company was ill prepared for the situation. Stakeholders' advisers could not access the information they needed. The additional support must have been given through gritted teeth, against the clock, and in the face of a much worse alternative. The lenders referred to the £140m additional facilities as emergency funding. They were largely unsecured and a significant element was a short-term bridge to a disposal.

The key stakeholder missing from the stabilisation effort was the biggest customer, the government. On the evidence of PwC, the government only began taking its advice in September. At that stage the company would have had no credible plan to share with the government in support of a request, because the previous one adopted in July was deemed not fit for purpose and work on a new one had not yet begun.

Unfortunately for the company and its stakeholders, the stability proved false, notwithstanding the earnest assurances by the board that it had rigorously scrutinised the forecasts and was confident that the additional headroom secured would be sufficient to keep Carillion afloat for at least the following 12 months. Within months, the company was again on the brink, with an incremental funding need of between £360m and £495m having been identified.

Liquidity management

Clearly, deeply flawed liquidity management was not confined to the early stages of the crisis, when the board's year-end expectation, announced on 10th July 2017, proved to be half a billion pounds out.

By early January, its assurances given in the half-year results announced on 29th September 2017 were shown to be wrong by as much as a further half a billion pounds.

We do not know what methodologies the company adopted or have any knowledge of the experience and skillsets of those who had responsibility for managing liquidity. Was it assumed that the receivables provided against would be turned into cash nevertheless? Was sufficient allowance made for the strain that the market reaction would exert on working capital? Was there a cash mitigation plan? Was somebody with suitable experience driving it?

Change of restructuring strategy?

In one sense, by the end of September 2017 the board had been forced by circumstances to adopt a revised roadmap – one that involved stabilisation and a financial restructuring – albeit with a delay while a business plan was built.

In another, it continued to make the case for self-help, in pursuit of an aggressive reduction in the net debt-to-EBITDA ratio of around 4 to between 1 and 1.5, within 15 months. That was shown to be futile in an announcement seven weeks later. When issuing the third profits warning on 17th November 2017, the board conceded that self-help had failed and it signalled the likelihood of a dilutive debt for equity swap. And less than two months after that, on the brink of liquidation, the board's proposal was for a full equitisation of debt.

Injection of experience

We can infer that what the lenders saw during September 2017 severely shook their confidence in the board. To urgently remedy the directors' restructuring inexperience, they requested the appointment of a non-executive director and the engagement of a different advisory firm to assist with the management of liquidity. In this day and age, with mainstream UK lenders so sensitive to conduct risk, it is a sign of how bad things were that Carillion's lenders 'requested' changes in personnel, particularly in a public company.

And in the business plan, we also see that a single senior battle-hardened independent restructuring professional was appointed to an execution role, just weeks ahead of the company going into liquidation.

The wider restructuring community watched the slow-motion car crash in amazement, wondering why more experienced specialist interim executives had not been parachuted in much earlier.

As restructuring veteran David Buchler commented in a Daily Telegraph article published two days after Carillion was placed into liquidation, it was baffling that 'the six to seven months between Carillion's major profit warning in mid-2017 and the company's eventual collapse did not feature a significant day-to-day involvement of professional, external turnaround specialists'.

In summary

. . .

The company did not survive long enough to attempt a financial restructuring because, over the course of six months, its board was unsuccessful in stabilising the existential crisis that, in the absence of committed new equity, the first profits warning had triggered.

By not instantly recognising liquidity as the key survival threat, which would surely have led it to identify stabilisation as an urgent priority, the board could sidestep the critical but thorny issues, namely: its own members' lack of restructuring experience; the gaps in people, skills and experience among the senior executives and in the finance team; the necessity of urgently developing reliable survival information; the need to appoint a Ringmaster to plan, resource and lead its management of the financial crisis and restructuring; and mobilising rapidly for an urgent dialogue with all financial stakeholders about true stabilisation.

Embarking instead on an ill-fated operational restructuring proved an enormous and ultimately fatal distraction. Vital time was spent rearranging the deckchairs as the Titanic sped towards the iceberg.

When reality interrupted and the board was forced to confront the deteriorating liquidity situation, unreliable analysis led to the illusion of stability. But thereafter, valuable time was spent on business planning which could have been started months earlier.

. . .

That left all of the financial stakeholders in a holding pattern, as they waited for the business plan to be produced. The under-resourced finance function was under enormous strain, but no interim resources with specialist experience were brought in.

The whole situation started to unravel. Performance deteriorated. Self-help produced little. A much larger funding need was identified. The stability achieved earlier proved to be false and further waivers from lenders were needed.

The survival of the company became wholly dependent on its biggest customer, the government. It was a big political call. When the business plan finally appeared, it confirmed the stakeholders' worst fears. Amazingly, it contained a proposal to retain all of the original non-executive directors.

After so many misjudgements, the board's credibility was in shreds. There was no Plan B. The SS Carillion hit the iceberg and sank quickly.

34

AN ALTERNATIVE ENDING

What might the outcome have been if the board had conformed with the guidance in this book?

Firstly, the board would have appointed a suitably experienced Ringmaster, ideally some time in advance of the first profits warning, but perhaps not if there was justified confidence that a rights issue would be going ahead.

The Ringmaster would immediately have focused on the liquidity analysis. Nothing I have seen suggests that liquidity was materially impacted by unforeseeable trading events after 30th June 2017 or by a materially misstated balance sheet at that date. By elimination, that leaves the connection between the contract provisions and the future cash flow being missed or misunderstood.

That would have set alarm bells ringing. Even before the process of building a timetable had begun, a Ringmaster would have identified the going concern sign off in late September 2017 as a red-letter milestone. Carillion was a public company, so a failure to resolve the issue would have been very visible and there were no palatable alternatives.

Funding would have been needed to last through a financial restructuring, with an adequate cushion to withstand the impact of adverse publicity and the low marketplace confidence. Relying on a two-stage fundraising – the first round to cover going concern in normal circumstances – would not have been feasible. Such a large need would have confirmed the destruction of the company's capital base and, in effect, the wipe-out of its existing shareholders. It would therefore have been deeply discounted and expensive to underwrite. And it would have needed one or more strategic investors to provide the cornerstone.

Time would have been of the essence. I have not seen any reason to suggest that, with a flying start, the correct priorities, adequate resources and leadership with deep and specialist crisis management and restructuring experience, a financial restructuring could not have been completed in the final quarter of 2017.

There are strong parallels with the situation in which Lonmin plc found itself in July 2015. The board rapidly appointed a Ringmaster, Ron Series, and he project-managed the twin, inter-conditional workstreams of a deeply discounted rights issue and a debt refinancing. A US$407m rights issue was launched in November, at a discount of almost 94%. To preserve jobs, South Africa's Public Investment Corporation sub-underwrote a material portion of the issue and increased its holding from 7% to 29.9%. The financial restructuring completed in the weeks before Christmas.

In such circumstances, it is important to produce a sensible, aspirational high-level plan very early on and to start talking to financial stakeholders as soon as possible. Their interests in stabilisation are symbiotic and there is a golden window within which to secure their mutual support. If they can be quickly convinced that, though dire, the situation is capable of being rescued with their support, then they are likely to rally round.

The four or five most senior lenders held the aces. A dialogue could have been established within days. The board update would have been no surprise. They would have been grateful for the opportunity to mobilise.

It would have been critically important for the Ringmaster to convince the board that their chosen course – embarking on an operational restructuring and relying on self-help to generate liquidity – would have involved enormous risks.

At that early stage, the strategic decisions agreed upon would pretty much have determined the restructuring roadmap. The backbone of the outputs would have been the 'key gating items' referred to in the Morgan Stanley letter – a liquidity review, a revised business plan and confirmation of management changes – which would have been common requirements of all financial stakeholders.

A timescale of 10 or 11 weeks to achieve stability would have been tight, but it would have been doable. The rights issue could have been announced with the half-year results.

That said, the one thorny issue was the management team. The specific grounds for the board terminating the CEO Richard Howson have not been made public, but I am confident that a Ringmaster, if involved early enough, would have made an argument for scaffolding him.

That would have allowed the decision on removing him to be deferred and left him *in situ* to be the face of the business plan. A search for a successor could still have gone ahead.

As for the CFO, a battle-hardened interim executive could have been brought in as one of the the Ringmaster's operations point people, ideally as a director, leaving the incumbent or his replacement free to concentrate on the day job.

The Ringmaster would have set several plates spinning: engaging with stakeholders, creating the essential survival tools, identifying triage candidates and setting up the workstreams. That would have required advisers and the right calibre of interim executives to be selected and engaged.

The company was already advised by Lazard (financial) and Slaughter and May (legal), both very high calibre firms with strong restructuring credentials.

The Ringmaster might have selected other advisers to fill two roles: stakeholder management point person and initial cash management set-up.

The operations point person would have been extremely busy in the finance team, diagnosing shortcomings and working out what resources and actions would be needed to produce the reliable numbers that survival would hinge on – always working on the principle that good is the enemy of best.

Other urgent priorities would have included improving cash management and identifying mitigation opportunities, establishing a PMO for cost cutting and setting up business planning. Instinctively, I believe an army of interims with situational experience would have been engaged, vacant posts in finance would have been filled rapidly and the finance team could have been invigorated and energised.

I also believe that the right Ringmaster and operations point person could have established productive partnerships with the senior operational managers, in order to unlock cash from the balance sheet.

I do not see how stability could have been achieved without the participation of the government, in its role as the company's biggest customer. One way of supporting stability could have been for reduced payment terms on outsourcing contracts. Another could have been a concerted joint effort, backed from the top of the government, to unlock the substantial amounts that Richard Howson drew attention to, which he said 'were properly due to Carillion under the contract from Government, or from Government-owned or majority-owned entities on a range of contracts'.

If all financial stakeholders had been approached within weeks of the first profits warning with requests to support stability, in order to provide a platform for a financial restructuring to be negotiated and agreed, it is hard to believe that any one of them would have declined. The risks – mainly through adverse publicity – would have been too high, both institutionally and personally.

The financial stakeholders all have big balance sheets and the request in relation to stabilisation would have been for bridging working capital support for a period of months, not for permanent capital. Their support could have been conditional on a deeply discounted rights issue. It could have been announced at the same time as the rights issue.

There would have been an awful lot to do and every day in those 10 or 11 weeks would have been needed to frantically stitch together a rescue deal supported by all financial stakeholders. Success would have seen an announcement in late September 2017 that true stability had been created and all parties would work towards completing a challenging financial restructuring by Christmas.

In parallel, alternative options could have been worked on, so that if it proved impossible to achieve stability, there would have been time to pursue them.

It is impossible to say with certainty, but that alternative approach would most likely have shored up confidence in the market and thus reduced the strain on working capital.

Perhaps a way could have been found to mitigate the future losses on the problem contracts if the government had been inside the tent and had had access to sensitive information from an early stage.

Maybe some cash could have been produced from the situation in Qatar if the strong support expressed by stakeholders had been publicly obvious.

An approach so very different from the one taken would necessarily have involved the board admitting upfront that the business was broken and that its survival was heavily reliant on its financial stakeholders. If the directors found that to be unpalatable, then either credible Ringmaster candidates would have bowed out of the selection process or there would have been a bruising scrap.

The ability of the lending banks to use their teeth might have been a determining factor. The workout leaders within the institutions involved are all highly experienced.

Unfortunately, in the present climate, conduct risk and the associated adverse publicity are significant concerns. As an independent restructuring professional I ask myself whether, if Carillion had happened in an earlier era, less fettered lender influence would have delivered a different outcome.

PART VII

Mitigation

35

MORE EFFECTIVE GOVERNANCE: PREVENTION AND CURE

I know dozens of senior professionals in the restructuring community. I would be surprised if a single one of them does not subscribe to the strong correlation between the quality of governance and value, in financial crisis and restructuring situations.

Clearly, weak governance puts a business at greater risk. But businesses in which governance is effective can still suffer a financial crisis. There are several reasons for including the next three chapters in this final section of the book: to help a board reduce the risk of suffering a financial crisis; to provide guidance to a board after a financial crisis has already been triggered; and to assist them to avoid a recurrence of a financial crisis.

And in the final chapter I share my views on what could be done to mitigate the impact of financial crises through improving and modernising the legal and regulatory framework in which they are managed and by encouraging those with influence to drive different behaviours.

36

THE FUNDAMENTALS OF GOVERNANCE

The shareholders, directors and executives are the main organs of a company. A company will comprise at least one business.

The legal and regulatory framework

In the UK, there is a well-defined corporate hierarchy of authority. Each company has a single (unitary) board to which its shareholders appoint directors, in accordance with its constitution, formally called its articles of association. The law does not distinguish between executive and non-executive directors.

Under principles developed in recent decades, it is considered good governance for: non-executive directors on a board to outnumber the executive directors; the non-executive directors to appoint the executive directors; and the chairman to be a non-executive director.

If set up in this way, the non-executive directors on a board will constitute a body that has authority over its executive directors. The latter are usually the CEO and the CFO at a minimum.

As a board, the directors have collective primary responsibilities which encompass: owning the strategy; appointing and incentivising the executives to deliver that strategy; signing off the executives' plans for delivering it; monitoring their execution (and thereby the delivery of the strategy); ensuring there is adequate funding; discharging a variety of administrative duties; and constantly reviewing opportunities to create and/or realise value for shareholders.

A board's main administrative duties are audit, risk, nominations and remuneration. It is customary for a board to delegate management of these issues to designated board committees, on which a subset of the directors is appointed to serve. The theory is that these committees have no authority to make decisions, rather they can make recommendations to the full board, which will have the final say. There is considerable coverage of this whole subject elsewhere.

On the boards of publicly listed businesses, one of the non-executives will be designated as the Senior Independent Director to support the chairman, to act as a conduit for major shareholders and the other executive directors, and to lead on reviewing the chairman's performance and on planning succession for the role of chairman.

Effective boards

It is said, although not prescribed, that on an effective board the CEO runs the business and the chairman runs the board.

Broadly, the role of the CEO should be to build a team

capable of delivering the strategy, manage individual performance and influence incentivisation. A CEO is expected to develop deep 'domain knowledge' and to maintain good relationships with key stakeholders, most particularly customers and suppliers, but also investors, funders, regulators and unions.

In addition to leading and organising the board, the chairman has to be engaged with the market, the business and the wider executive team. To ensure that the chairman and the CEO can each perform their separate but complementary roles to a high standard, they have to form a mutually supportive alliance.

It falls to the chairman to influence the selection of able non-executives and to manage them, both individually and as a group, so as to create synergy rather than divisions on the board. This may not suit introverts or those to whom managing relationships does not come easily.

Running a board is a serious business and to achieve a high standard the chairman needs to be an excellent organiser, supported by a competent secretariat, to ensure that all activities are planned well in advance, that the directors receive high quality information in good time, that agreed actions are followed up and that, in a constitutional sense, all responsibilities are identified and discharged as appropriate.

Effective boards conduct all of their business and make all of their decisions 'in the boardroom'. As a group, the directors feel comfortable with healthy disagreements and as individuals they feel safe expressing their views, and do so without rancour. But if they end up in the minority on a specific issue they accept and support the decisions of the majority.

Non-executives have access to the executives and to the business, and they maintain bilateral contact with each other outside the boardroom. The chairman ensures that the non-executive directors regularly meet as a group without the executive directors present.

Bad boards

At their worst, boards can be political cesspits of hopelessly divided factions, driven by greed and fear and rendered unworkable by personal agendas and outsized egos.

There are many and varied signs that a board is bad.

Does the board have a strategy? Is it written down? Is there a recently updated business plan covering at least three years that both reflects the current strategy and demonstrates that there will be adequate funding? Does the current budget align with the forecasts for the same period in the business plan?

Is the board report useful? Is it succinct? Does it provide the reader with a ready understanding of what is going on in the business? Do the appendices contain detailed data to support the main report? Does it focus on the key issues and highlight any areas of underperformance and remedial actions to address them? Does it contain a balance sheet and sensible information about cash, working capital, funding and covenants?

Or is the report designed to downplay inconvenient truths and support the executives' assertions that they are managing the business well? Does it contain numerous colourful graphs of questionable value? Is it delivered to the board so late that the non-executives have little or no time to study it? Are the various appendices delivered piecemeal by their authors? Are these verbose? Is the early part of every meeting conducted to the sound of turning pages, as attendees read the papers for the first time?

Is there a prevailing culture of restricting meeting time to a minimum, so as not to unnecessarily 'take up the busy executives' valuable time'? Does the chairman kick off by telling the meeting what time the train home is? In the meetings, is the chairman habitually unrealistic about the time planned for each agenda item? Are the early parts of the agenda routinely allowed to run well over time so that the rest has to be shoehorned into an implausibly small time slot?

Are non-director executives with only cameo roles routinely permitted to sit in on the whole meeting? Are they present when sensitive issues are raised? Does this suppress a free discussion?

Is there a running list of agreed action points? Are they followed up regularly between meetings? Or is the bare minimum done just before the next meeting?

Is the chairman a good manager of the non-executives and respectful of them as individuals? Do all of the non-executives meet without the executives present, ahead of every board meeting? Is executive performance formally assessed by the non-executive directors? Are targets formally set and is performance properly reviewed and used as the basis for deciding on rewards earned?

Or does the chairman (and the shareholders if the

businesses is privately owned) confer with the senior executives in between board meetings and then announce to the non-executives what has been decided, with little or no opportunity for debate? Do some of the non-executives consider they have a higher status and form a cabal with the chairman and possibly the executive directors too? Do they routinely hold de facto board meetings separately, possibly involving others who are not registered directors?

Executive rewards

It is customary to incentivise the CEO, CFO and other key executives – but not the non-executive directors – using a combination of short-term bonuses related to performance and long-term schemes that enable them to share in the growth in value of the business.

A thoughtfully designed and well-managed incentive programme will encourage executive behaviours that are aligned with the interests of the business and enhance its value.

But, human nature being what it is, a board that gets this issue wrong increases the risk that financial information reported to the board and to the outside world will be distorted, potentially sowing the seeds of a crisis.

37

THE BOARD'S MONITORING OF FINANCIAL PERFORMANCE

The standard to which boards monitor the company's performance is vitally important, not only to evaluate how the business is currently doing but also to deter, detect and remedy financial misstatements and irregularities.

For the board to be an effective monitor, information should be flowing more or less continuously from the board down to the second tier of management and back up to the board, in both directions via the senior executive team, in a way that is similar to the operation of a builder's continuous bucket elevator.

The cornerstone of performance monitoring is the annual budgeting process. It is logical to start this process with a strategy review by the board, which should result in planning parameters flowing down to the managers who are responsible for preparing their subsidiary, divisional or departmental budgets. They should submit their raw forecasts up to the executive, for review and finalisation. The aggregated budgets should then be presented to the board for review. And the final, approved budgets should be sent down for the managers to deliver.

That is also the logical time to refresh the business's three-year business plan, by updating the strategy, incorporating the latest approved annual budget and extending it into the second and third years. That provides a useful basis for reviewing the adequacy and cost-effectiveness of the business's funding and, if necessary, agreeing plans to modify it.

For a second-tier manager, the principle of a trading budget is straightforward: do you know the bit of the business that you control well enough to predict how it is going to perform?

Some industries should, by their nature, be easier to predict. Take, for example, mining. If the mineral resource to be mined in the period has been evaluated with confidence and the methods of extraction are reliable, it should be possible to build up week by week an annual budget from five or six non-financial KPIs.

Obviously, to avoid false precision, the senior team and the board have responsibility for making adjustments for issues outside of the control of those managers at the coalface. Such an approach ensures that performance reviews are focused on what the budget holder can control, by reference to the KPIs on which the budget for that bit of the business was constructed.

It is vital for the board or, at the very least, the audit committee to be familiar with the details of how the most senior executives run the process of reviewing monthly performance across the business. One of the core jobs that managers at every level are paid to do is to understand and explain the performance of the bits of the business that they control.

Boring and frustrating – and at times uncomfortable, embarrassing and possibly even threatening – as such activity may be, there is no better reminder of what a manager is employed to do, and with what priority, than the time taken to formally analyse, understand and articulate both performance in relation to what was expected and remedial actions.

As a good friend and colleague is fond of saying: 'You won't get what you EXpect, only what you INSpect'.

Being vague at the budgeting stage, or budgeting and reporting on different bases, dilutes the effectiveness of the review process.

To facilitate and support both budgeting and effective monthly reviews, it is important to have a Financial Planning & Analysis (FP&A) team, close to the CFO, whose members are custodians of all the detail underlying the budget submissions from all the different bits of the business. That team should be involved in the monthly reviews and should be doing the heavy lifting on the calculation and analysis of variances and the commentaries. This provides a link between the central hub and the business unit spokes and should keep the owners of the numbers honest and their feet to the fire.

Each month, the CEO and the CFO should have a call with, or meet, the various owners of the numbers and those conversations should be high-level and tightly scripted in advance to cover the key variances, including analysis already provided, as well as any remedial actions that the CFO and team have already established. In parallel, the remedial actions agreed previously should be reviewed at least once between monthly reviews and then updated at the next one.

A poor quality back office will have a corrosive effect on the monthly review process. Whether the people being subjected to review are bluffers, duckers or paragons of conscientiousness, there is not much anyone can do with duff information and inevitably a sizeable chunk of the review call or meeting will be spent arguing about where the figures have come from. *In extremis*, conscientious managers will try to keep their own records!

All of the outputs from the monthly reviews provide the raw material for the performance section of the board pack and preparing it involves distilling the information accurately, rather than taking artistic licence to be creative in the service of some other agenda. It is common to have a reporting manager or team, managing the compilation of the pack.

In the course of the board pack preparation process, the CEO and CFO should set aside quality time to have their own conversation in order to agree what information should be in the pack, including the commentary. This is the very essence of stewardship: explaining to the board appointed by shareholders how the business is performing and what actions will be taken to improve it.

As a young CEO, it took a while before I appreciated the value of carving time out of my busy schedule to concentrate on understanding how the business had been performing and to articulate this to the board. Taking time out to do this helped me to rise above the day-to-day and tweak my short-term priorities with a clear head.

As all of the information is perishable, a compact monthly timetable is important. Ideally the board should meet in the middle of the following month. To do this, all of the review and board reporting activity needs to take place within a relatively small window.

A succinct and coherent board pack is essential. It should be delivered to the non-executive directors in the appropriate format in good time. A balance sheet with supporting analysis and details of cash flow, funding and covenants is both a good defence against financial shocks and a sound preparation for any financial crisis, no matter how improbable one may seem at the time.

I find it very helpful to have a 'data pack' in the appendices detailing the finances of individual bits of the business. This enables me to get behind the high-level numbers in my own time.

For reasons that I expand on later, I believe the CFO, rather than the CEO, should own both the performance section of the board pack and the related agenda item in the board meeting.

Of course, the CEO should be fully conversant with all the numbers and be responsible for any promised remedial actions. If the CEO adopts the stance of a non-executive and starts grilling the CFO about performance – and I have seen it happen! – then that should scare the non-executive directors.

In my experience, the CEO can be far more effective in the board meeting by covering value creation and realisation, encompassing updates on the market, customer and competitor activity, order book status, supplier news, regulatory challenges, M&A and organic growth opportunities, product and margin issues, and so forth.

Something a non-executive should work out soon after joining the board is how and when to query financial information. As a CFO, I preferred a call or an email beforehand, not only because it helped to keep meetings efficient but also because it eliminated opportunities for recent appointees to mount an ambush in an attempt to make an early impression on their new paymasters!

38

THE BOARD'S INFLUENCE ON THE QUALITY OF FINANCIAL MANAGEMENT

There is a limit on what non-executive directors can do directly to strengthen financial management.

If two or more non-executive directors feel strongly about these issues, and they agree a mutual position, they will likely have more influence. It very much depends on the politics, in particular the philosophy of the shareholders (if the business is privately owned), the chairman's attitude and to what extent the senior team is hero worshipped.

Over time, the board will, as a group within the political framework that has evolved, develop standard views with respect to various aspects of finance. Someone new coming in may not be made very welcome if they start challenging these views. If a non-executive does not have a finance background, they would be less likely to have the confidence to do so.

So there is a danger of groupthink and a fear of being pigeonholed as a member of the awkward squad. This can be diluted and then overcome if an axis two- or three-strong gets the bit between its teeth and patiently builds a case. If the CFO becomes an ally, such a group's concerns are more likely to be taken more seriously, but that risks making the whole issue very political and thereby impacting the overall effectiveness of the board.

However, there are specific areas in which boards can exercise greater influence over the quality of financial management in a business. These are outlined below. Unavoidably, they are interwoven. The audit committee can be a good place through which to bring this influence to bear.

Tone

To be good at planning, reporting, transactional management and record keeping, it is essential that a business has a well-led back office with high calibre people, processes and systems. There is no getting away from this; it is a fallacy that maintaining a back office in a state of disrepair and disarray saves costs.

Mature, experienced business people understand that there is a direct correlation between a high quality back office and value. That is particularly pertinent to a business owned by professional investors because, at exit, a business capable of producing reliable information (so that due diligence can be a quick and easy process) will attract a crop of quality buyers in a short and competitive process.

If non-executive directors share this view, they should not shrink from making clear their position, in a constructive fashion.

Hiring the CFO

Appointing a team capable of delivering the strategy is one of the primary responsibilities of the board. The non-executive directors should be fully involved in both appraising the incumbent CFO and selecting a replacement.

In the recruitment process, they should be directly involved in recruiter selection, candidate specification, final interviews and the choice of candidate.

Traditionally, the finance director was a technical individual who spent long hours immersed in number crunching. And it was joked that you could tell the ones with personality, because they looked at your shoes, as well as their own.

However, an effective CFO today ought to be a strategic co-leader of the business, in harness with – but independent from – the CEO. Yet some CFOs are regarded by professional investors as no more than flunkeys to 'brilliant' CEOs: shareholders and boards that have an innate desire to remove as many obstacles as possible for the CEO and the sales team are very seriously putting value at risk.

To enable an independent CFO to provide an effective check and balance on the CEO, it is vital that the CFO can exercise robust independent judgement on the board, primarily through owning the performance monitoring section of the board report and then presenting that agenda item in the meeting.

In my book, to be effective, a CFO must be capable of: building a high quality finance team and back office (people, processes, systems); supporting board and first-tier management colleagues on all matters relating to finances and funding (without being immersed in the detail); maintaining good quality relationships with key stakeholders, particularly capital providers and regulators; continuously overseeing a variety of project-type activities that a modern business undertakes; and being a pillar of good governance, most particularly by supporting the board to do its job effectively.

A good CFO should be capable of mastering any sector within months. Sector experience is essential only if an operational finance director, who will be immersed in the numbers, is being hired in preference to a strategic CFO. In a business of any size, the CFO's direct reports will between them have the responsibilities of an operational finance director and the CFO will provide leadership. In some sectors, the major players' back offices suffer from similar weaknesses, hence a fresh pair of eyes in a new leader who brings experience from other sectors can offer significant benefits.

Supporting investment in people, systems and processes

There is a popular, but ill-founded, notion that finance, IT and the back office are great places to cut costs.

The problem with this approach is that layer upon layer of tasks done ostensibly on the cheap in combination with continuous indiscriminate cost cutting produces an inefficient back office and an unproductive environment: manual systems, over-staffing, poor leadership, weak standards, low morale, high staff turnover and excessive recruitment costs.

Before long, the cost differential becomes adverse and it keeps growing. And the problem is compounded when all manner of external consultants are hired to discover what the problems are and to suggest fixes. In my experience they tend to produce a lot of reports but deliver little.

The non-executive directors are in a position to influence the quality of a business's back office. Their overt support may have to be provided despite resistance from the CEO (and acolytes), typically because the issue is not considered a high priority or because the CEO is part of the reason why there are problems in the first place.

Leadership in this area has to come from the CFO who needs to be strong enough to withstand pressure from the CEO and other colleagues for indiscriminate cost cutting. Ideally, the CFO will diagnose the standards and have a long-term plan for improvement. Hence demonstrable experience appropriate to the circumstances ought to feature in the candidate specification when hiring a new CFO.

An improvement programme need not involve expensive outside consultants. Leading from the front, maintaining a high-level perspective and having the support of the board are essential for success. If the CEO's support is lukewarm, that of the non-executives needs to be stronger to compensate. Occasionally, the benefits will be evident, for example a much improved board report. However, the fact that value is difficult to discern makes it important that progress reports to the board are based on at least some tangible indicators, usually operational.

The big prize is a much improved back office that costs significantly less. Clearly, there will be upfront costs and the board needs to ensure that these and the benefits are reported rigorously. The financial benefits may well include improvements in the balance sheet, for example, in reduced working capital lock-up.

It is easy to think that the issues are highly complex. However, the fundamentals are usually straightforward. Despite enormous technological advances in recent decades, the basics of bookkeeping have remained the same since Luca Pacioli wrote the first book on double-entry accounting in 1494. No matter how big or small the business, whether a family-run newsagent or the Tesco supermarket chain, the key 'books of prime entry' are the same – cash book, sales and purchase journals, payroll and journal – and they are all posted to the general ledger, from which the accounts are extracted.

There is a gold standard that every business can achieve, the cornerstone of which is: 'Update the bank balance and cash book by 10 am, allocate the sales receipts by midday and after lunch have credit control chasing the debts that became overdue this morning.' Much that is good can be built on such simple foundations.

Systems and processes can be designed to ensure that numbers march smartly and in time. Although some aspects can involve IT people writing code, implementing applications and upgrading hardware, which can be expensive and disruptive and involve quite serious downside risks, much of the change involves the tasks that people perform between 9 and 5 every working day.

The key is unlocking the enthusiasm of the employees for improvements, feeding in experience of change principles to design a programme that is practical and realistic with minimal outside help and getting them to work collaboratively to effect change. I have seen it done and done it myself, in businesses of different sizes in a variety of sectors. To lead a business to that state does not require immersion in the numbers or long experience in the sector. Nor does it require consultants with whizzy diagrams, snazzy buzzwords and turgid red-amber-green project updates.

My first job within six weeks of leaving school was as a conscript in the armed forces during the civil war in Zimbabwe. Although boot camp was the toughest eight weeks of my life (so far, anyway), through the pain and the exhaustion I could not help but admire how the military used tried and trusted methods, developed all around the world over the course of centuries, to turn hundreds of long-haired, callow youths into a slick squad on the parade ground – in just six weeks. And it was all delivered by non-commissioned officers, most of whom possessed limited intellect.

If a business's back office is in a mess, the data flying around could be thought of as the callow youths arriving at boot camp. And the board report as marching soldiers. With poor processes, systems and people the numbers in the board report will resemble the youths trying to march in their first week on the drill square. But with good ones, the numbers the board sees will resemble the slick squad, marching smartly in time at the end of week six.

It should be perfectly possible for the board's audit committee to concern itself with these matters, to ensure that they have a candid evaluation of their condition and status and to have the right CFO in place both to identify essential improvements and to provide the leadership required for them to be delivered. If the committee's existing terms are restrictive in this regard, they should be amended.

Integrating acquisitions

The making of acquisitions provides a fertile breeding ground for financial misstatements and irregularities. In my experience, there are several key reasons why this is so, which I outline below.

The non-executive directors should insist that every acquisition proposal coming to the board should be specific about integration and they should ensure that henceforth board reports both monitor progress and provide adequate visibility of the performance of the new acquisitions.

Firstly, a management team can lose its focus on managing the business by becoming deal junkies. The temptation will be to spend more and more time in board meetings on acquisition-related matters. And that will make it more difficult for non-executive directors to provide challenge, more so if the senior team becomes hubristic.

Secondly, it becomes harder to understand the numbers because a bigger and more complex business is being reported on. If acquisitions are made frequently, comparisons become very difficult.

Thirdly, acquisitions present opportunities to play games with the numbers by understating assets in order to overstate goodwill at acquisition and thereby falsely boost profitability in the early stages of ownership.

Fourthly, if an acquisition is left with the autonomy to simply send its finalised budgets and reports up to the 'group', it becomes harder and takes longer to produce the consolidated numbers – and if a crisis is triggered that will directly affect the quality and responsiveness of the forecasting.

Fifthly, as the acquiring business becomes a group, management of its finances becomes more complex so that any failure to invest at the appropriate pace in group finance capabilities and additional technical expertise poses serious risks.

A roll-up strategy

The risks that attend acquisition-making businesses are magnified by a roll-up strategy. To keep delivering growth, such businesses have to continuously make ever larger acquisitions. As the market becomes aware of this, bargaining power shifts to the sellers and the risk of overpaying increases.

Their management teams get sucked into M&A at the expense of running the businesses they already have. And if their strengths lie in making acquisitions, they will be oblivious to the necessity to invest in central finance capabilities as the group grows.

The temptation to play games with the numbers is even greater once they have started to get away with it. And they delay integrating the businesses acquired 'until the earnouts can be determined'.

The ever-climbing share price in the growth phase makes a Midas of the key executive: untouchable, squashing every challenge and quickly silencing or dismissing anyone foolhardy enough to make one.

By the time the share price succumbs to gravity, often in

dramatic fashion, the board is in Midas's pocket, the first- and second-tier managers are valued for their loyalty and not their ability, and a fortune is paid for advice to help prolong the whole crew's stay at the top for as long as possible.

39

CHANGES IN LAWS, REGULATIONS AND BEHAVIOURS

Clearly, financial crises and restructurings that have suboptimal outcomes cause the loss of jobs, receivables, supply contracts, rental income, pension benefits, taxes, debt and investment.

I am very hopeful that the guidance in this book will equip directors to achieve better outcomes, principally through being better informed.

However, even if I were to be spectacularly successful in achieving that ambition, many pitfalls, obstacles and bear traps will remain. Politicians and regulators could act to reduce or remove these. And investors, lenders and business leaders could direct or encourage changes in behaviour.

The backdrop to this situation is that in the UK we have an insolvency legal framework that was last overhauled between 30 and 40 years ago – off the back of the second Cork Report that was commissioned in 1977, published in 1981 and enacted into legislation in 1986 – when the capital of businesses was funded in very different ways, incentivisation did not have such a malign influence on the moral compass of business people, and society was concerned about a range of associated issues that are now no longer of serious concern.

To hop on my soapbox for a few seconds, this has led to a situation in which an increasingly important system for the preservation of value sits in a dark corner and offers opportunities for the rapacious to arbitrage the ignorance of the frightened and inexperienced.

How can it be fair that advisers with different agendas can watch directors going through their first restructuring make many mistakes and then clean up when those come home to roost, as the business either dies an agonising death or narrowly avoids it? If it succumbs, is that advice not in reality expensive palliative care?

It is all very well to advance the defence that they were taking instructions from their clients. But which advisers provide coaching for boards facing their first crisis or restructuring, to help them make sounder judgements and give better instructions? It is not in their interests to do so.

And where is the justice in those same advisers facing no risk of redress when the directors who engaged them will, in the event of an adverse outcome, suffer financial and reputational loss and a great deal of stress, possibly lasting years? Does society not need to both encourage and frighten inexperienced directors to bring in and/or make way for those with experience, when a crisis hits?

I am not tarring all advisers with the same brush, or

suggesting an asymmetry of Little Red Riding Hood and Big Bad Wolf proportions. Many directors are no angels either, and their inexperience and conflicts can create enormous problems and destroy material value.

But I do think that changes could be made, and I outline my thinking below (without regard for how difficult they may be to implement, in practice).

Transparency

Louis Brandeis, an early 20th Century US lawyer, Supreme Court judge and crusader for social justice, wrote that 'sunlight is said to be the best of disinfectants'.

What happens in insolvency is the antithesis of this. A thick veil is thrown over a failed company. By lifting that veil in the case of the insolvency of Carillion the parliamentary inquiry created a rare but welcome exception.

I advocate building upon that foundation, by introducing a form of public inquiry when a financial crisis and restructuring has had an outcome that adversely impacts on the stakeholders of a business.

Until the early 2000s, UK company law provided for public inquiries and it seems to me there would be enormous benefits if they were to be re-introduced, in hybrid form.

Speed is a vital aspect: the sooner oral and documentary evidence is gathered the greater its value, particularly if opportunities are reduced for well-funded participants to airbrush history with the benefit of legal advice.

I believe the introduction of such inquiries would be essential to the success of the other reforms I am suggesting.

And that their deterrent threat would encourage helpful changes in behaviours.

Consensual development of a methodology

There is considerable evidence that restructuring activity has grown exponentially in recent decades, including a stream of high-profile names in distress, a proliferation of capital providers seeking distressed investment opportunities, and an abundance of specialist professional advisers.

This is no accident: professional investors thinly capitalise the businesses they acquire and when lenders advance acquisition debt to them, restructuring activity is anticipated, and built into the loan documentation if the performance of the acquired business deviates materially from the plan that is being funded.

That is necessary to ensure that the sale of the business acquired can be forced, in the absence of other solutions, because the lenders have lent principally against the cash flows generated by the business, not hard assets. That cash will only keep flowing if the business keeps operating in the hands of a new owner, whose payment to acquire it will thus provide the means to repay the acquisition loans.

These principles have permeated all term lending. They simply did not exist when the insolvency law was last overhauled, because at that time is was illegal for a company acquired to give security over its business and assets. And an acquirer could not get tax relief on the costs of borrowing.

Despite that important evolution, there is no mention of restructuring in legislation, regulations or corporate codes.

This should not come as a surprise, because the history of emerging fields of specialist activities in the sphere of business shows that it takes decades for codification to evolve.

Audit and insolvency provide good examples of this. Both were first legislated for in the mid-19th century. Yet for over 50 years anyone could conduct an audit and it took a further 80 years before the first standards and guidelines were published. Prior to 1986, insolvency practitioners required no licence. And insolvency standards did not appear until the mid-1990s.

I believe that restructuring has evolved into a distinct specialist activity. I hope that this book evidences that, and that it can provide a contribution to the development of a methodology, if my suggestion is taken up.

It is interesting to contemplate whether the Carillion situation would have had a different outcome if such a methodology had existed.

An accepted methodology would: create a framework for directors to assess the risks of their inexperience; offer guidance to help them manage a financial crisis and restructuring; and provide a benchmark against which the conduct of boards and advisers could be evaluated by subsequent inquiries.

Enhanced reporting

Where the outcome of a financial crisis and restructuring is a formal insolvency process, the insolvency office holder appointed to manage it has to provide public progress reports.

It is typical for these reports to be prepared 'solely to comply with statutory requirements'. Hence they provide very limited information about the way in which the directors managed the financial crisis and restructuring and no information about the costs that they caused the business to incur.

The existence of a methodology and the possibility of a subsequent inquiry would provide the framework for this opacity to be remedied.

Scrutiny of advisers' costs

A methodology and more transparency in reporting would provide the basis for subjecting to scrutiny the costs borne by the borrowers' advisers, as happens in an adversarial legal trial.

The costs would have to be itemised and a refund could be sought in respect of elements deemed excessive or unreasonable.

In the absence of a consensual settlement, the insolvency office holder would have the ability to pursue a claim using the courts. The defences available to an adviser would include that the board ignored advice.

Recoveries would benefit the insolvent estate. All aspects would be reported on by the insolvency office holder.

Mis-alignment of incentives

In my view, the health and survival of their borrower clients should demonstrably be the only interest of firms that provide them with restructuring advice.

If these changes, or contemplation of them, produce evidence that the interests of borrower-side advisers, on the one hand, and of the board and all the stakeholders on the other, can diverge when things start to go badly wrong, then, clearly, eradicating the causes would be in the public interest.

The suggestions so far would be helpful in this regard, but additional measures would be necessary.

Restructuring advisory firms should have to choose between, on the one hand, providing insolvency and lender advisory services and, on the other, advising borrowers. Specific technical insolvency advice required by boards, such as CVAs or the insolvency of a subsidiary, could be carved out.

With such restrictions in place, it would be reasonable to expect borrower-side advisory firms to take a strong interest in some of the key issues raised in this book. For example, the inexperience of their client boards, the value of appointing a Ringmaster, the reliability of liquidity analyses and restructuring roadmaps that are not fit for purpose.

And it would be in their interests to ensure that a clear trail existed of their advice being offered and of a board ignoring it.

Changes such as these would make it much more straightforward for the professional bodies and their regulator, the Financial Regulatory Council, to enforce the ethical requirement that a borrower-side adviser should not take on a role for which he or she does not possess adequate qualifications or experience.

Such ethics are a cornerstone of public trust in the professions and in recent times that has been corroding.

Breaking up the Big Four

At the time of writing, this is a high-profile topic in political, regulatory and business circles.

A Sunday Times article on 19th August 2018 provides a flavour of this: 'Auditing, something that sounds dry and uncontroversial, is proving to be the subject of heated debate. The big four are in the line of fire ... What few deny is that change must come. Earlier this year, the Commons business and work and pensions committees delivered an excoriating verdict on the role of KPMG in the collapse of outsourcing group Carillion.'

In their report, the committees also recommended that 'the Government refers the statutory audit market to the Competition and Markets Authority. The terms of reference of that review should explicitly include consideration of both breaking up the Big Four into more audit firms, and detaching audit arms from those providing other professional services.'

My very limited contribution to this debate is that an auditor's sole interest ought to be its audit client: primarily the shareholders, to whom its audit report is addressed, but also those parties who will be relying on it.

It should not have a vested interest in its relationships with its client's lenders. Or in maximising its own firm's fees, generated by colleagues in other service lines.

My suggestion, to give effect to this, is that if restructuring advisory firms are compelled to choose between advising borrowers and lenders, as suggested earlier in this chapter, then if audit practices are spun off it would make sense for borrower-side advisory practices to be bundled in with audit.

Liquidators: independence and inquiries into conduct

Separating lender- and borrower-side advisers would enhance the independence of liquidators. And the other suggestions above would incentivise them to scrutinise the conduct of both the directors and the borrower-side advisers, and to report on it.

That would put them in a position to provide much more useful reports into conduct. Presently, those reports focus on criminal conduct and prejudices to creditors. Modern-day non-executive directors of a large business are unlikely to have a case to answer, given how far removed they are from any levers of power and the copious advice that boards typically receive when in the zone of insolvency.

The excellent autobiography of the late Sir Kenneth Cork, doyen of UK insolvency and author of the Cork Report that formed the basis for the Insolvency Act of 1986, explains that the current reporting regime on directors was introduced primarily because society had lost faith in the insolvency laws of the 1970s and the legal concept of wrongful trading was designed to address that.

In that era, if a sizeable business collapsed it was a black swan event and the government or the Bank of England acted quickly to recapitalise it. But nowadays, such collapses are more commonplace, in large part because they are failed gambles on thin capital that go wrong.

Once in crisis, firms are managed by the directors who were

hired pre-crisis for many reasons, but seldom for their restructuring experience. With apologies for the mixed metaphors, it might be said that it is an accident of history that they are in the hot seat when the balloon goes up!

With the changes I am suggesting, the scope of independent liquidators' reports could be expanded to include an assessment of the way in which directors managed financial crises and restructurings, by reference to benchmarks founded in an accepted methodology.

The Financial Reporting Council (FRC)

In the words of the joint committees, 'The Financial Reporting Council (FRC) is the regulator of accountants, auditors and actuaries. It has a responsibility for maintaining high standards of financial reporting and auditing, and for pursuing sanctions against those who fall below established professional standards. It also has a wider mission to promote the integrity of UK business through its Codes on Corporate Governance and Stewardship.'

Reforming the FRC is another high-profile topic at the time of writing. The same Sunday Times article quoted above said the committees' report branded the FRC ... as 'toothless' and 'useless' and added that an inquiry led by Legal & General chairman Sir John Kingman was 'looking at the way the FRC is run'.

The joint committees' report went on to say: 'We welcome the Government's review of the FRC's powers and effectiveness. We believe that the Government should provide the FRC with the necessary powers to be a much more aggressive and proactive regulator: one that can ... through the judicious exercise of new powers, provide a sufficient deterrent against poor boardroom behaviour to drive up confidence in UK business standards over the long term. Such an approach will require a significant shift in culture at the FRC itself.'

In its submission to the Kingman review, the Institute of Directors advocated the establishment of a new independent Corporate Governance Commission to oversee the UK's corporate governance framework.

My contribution to this debate is that, if there is going to be a restructuring methodology adopted as I have suggested earlier in this chapter, it is logical that the FRC, or any successor body, should be its regulatory owner.

Standards of corporate governance

I have not spoken much about my experiences, but they have led me to form a strong view that, nowadays, there is far less appreciation in business of the causal link between effective governance and the value of a business.

I am not referring to box-ticking, of which there is a surfeit, but to the matters covered in the preceding chapters on good governance. Twenty or so years ago, Patrick Dunne wrote some excellent books on the subject. But nowadays they are rarely talked about.

Although banks can still make the odd howler in lending to a business with a dysfunctional board, I think the issue is particularly pertinent for both professional investors and non-bank lender funds, who are deploying enormous sums entrusted to them by insurers, pension funds, high net worth families and others.

The individuals such funds employ tend to be sourced from

the same gene pool of accountants, lawyers, investment bankers – some with MBAs and some without.

Typically, these individuals' work experience comprises moving to a big city after they graduate and over the ensuing years working for a variety of employers in a succession of high-rise buildings. They are surrounded by peas from the same pod and very few rub shoulders with managers and workers in real operating businesses.

When they get appointed to a board, how are they expected to be a force for effective governance? I find it amusing when they arrive at a company's premises for a board meeting and appear terrified that they might actually meet a real live worker – or worse, take a wrong turn en route to the boardroom and find themselves in a room full of employees!

And once the meeting starts, what value can they add? If the CEO is a domineering force that the investor is convinced is going to make them all wealthy upon exit, they gaze in wonder with pound signs in their eyes. At some point they will ask the token question and, like a cat having fun with a mouse, the CEO will humour them with an answer that may or may not be garbage.

Almost all of the companies I have been engaged by in the past ten years have suffered from dysfunctional finance functions. Not only do the senior people have no idea what good looks like, but the vast majority of board members exhibit no curiosity and seem to think the situation can no more be influenced than the weather.

These situations are crying out for adult supervision and I expect they are replicated across the land. Cynical professional investors may take the view that it will be a buyer's problem, if only they can get a sale away – but that is wasting value that could be theirs and their investors'.

Until the bank lenders became consumed by fears of conduct risk, they at least used their teeth to provide a backstop in the most egregious cases.

Is part of the reason that, in recent decades, corporate codes have been blindsided by 'blue chip bias'? That the code setters have made misplaced assumptions about the way that all businesses are run? Because the businesses they worked in were very different from the situations and conditions that I come across?

Do politicians and regulators assume that professional advisers are experts in how boards should be run? Speaking from experience, only after leaving a profession and spending years in real businesses will anyone know what good looks like in the boardroom.

Whatever the historical reasons, my very limited contribution to this debate is that, for the sake of business and society more widely, a way needs to be found to: balance the box-ticking with more practical governance matters; put much greater emphasis on defining what good looks like in the areas of approving plans and monitoring performance; make the rigorous evaluation of back offices compulsory and more transparent; and ensure that post-acquisition integration remains visible both before and after acquisitions are made.

One friend, a Big Four audit partner with whom I have spent time in the trenches, wonders whether the day will come when auditors are required to present, in person, a warts-and-all report to company AGMs.

Whatever measures are adopted, in order to improve the effectiveness of governance a way needs to be found to educate non-executive directors on matters other than box-ticking. And to routinely allow them more independent access to the second- and third-tier managers.

Formal valuations

The ability of professional investors to retain their shareholders' authority over board and senior management appointments long after they have de facto been disenfranchised can, if abused, lead to the unnecessary destruction of value. This is outlined in Chapter 7.

One way to take away this authority is to make it mandatory for a formal valuation of the business to be confirmed by a court early on in a financial restructuring process.

For at least the past decade or so, investors and lenders have lobbied for a change of this sort.

Recognising the greater influence of lenders

One area in which the current laws, regulations and codes would benefit from updates is in recognising that the trend towards thin capitalisation can cause de facto control to shift more quickly and easily from shareholders to lenders.

Since Victorian times, successive Companies Acts have comprehensively covered what shareholders can and cannot do and prescribed related disclosures. But there is comparatively little coverage of lenders.

When a company is in difficulty, it is not easy for interested parties to discover the identity of the lenders and the terms of their loans.

Public information filed at Companies House will show the identity of the chargeholder, but not of the lenders in the syndicate. And if the debt and security has been sold the chargeholder may simply be acting as security agent, without any influence.

The accounts have to show more detail, but even that is seldom of much use. Particularly in the case of private companies, which are permitted to file their annual accounts nine months after their financial year-ends.

But it is typical for companies in difficulty to be late in doing so, because completion of their audits is delayed on account of going concern uncertainties. And if a company decides to mitigate the problem by lengthening its financial year, that increases the delay.

Publicly listed companies provide additional opportunities for discovery, but often their announcements are less forthcoming than they might be about the realities of the current state of the lending relationship.

The UK's corporate and stewardship codes are framed on the assumption that shareholders will always be in the money. The latest versions can be found online. But note that searching the documents for the term 'lenders' will return the result 'not found'.

Curb indiscriminate banker bashing

The largest UK banks employ a small cadre of people who are not particularly well paid but who nevertheless save their institutions billions.

Being a senior workout manager is a stressful job, but the individuals who do it are highly motivated experts with deep experience and rare expertise. Since the recession of the 1990s, they and their predecessors have been at the forefront of making the rescue culture work.

That recession featured the wholesale use of formal insolvency processes. In a variety of ways, the approach needlessly destroyed value. Those who worked through it concluded that there must be a better way and that was the catalyst for recognising the value that independent restructuring professionals could protect when businesses get into difficulty.

They sponsored and fostered the development of a professional culture and the adoption of standards for independent restructuring professionals. And they demanded that the insolvency and advisory firms consider the option of introducing them to borrowers, in preference to formal insolvency.

It seems to me that, unfortunately, they have been caught in the crossfire of the wider debate in society that has led to all banks and bankers being bashed.

The resultant sensitivities over conduct risk and the significant increase in compliance have led to workout bankers having their wings clipped. In practical terms, that has blunted their ability to influence boards and thereby steer them towards better outcomes.

Anecdotally, I am aware of dedicated and very effective workout bankers who have left their profession in frustration that their institutions would rather lose money than risk being subjected to any public criticism, justified or not.

Leadership will be required if a sensible balance is to be restored.

Directors staying or going: carrot and stick

I have articulated in some detail, in Chapter 21, the dilemma that all directors face when they are *in situ* at the time that a financial crisis is triggered.

Even before changes to the current laws and regulations are contemplated, I believe that the benefits of directors resigning should be made clearer. And if, legally, there are any overt reasons why they would be disadvantaged if they did so, those should be clarified and, if feasible, addressed.

In terms of changes, those that I have suggested would provide: a methodology for directors to refer to; an incentive for advisers to get them up the learning curve; a benchmark against which their conduct could be assessed; transparency in relation to whether their appointed advisers provided value for money, and whether they took the advice; and for the public to be informed about how the directors conducted themselves.

That would incentivise those willing and able to make the necessary contributions to stay, more so if shareholders could be seen to make it worth their while financially. And encourage those who could not to resign.

Financial non-executives

I came across a concept that I believe has the potential to remedy many common failings in governance that are rooted in the sphere of finance in a business.

A financial non-executive has specific additional responsibilities that are best discharged on a quasi-executive basis by an individual who is appointed as chairman of the audit committee.

Ongoing responsibilities would typically involve the financial non-executive being the board's eyes and ears, spending time ahead of board meetings reviewing planning, reporting, liquidity management and covenant reporting.

Ad hoc responsibilities would include being the point person on recruiting a new CFO and senior finance personnel and oversight of projects to strengthen people, processes and systems.

It would be typical for a financial non-executive to be a participant in the management incentive plan for senior executives.

Professional investors already have the authority to appoint financial non-executives to boards of their investee businesses. Lenders would have the option to request such an appointment as a condition of their continuing support of a borrower in financial difficulty.

The government's response

In the aftermath of Carillion's liquidation, BEIS, the government department responsible for Business, Energy & Industrial Strategy, published a white paper. In August 2018 it published a response to both that and an earlier white paper, published in 2016.

The response can be found here:

https://assets.publishing.service.gov.uk/government/uploads/system/uplo _Government_response_doc_- _24_Aug_clean_version__with_Minister_s_photo_and_signature__AC.pdf

The views of lawyers I have heard is that few of the proposals are likely to make it into legislation and the primary motivation for publication was political.

Aside from potentially making it mandatory to have formal valuations of the business confirmed by a court early on in a financial restructuring process, there is little overlap between my suggestions and the published response.

ads/attachment_data/file/736163/ICG_-

APPENDIX

The Final Report of the Business, Energy and Industrial Strategy and the Work and Pensions Committees of the House of Commons, 16 May 2018

https://publications.parliament.uk/pa/cm201719/cmselect/cmworp

Oral evidence: Tuesday 30 January 2018

http://data.parliament.uk/writtenevidence/committeeevidence.svc/evidencedocument/work-and-pensions-committee/carillion/oral/77681.pdf

Oral evidence: Tuesday 6 February 2017

http://data.parliament.uk/writtenevidence/committeeevidence.svc/evidencedocument/work-and-pensions-committee/carillion/oral/78103.pdf

Oral evidence: Thursday 22 February 2018

http://data.parliament.uk/writtenevidence/committeeevidence.svc/evidencedocument/work-and-pensions-committee/carillion/oral/79121.pdf

Oral evidence: Wednesday 7 March 2018

http://data.parliament.uk/writtenevidence/committeeevidence.svc/evidencedocument/work-and-pensions-committee/carillion/oral/79969.pdf

Oral evidence: Wednesday 21 March 2018

http://data.parliament.uk/writtenevidence/committeeevidence.svc/evidencedocument/work-and-pensions-committee/carillion/oral/80775.pdf

Responses from Interested Parties, published on 12 July 2018

https://publications.parliament.uk/pa/cm201719/cmselect/cmworpen/1392/1392.pdf

Carillion's final business plan, January 2018

https://www.parliament.uk/documents/commons-committees/work-and-pensions/Carillion-Group-Business-Plan-January-2018.pdf

Letter from Simon Willes to the Chair, 29 March 2018

https://www.parliament.uk/documents/commons-committees/work-and-pensions/Carillion%20report/Letter-from-Simon-Willes-Executive-Chairman-Gazelle-re-Carillion-290318.pdf

Project Ray, FTI Consulting, 15 January 2018 ('the FTI Consulting IBR')

https://www.parliament.uk/documents/commons-committees/work-and-pensions/Carillion/Project-Ray-FTI-consulting-15-January-2018.pdf

Letter from Ernst & Young (EY) Chairman to the Chairs relating to Carillion, 2 February 2018

https://www.parliament.uk/documents/commons-committees/work-and-pensions/Correspondence/Letter-from-EY-Chairman-to-the-Chairs-relating-to-Carillion-2-February-2018.pdf

Appendix to letter from EY Chairman to the Chairs relating to Carillion, 2 February 2018

https://www.parliament.uk/documents/commons-committees/work-and-pensions/Correspondence/Letter-from-EY-to-the-Chairs-relating-to-Carillion-25-January-2018.pdf

Letter from Nicholas Shott, Vice Chairman, Lazard & Co Limited on Carillion inquiry, 20 February 2018

https://www.parliament.uk/documents/commons-committees/work-and-pensions/Carillion/180220-Letter-from-Lazard-to-Chairs.pdf

Letter from Slaughter and May to the Chairs on Carillion, 20 February 2018

https://www.parliament.uk/documents/commons-committees/work-and-pensions/Carillion%20report/180220-Letter-from-Slaughter-and-May.pdf

Carillion Board minutes, 5 July 2017

https://www.parliament.uk/documents/commons-committees/work-and-pensions/Correspondence/Carillion-Board-minutes-5-July-2017.pdf

Carillion Board Minutes, 22 August 2017

https://www.parliament.uk/documents/commons-committees/work-and-pensions/Carillion/Carillion-board-minutes-22-August-2017.pdf

Joint presentation by Morgan Stanley and HSBC to the Audit Committee, 22 August 2017

https://www.parliament.uk/documents/commons-committees/work-and-pensions/Carillion%20report/Joint-presentation-by-Morgan-Stanley-and%20-HSBC-to-the-Audit-Committee-22-August-2017.pdf

Extract from EY presentation to Carillion Board, 22 August 2017

https://www.parliament.uk/documents/commons-committees/work-and-pensions/Carillion/Extract-from-EY-presentation-to-Carillion-Board-22-August-2017.pdf

Letter from Morgan Stanley to the Chairs regarding Carillion, 21 February 2018

https://www.parliament.uk/documents/commons-committees/work-and-pensions/Correspondence/Letter-from-Morgan-Stanley-to-the-Chairs-regarding-Carillion-21-February-2018.pdf

Letter from Kiltearn Partners LLP to the Chairs regarding Carillion, 2 February 2018

https://www.parliament.uk/documents/commons-committees/work-and-pensions/Carillion/Letter-from-Kiltearn-Partners-LLP-to-the-Chairs-regarding-Carillion-2-February-2018.pdf

Letter from Patricia Halliday, Chief Risk Officer, Santander, regarding Early Payment Facility programme, 5 February 2018

https://www.parliament.uk/documents/commons-committees/work-and-pensions/Carillion/050218-santander-patricia-halliday-epf-carillion.pdf

Letter from Carillion to the Permanent Secretary for the Cabinet Office regarding Carillion, 13 January 2018

https://www.parliament.uk/documents/commons-committees/work-and-pensions/Correspondence/Letter-from-Carillion-to-Permanent-Secretary-for-the-Cabinet-Office-regarding-Carillion-13-January-2018.pdf

Carillion: Summary of short-term funding proposal, 13 January 2018

https://www.parliament.uk/documents/commons-committees/work-and-pensions/Correspondence/Carillion-Summary-of-short-term-funding-proposal-13-January-2018.pdf

Carillion: Response from former CEO Richard Howson, 12 July 2018 (Page 42)

https://publications.parliament.uk/pa/cm201719/cmselect/cmworpen/13

Carillion (DB) Pension Trustee Limited Covenant Report, May 2017

https://www.parliament.uk/documents/commons-committees/work-and-pensions/Draft-covenant-report-for-Trustees-May-2017.pdf

Additionally, the various Carillion announcements to the market can be found at:

https://www.londonstockexchange.com/exchange/prices-and-markets/stocks/exchange-insight/company-news.html?fourWayKey=GB0007365546GBGBXSET3

Some of these announcements have links to much more detailed supporting documents.

Printed in Great Britain
by Amazon